# Post-Colonial Literatures in English

# Post-Colonial Literatures in English

## History, Language, Theory

Dennis Walder

BLACKWELL
*Publishers*

First published 1998

Blackwell Publishers Ltd
108 Cowley Road
Oxford OX4 1JF
UK

Blackwell Publishers Inc.
350 Main Street
Malden, Massachusetts 02148
USA

*British Library Cataloguing in Publication Data*

A CIP catalogue record for this book is available from the British Library.

*Library of Congress Cataloging-in-Publication Data*

Walder, Dennis.
    Post-colonial literatures in English : history, language, theory /
Dennis Walder.
        p.      cm.
    Includes bibliographical references and index.
    ISBN 0-631-19491-6. — ISBN 0-631-19492-4 (pbk)
    1. Commonwealth literature (English) — History and criticism.
2. Literature and society — Commonwealth countries — History — 20th
century.   3. Decolonization in literature.   4. Colonies in
literature.   5. Blacks in literature.   I. Title
PR9080.W25   1998
820.9'9171241—dc21                                        97-42235
                                                              CIP

Typeset in 10½ on 12½ pt Bembo by Ace Filmsetting Ltd, Frome, Somerset
Printed in Great Britain by MPG Books Ltd, Bodmin, Cornwall

This book is printed on acid-free paper.

# Contents

# Preface and Acknowledgements

Much of the most exciting and important creative writing in English in recent decades has its origins in former British colonies, all independent nation states which, in one way or another, retain political, cultural and linguistic ties with Britain, itself now increasingly understood to be a construct of varying identities – including, for the time being and most contentiously, that of the north of Ireland. Many people have now come across such writing, or at least have heard of the work of Nobel Prizewinners such as Wole Soyinka of Nigeria, Nadine Gordimer of South Africa and Derek Walcott of St Lucia – and indeed, who can have escaped knowing about the unfortunate Salman Rushdie? An increasing number of educational institutions worldwide (including non English-speaking countries), are adopting texts by writers from the English-speaking diaspora, not only on English Literature courses traditionally conceived, but as part of World Literature, Area or Cultural Studies courses. There is no question of the large and growing interest in Literatures in English (as the subject should now be described) and of the influence they exert.

The aim of this book is to engage with this relatively new and fast-growing area of literary endeavour, and the criticism or 'theory' which increasingly – with varying degrees of success – attends it. I do not pretend to offer an objective, or even agreed approach. I have my own agenda, as an ex-colonial (South African) long based in the UK, with particular links in Southern Africa, India and South East Asia. Nor am I trying to speak on behalf of others; rather, I want to suggest what one position, developed I hope with a proper sense of its limitations as well as advantages, may provide. I also see it as part of my brief to alert the reader to the most well-known or current trends, insofar as they strike me as relevant; while I attempt to generate new thinking about the nature and practice of literary study today. The parochial, ethnocentric if not merely unexamined nature of what passes for literary study in many quarters makes me feel some justification in going over ground that will be familiar to fellow toilers in the field; my hope is that what I have to say, and the way I have set out on this occasion to say it, will remind them – as it has reminded me – of some of the basics we are liable to forget in the heat of debate.

The contemporary nature of what have come to be called 'post-colonial' literatures in English, their focus upon matters of broad yet immediate interest – matters of history, language, race, gender, identity, migration and cultural exchange – has ensured a dramatic impact upon traditional literary studies, despite the apparent lateness of their arrival. I say 'apparent' because not only do the writings which may be thought of as post-colonial go back a long way (some claim to the first moment of colonization); but also because the roots of thinking about or 'theorizing' the post-colonial go back some distance too – certainly further than the work of the three most well-known representatives of that theorizing, Edward Said, Gayatri Spivak and Homi Bhabha. A mere glance at, for example, Aimé Césaire's *Discourse on Colonialism*, first published in 1955 and one of the most powerful accounts of the barbarism of the colonizer, and the unhappiness of the colonized, I have ever read, should lead those who begin their study of the subject with the aforementioned threesome to look a little further back.

I do not have the space to do so here, although I do go back to Frantz Fanon, who raised most of the important questions, even if he did not stay to answer them. I have organized this book as follows. After providing an Introduction to the shift in perspective these writings demand, based on a reading of Achebe's great novel *Things Fall Apart* (1958), I develop an approach to the relevant strands of history, language and theory, which I have separated out into three chapters, as Part I. The second Part introduces a range of literary texts by means of three case studies, each focusing on a different cultural-geographic area and genre or group of genres, organized to suggest an accumulating complexity of debate around a number of central issues. The idea of a case study is familiar as an educational and ethnographical tool; my use of it here is intended to balance inductive generalizations from my chosen texts on the one hand, with an awareness of the unavoidability of pre-knowledge on the other.

All three studies draw on the issues of history, language and theory broached in Part I: the first study, of Indian fiction in English, suggests how the historic question of authority is dealt with by fictions which engage with the most serious crisis of the post-independence state, the 1975 emergency in India; the chapter (6) on Caribbean and Black British Poetry inevitably foregrounds language; while South African Literature in the Interregnum, including fiction, poetry and drama, offers a position designed to expose the fuller understanding of history, language and theory which using the term 'post-colonial' in relation to literatures in English now demands. I conclude with 'After Post-Colonialism?' since, even if we accept the periodization implicit in the term, it is no longer possible to pretend that its defining moment of resistance and transformation has left us with a stable signifier. Rather, the literary products which now appear to supersede while implicating post-colonialism – texts as diverse as V.S. Naipaul's *The Enigma of Arrival* (1987) or Ariel Dorfman's *Death and the Maiden* (1991) – propose emerging and new representations of power relations which suggest that the post-colonial is what Stuart Hall calls 'an episteme-in-formation'.[1] In other words, a kind of knowledge-inducing, but changing, historicist paradigm.

My case studies deliberately focus on a number of more or less widely available texts or anthologies, from Nadine Gordimer's *The Conservationist* (1974) to R.K. Narayan's *The Painter of Signs* (1976), from Gcina Mhlophe's *Have You Seen Zandile?* (1988) to E.A. Markham's *Hinterland: Caribbean Poetry from the West Indies and Britain* (1989). In such a relatively new area of study, however, literary and critical material has not always made its way sufficiently for such purposes, and I refer to many other, less easily available texts. Those of us who have long pursued Commonwealth (as they used to be, and sometimes still are called) or post-colonial literatures in English, are familiar with the obscure corners of libraries and bookshops, are used to relying upon friends' and writers' generosity. Like others, I have had to persuade publishers to publish, or allow me to edit for publication, the texts I wish to read, or make available. Things are improving, with the growth of interest worldwide, and publishers (intermittently) responding; hence the arrival of books like Victor Ramraj's *Concert of Voices: An Anthology of World Writing in English* (Broadview Press, 1995), or John Thieme's more hefty collection of (all too brief) extracts, *The Arnold Anthology of Post-Colonial Literatures in English* (Arnold, 1996). These are at best tasters.

I have eschewed the globalizing ambitions of many who have entered this field, although it is impossible to avoid some very large generalizations, given the enormous range and variety of writings. I think it is time to be both more selective and text-based. In any case, the uneven pace and development of colonialism from one place to the next, as well as the different intensities of decolonization in those places, have important consequences in terms of the kind of writing – the form, language and genre – that is produced. Unlike the Australian authors of the first critical-theoretical book to consider the 'post-colonial' rubric adequately, Ashcroft, Griffiths and Tiffin's *The Empire Writes Back: Theory and Practice in Post-Colonial Literatures* (Routledge, 1989), my use of the term involves writings in English from peoples whose experience of colonization is relatively recent; excluding the Americans, Irish (although arguably their experience of colonization continues) or Scots; but including Indians, Trinidadians, South Africans – and, within the post-colonial nation from which this is written, Black Britons – insofar as these labels are accepted or acceptable to those who inhabit them. I use 'post-colonial' to identify recent writings in English which have come into being as part of the processes of decolonization. This is not to suggest that the works of, say, Toni Morrison, Brian Friel or Ian Crichton Smith are not relevant in this context; rather, that my chosen areas enable me to develop an approach which can best be clarified without following them up.

Finally, I should add that the structure of this book and the selection of material, is derived to some extent from a course I designed and have run since 1992 for Open University students, many with diasporic back-grounds, whose responses and comments have been invaluable. I would also like here to acknowledge the advice of colleagues who helped write the material for that course, Cicely Palser Havely and Michael Rossington (now of the University of Newcastle), as well as that of the course assessor, Lyn Innes of the University of Kent. I have benefited from specific discussions with members of my Post-Colonial Literatures Research Group, especially Richard Allen, Marcia Blumberg, Ban Kah Choon, Ganeswar Mishra, Mpalive Msiska, Vrinda Nabar, Rajeev Patke and Stephen Regan (who also read the book through in draft for me). The presence of Fatima Dike and Jack Mapanje as Writers in Residence in 1996 and 1997 ensured I would not forget where writers see themselves coming from. I dedicate this book to the memory of Paul Edwards, who introduced me to the pleasures of the post-colonial at Edinburgh University long before the term had been heard of.

## Note

1 'When was "the post-colonial"? Thinking at the limit', *The Post-Colonial Question*, eds Iain Chambers and Lidia Curti (Routledge, 1996), p. 255.

Literature is necessary to politics above all when it gives a voice to whatever is without a voice, when it gives a name to what as yet has no name, especially to what the language of politics excludes or attempts to exclude.

Italo Calvino, 'Right and wrong political uses of literature', *The Uses of Literature: Essays*, 1982, transl. Patrick Creagh

despite your Empire's wrong,
I made my first communion
there, with the English tongue

Derek Walcott, 'Eulogy to W.H. Auden', *The Arkansas Testament*, 1988

There are powerful winds blowing through English literature. English is being assaulted by cross-currents of racial experience, by a vast expansion of its frame of reference, by new uses of imagination and language.

Nayantara Sahgal, 'The schizophrenic imagination', Silver Jubilee Conference of the Association for Commonwealth Literature and Language Studies, University of Kent, Canterbury, 1989

My own preference is for a story which is kaleidoscopic, with a number of different voices rather than one character speaking for the entire novel. I suppose it may be a post-colonial viewpoint.

Fred D'Aguiar, interview, *Independent on Sunday*, 23 July 1995

# 1

## Introducing the Post-Colonial

Well-bred post-colonials much like myself, adrift in the new world.
Bharati Mukherjee, *Darkness*, 1985

### The Arrival of the Post(-Colonial)

The aim of this book is to offer an approach to recent literary texts in English which, for want of a better term, have come to be called post-colonial. All literary or cultural labels are questionable to some extent, and 'post-colonial' is no exception. Indeed, nothing is more likely to enrage certain writers than to hear themselves described as 'post-colonial'. Who can blame them? To write is usually an attempt to express the particularity of your self or your situation, an attempt to engage an audience with what you have to say. To find yourself then lumped together with authors from around the globe whose only connection with you appears to be that they also happen to use one of the world languages, and come from a country once colonized, is not going to leave you with the feeling of being attended to for what *you* wrote, or the way you chose to write it.

As the novelist Nayantara Sahgal remarked to the Silver Jubilee Conference of the Association for Commonwealth Literature and Language Studies at the University of Kent, Canterbury, in August 1989:

First we were colonials, and now we seem to be post-colonials. So is 'post-colonial' the new Anno Domini from which events are to be everlastingly measured? My own awareness as a writer reaches back to x-thousand BC, at the very end of which measureless timeless time the British came, and stayed, and left. And now they're gone, and their residue is simply one more layer added to the layer upon layer of Indian consciousness. Just one more.[1]

Yet that residue, that additional layer of British colonial culture, *is* there, and it has shaped the thematic and formal preoccupations of Sahgal's novels. What she is resisting is the assumption that this is the only, or indeed always the most important thing to notice about her work. Sahgal is a writer interested in the complexities of time and history; as such, she is also concerned to oppose the reductionism implicit in periodizing labels such as 'post-colonial'. Yet her claim upon the historical sense itself implies the importance of the label. To read and respond to her work with understanding is to acknowledge, amongst other things, the intricate and intriguing ways in which the colonial inheritance operates in her specific context.

In its simplest, and indeed most familiar meaning, the hyphenated term 'post-colonial' means post, or after, the colonial period. It has its obvious and widely accepted use as a way of indicating something that happened after the end of formal colonization; hence, in this context, it can be taken to refer to the writings which emerged in the post-colonial period. Yet that is not as straightforward a matter as it seems: at what point, for example, can one reasonably say South Africa became 'post-colonial'? The Union of 1910 marked the country's formal release by Britain into self-governing status; but the white Afrikaner Nationalists thought of the country's departure from the Commonwealth in 1961 as a more final marker of its independence, which they identified as their own independence from British influence; while most South Africans nowadays think of the achievement of multiracial, democratic elections in 1994 as the turning-point at which the colonial structures of the past – reinforced during the postwar period with unique ferocity by the apartheid system – were at last being dismantled. Does this mean that it is inappropriate to call any literary product from before that *annus mirabilis* post-colonial?

I will return to the question of South Africa later in this book. The point is that as soon as you begin to pursue the relevance and applicability of 'post-colonial', you run into – not just difficulties, but questions. However, this is also what makes using the term worthwhile. 'Post-colonial' is useful because the questions it raises are large, and important. It carries with it the implication that what we are talking about has to do with large-scale historical phenomena, phenomena involving shifting power relationships between different parts of the world, as well as between people within particular territories. It demands a kind of double awareness: of the colonial inheritance as it continues to operate within a specific culture, community or country; and of the changing relations between these cultures, communities and countries in the modern world. For those interested in the literary mediation of social process and change, this opens up a wider range of study – on an international as well as national and personal scale – than is usual.

It provincializes much of what passes for the latest critical or theoretical fashion.

How did the term arise? The OED records the first use of 'post-colonial' in a British newspaper article of 1959, referring to India, the jewel in the crown of Empire, which achieved independence in 1947; since when 'post-colonial' has referred mainly to the former colonized areas of Asia and Africa as they became self-governing states during the 1950s and 1960s – states as different yet related by their pasts as, say, Ghana and Singapore, or Pakistan and Sierra Leone. More recently, 'post-colonial' has come to be thought appropriate, because of the implication that the colonial experience persists despite the withdrawal of political control, as a result of the continuing strategic and economic power of the former colonizers, the new global dispositions which keep groups of poorer states in thrall; and because, as Sahgal admits, however minimal the impact of empire upon a particular people in the long perspective, it has always left its imprint.

This development of meaning has led critics and theorists to shift the terms of debate, from a fairly straightforward notion of the post-colonial as a linear historical development, towards a much broader and more varied sense of the term as a marker of historical and cultural change. One such change has been the decline of Britain as a world power since the last world war – a decline marked by an increasing preoccupation with domestic affairs, and a disillusion with the country's former imperial role. It is often argued that, while losing political and economic leadership, Britain has maintained a certain cultural predominance through such institutions as the Commonwealth, a loose collection of countries which before 1947 formed part of the British Empire; and by the growth of English as a world language. But, since the early 1960s, British influence within the Commonwealth has also declined, and its focus has switched towards its European continental neighbours; while the spread of English has had more to do with US power than British.

These facts are familiar, but they help explain the tunnel vision of much UK creative writing and its attendant critics, to the extent that even apparently subversive thinkers such as the Marxist Terry Eagleton, who aim to undermine the traditionally accepted 'canon' of literary works, still silently assume the only texts worth discussing are those produced solely within the British Isles, if not also by dead white males. Eagleton's recently revised *Literary Theory* (1996) admits the two areas most conspicuously absent from the earlier (1982) book, 'feminist criticism' and 'post-colonial theory' in an Afterword, without so much as a place in his Bibliography for the latter. There is of course nothing wrong with continuing to interest yourself in the familiar 'classics' of the English literary tradition, continuing to read, enjoy and study all those great, so-called canonical works by Shakespeare, Milton, Keats, the Brontës and Dickens. But these works require a new sense of their place in the changing world, the modern multicultural world of today, if they are to retain their freshness and relevance; and there are also strong arguments for attending to the torrent of creative writing which has emerged in English from around the world. Umberto Eco has suggested it takes twenty years for an idea to penetrate beyond the specialized group in which it originates. This may explain how it is that the writings of left-leaning Oxbridge critics such as Eagleton, or indeed his mentor Raymond Williams (both from non-metropolitan, 'peripheral' backgrounds, in fact) who did most to challenge establishment views from within, concentrated their analyses upon the familiar monuments of English literary expression.

Williams did once respond to creative writing from outside the familiar territory, in *The Country and the City* (1973), where the classic example of such writing, Chinua Achebe's *Things Fall Apart* (1958), received a sympathetic, brief critique. Achebe's own penetrating and influential (outside Oxbridge and London) critical essays on, for example, 'Colonialist criticism' (1974) were, as they often still are, ignored. A footnote to Eagleton's Afterword on 'post-colonial theory' refers us to the three most well-known representatives of 'post-colonial' theorizing (too abstract and general to be called criticism), Edward Said, Gayatri Spivak and Homi Bhabha, the authors, respectively, of the influential *Orientalism* (first published 1978); *In Other Worlds: Essays on Cultural Politics* (1987) and *The Post-Colonial Critic* (1990); and *The Location of Culture* (1994) – to all of whom I shall return. He also refers to his Oxford colleague Robert Young, whose *White Mythologies: Writing History and the West* (1990) has little if anything to do with literary texts, but offers a critique of Western historiography from Hegel and Marx to – again, Said, Spivak and Bhabha, who have by now become the three police officers of the post-colonial.

Eagleton's scathing summary of what he thus narrowly defines as 'post-colonial discourse' confirms its derivation from global historical developments such as the collapse of the European empires and their replacement by American hegemony, alongside an increase in mass migrations, and the creation of multicultural societies. But, he argues, the presence of this discourse has led to a politics in which issues of race, language and identity obscure the 'vital material conditions which different ethnic groups have in common'.[2] He aligns himself with Aijaz Ahmad's bluntly Marxist *In Theory: Classes, Nations, Literatures* (1992), in which post-colonial theory is viewed as the creation of a class fraction of guilt-ridden Western intellectuals and their 'Third World' incorporated colleagues (Ahmad himself meanwhile taught in the USA before returning to India), who recycle 'primary' cultural products from abroad for their own consumption, while neglecting more 'independent' local literatures in Urdu or Zulu.

There is an obvious truth in this position, whatever its origins. The best anyone can do, however, is work critically from their own position. Mine is derived from that of the radical thinker from Martinique and Algeria, Frantz Fanon (1925–61), who observed that 'Marxist analysis should always be slightly stretched' when dealing with the colonial problem; 'stretched' being a nicely ironic understatement.[3] As A. Sivanandan, a Sri Lankan long settled in the UK, has pointed out, 'Marxism, after all, was formulated in a European context and must, on its own showing, be Eurocentric'; hence for European Marxists to understand fully the 'burden of blackness, they require the imagination and feeling systematically denied them by their culture'.[4] Where to find the sources of that imagination and feeling? Among the creative writings and other cultural products which address the issue of 'difference', without losing the particularity and presence generalized out of existence by many so-called 'theorists'. Edward Said is one of those who attends to the voices of writers whose availability and quality should long ago have alerted those claiming to have an interest in knowing where we are, and who we are, in the world today. But his most extended development of the subject in *Culture and Imperialism* (1993), for all its range and brilliance, focuses upon the earlier writings of the colonial era, from Austen to Dickens, from Conrad to Kipling. My own focus is more recent, and questions that canon: not merely in theory, but in practice, through particular analyses.

If literature is more than an escapist pastime, then it should be understood to offer a testimony to what concerns us as alive and thoughtful people hurtling towards the second millennium, when we will all be linked together by forms of communication and politics which we will not be able to grasp without a grasp of the present, and the past – including the colonial past.

In this sense, it may be appropriate to consider all the writings which have emerged since colonization began as post-colonial. Influential critics, such as the authors of the first 'theorized' account of the subject, Bill Ashcroft, Gareth Griffiths and Helen Tiffin's *The Empire Writes Back* (Routledge, 1989), have taken the first writings from settler colonies of the seventeenth century to mark the start of the 'writing back' process, which they assume the most important aspect of the 'post-colonial'. But, as Laura Chrisman and Patrick Williams point out in their Introduction to a more recent anthology, this presumes a seamless, homogenized continuity of historical process which is highly questionable.[5] Like them, I prefer to distinguish 'colonial' and 'post-colonial', so as to start off by respecting the range and historical and geographical specificity of the associated forms of discourse, since after all, there _was_ (and continues to be) a sea change in power relations within cultures becoming independent of the colonizer.

Of course there is overlap and continuity, and no boundary is secure or impermeable here. Above all, the persistence of 'neo-colonial' forms of control across and within national boundaries makes it dangerous to over-emphasize the changes attendant upon independence. The writings that I focus on are relatively recent, because these seem to me to offer the survival kit for the twenty-first century that we need – 'we' including all of us aware of the accelerated connections between every part of the world linked as much by economic and technological change as by the politics of modernity. These writings deal with pressing matters of language, race, gender, history and identity, in terms of the peculiarly felt and shaped particularity which it is the special genius of literary forms to offer. It is my purpose to show that despite the problematic status of the term 'post-colonial', the writings it foregrounds and the issues it raises, introduce readers to new and exciting texts and vital contemporary debates, while suggesting a particular perspective upon them. For this reason, I place less emphasis upon the post-colonial reading of earlier, canonized texts, like _The Tempest_ or _Robinson Crusoe_, to name two obvious examples, or upon the resuscitation of the neglected writers of Empire, such as Meadows Taylor, Thoru Dutt or even Kipling (to take 'just' the Indian subconti-nent), a job which is nowadays being well enough done by others. On one level, my use of 'post-colonial' is simply an acknowledgement of its increasing currency in contemporary literary and cultural theory. But it is also because I believe that, whatever its limitations, the implicit claims of the term are of importance to anyone interested in literature and the arts today. And of course, I am offering my own particular spin upon it.

### _Changing Perspective:_ Things Fall Apart

At the risk of grossly oversimplifying, then, I would say that the basic claim implied by the use of 'post-colonial' in relation to literature is twofold: on the one hand, it carries with it the intention to promote, even celebrate the 'new literatures' which have emerged over this century from the former colonial territories; and on the other, it asserts the need to analyse and resist continuing colonial attitudes.

The term implies a shift of perspective on the part of writers and readers.

It is a shift which the Nigerian writer Chinua Achebe has very clearly identified. This is what he says about how he first came to write:

> The Nationalist movement in British West Africa after the Second World War brought about a mental revolution which began to reconcile us to ourselves. It suddenly seemed that we too might have a story to tell. 'Rule Britannia!' to which we had marched so unselfconsciously on Empire Day now stuck in our throat.
>
> At the university I read some appalling novels about Africa (including Joyce Cary's much praised *Mister Johnson*) and decided that the story we had to tell could not be told for us by anyone else no matter how gifted or well intentioned.[6]

Why did Achebe find novels like Joyce Cary's *Mister Johnson* appalling? First published in 1939, *Mister Johnson* depicts with great comic zest the life of a semi-educated clerk who helps his white district officer to build a road in remote northern Nigeria in the name of progress, only to end up shot like a dog. It was an advance upon the belittling stereotype of black people to be found in earlier fictions of Africa, such as Rider Haggard's *King Solomon's Mines* (1885) or even Conrad's *Heart of Darkness* (1899), for all the latter's dismay at the impact of Belgian imperialism in the Congo. But Cary's novel, although based (like these other works) on the author's first-hand experience in Africa, could not tell, in Achebe's repeated phrase, the story the Africans themselves had to tell. It is by listening to this story, that readers may change their perspective, their sense of what counts in literature today.

As Achebe's remarks indicate, until the withdrawal of colonial rule, the colonized seemed to accept that they were always the objects of someone else's story, indeed, someone else's history. It was precisely the project of *Things Fall Apart* to resist and reject this assumption; by telling the story of the colonized, to retrieve their history. And more than that: by retrieving their history to regain an identity. This is why autobiography has been a favoured subgenre among the 'new' African (and indeed Caribbean) writers; and it is an important and complex element in *Things Fall Apart*, of which the author said that 'although I did not set about it consciously in that solemn way', the novel was 'an act of atonement with my past, a ritual return and homage of a prodigal son'.[7]

The novel recounts events that took place in Achebe's grandfather's lifetime, towards the end of the nineteenth century, when white missionaries first came into close contact with the Igbo people of eastern Nigeria. This man's son, Achebe's father, was converted to Christianity, also taking on the Christian name Isaac. Isaac Achebe thereafter became a school-teacher and evangelist, while many relatives and neighbours remained attached to Igbo custom and belief – as some continue to do. Achebe was, as he puts it himself, a man 'born into two cultures'. What, then, does his writing look like? What distinguishes *Things Fall Apart* from that Cary novel? To answer these questions, it is worth looking closely at their opening paragraphs for a moment:

> The young women of Fada, in Nigeria, are well known for beauty. They have small, neat features and their backs are not too hollow.
>
> One day at the ferry over Fada river, a young clerk called Johnson came to take passage. The ferryman's daughter, Bamu, was a local beauty, with skin as pale and glistening as milk chocolate, high, firm breasts, round, strong arms. She could throw a twenty-foot pole with that perfect grace which was necessary to the act, if the pole was not to throw her. Johnson sat admiring her with a grin of pleasure and called out compliments, 'What a pretty girl you are'.
>
> Bamu said nothing. She saw Johnson was a stranger. Strangers are still rare in Fada bush and they are received with doubt. This is not surprising, because in Fada history all strangers have brought trouble; war, disease, or bad magic. Johnson is not only a stranger by accent, but by colour. He is as black as a stove, almost a pure Negro, with short nose and full, soft lips. He is young, perhaps seventeen, and seems half-grown. His neck, legs and arms are much too long and thin for his small body, as narrow as a skinned rabbit's. He is loose-jointed like a boy, and sits with his knees up to his nose, grinning at Bamu over the stretched white cotton of his trousers. He smiles with the delighted expression of a child looking at a birthday table and says, 'Oh, you are too pretty – a beautiful girl'.[8]

Okonkwo was well known throughout the nine villages and even beyond. His fame rested on solid personal achievements. As a young man of eighteen he had brought honour to his village by throwing Amalinze the Cat. Amalinze was the great wrestler who for seven years was unbeaten, from Umuofia to Mbaino. He was called the Cat because his back would never touch the earth. It was this man that Okonkwo threw in a fight which the old men agreed was one of the fiercest since the founder of their town engaged a spirit of the wild for seven days and seven nights.

The drums beat and the flutes sang and the spectators held their breath. Amalinze was a wily craftsman, but Okonkwo was as slippery as a fish in water. Every nerve and every muscle stood out on their arms, on their backs and their thighs, and one almost heard them stretching to breaking point. In the end Okonkwo threw the Cat.

That was many years ago, twenty years or more, and during this time Okonkwo's fame had grown like a bushfire in the harmattan. He was tall and huge, and his bushy eyebrows and wide nose gave him a very severe look. He breathed heavily, and it was said that, when he slept, his wives and children in their outhouses could hear him breathe. When he walked, his heels hardly touched the ground and he seemed to walk on springs, as if he was going to pounce on somebody. And he did pounce on people quite often. He had a slight stammer and whenever he was angry and could not get his words out quickly enough, he would use his fists. He had no patience with unsuccessful men. He had had no patience with his father.[9]

At first glance, the opening of Cary's novel may seem fairly sympathetic, offering a value system foreign to its presumed reader at once: 'The young women of Fada, in Nigeria, are well known for beauty.' Well known, we take it, in Fada and the surrounding territory. And yet, by going on to describe the ferryman's daughter in terms of her 'skin as pale and glistening as milk chocolate' and her 'high, firm breasts', the narrator invites (and constructs) a European, heterosexual male reader to share that system of values on terms that incorporate it within his own. The young woman is like a European delicacy and, note, not too black. Johnson, on the other hand, we are invited to think of as a pathetic clown, 'like a child', his body resembling 'a skinned rabbit's' and, 'as black as a stove'. An idealizing, exoticizing tone has crept into the description of Bamu; Johnson is characterized in the equally stereotyping, but more patronizing tone of the amused European encountering a half-educated black man. Either way, the Africans are rendered as less than human, their history a matter of 'war, disease, or bad magic'.

By contrast, the opening of *Things Fall Apart* nowhere idealizes, exoticizes, belittles or undermines the values of the specific African culture it is describing. It is quietly but firmly positive about the world it is offering to its reader, confident that its (different) audience will understand, if not necessarily sympathize with, its values. Okonkwo's fame 'rested on solid personal achievements' the nature of which – bringing honour to his village by wrestling – is far from familiar in the culture which has produced the voice of Cary's narrator. In place of the presumption and arrogance of that narrator, we have here an accepting intimacy that does not – very important in the light of what's to come – preclude criticism. The overriding factor is that the perspective adopted by Achebe's narrator is *from within*: we are being introduced to the traditions, the way of life of a community by a voice that, apparently, belongs to it.

This is conveyed by a series of short, syntactically simple and repetitively structured sentences, and by the comparisons that reflect an oral rather than a literate culture. Okonkwo's fame has evidently been transmitted by word of mouth; Amalinze was 'called the Cat'; and 'the old men agreed' their wrestling-match was one of the fiercest since the founder of their town engaged a spirit of the wild 'for seven days and seven nights' – in other words, since the earliest times, whose history is transmitted as a myth or legend by the elderly men deputed to carry it on. The continuity of earthly and spiritual experience is implicitly accepted from the start; so, too, are such 'pagan' customs as a man having several wives. The narrator of the Cary passage invariably relates what is described in terms of Western cultural norms, confirmed by such detail as the 'milk chocolate' and 'birthday table' the reader is invited to think of in relation to Bamu and Mr Johnson; Okonkwo's fame, however, is compared with the growth 'of a bushfire in the harmattan' – a comparison from inside the world being described, reinforcing the reader's sense of close contact with another culture, and one that has its own frame of reference, yet which can be mediated to us by a narrator familiar with it. A colleague reading this passage for the first time thought 'harmattan' was a place; in the next paragraph but one, the narrator – characteristically in this novel – explains, as if merely in passing, that it is a cold and dry wind 'blowing down from the north'. It descends from the Sahara each year during the dry season, drying everything out so that fires are frequent.

### Language, Audience and Genre

According to Achebe, his wife

> who teaches English in a boys' school, asked a pupil why he wrote about winter when he meant the harmattan. He said the other boys would call him a bushman if he did such a thing . . . I think it is part of my business to teach that boy that there is nothing disgraceful about the African weather, that the palm-tree is a fit subject for poetry.[10]

The choice of 'harmattan' in the opening of *Things Fall Apart* is a deliberate step towards overturning the assumptions of cultural and racial inferiority imposed by the colonizers and accepted by the colonized, a step towards showing that the African words, their languages, their ways of life, have their own integrity. But if 'harmattan' was not a new word for Nigerians, why should the text explain its meaning after its first introduction? Does this suggest that this novel was written *primarily* for an overseas audience, if not for the same audience as Cary's *Mister Johnson*?

This is an important question, and the immediate answer must be, yes. This appears to be confirmed by the fact that *Things Fall Apart* was first published in Britain, by a British publisher, Heinemann, at a price few Nigerians could afford – fifteen shillings; and at a time (1958, two years before independence) when the local market for novels was severely limited – that is, even for novels whose status as set books in the colonial school system ensured some readership. Only a tiny minority of Nigeria's enormous, multilingual and multicultural society was literate in English. But the answer is not quite so straightforward.

Achebe's manifest concern that Nigerian schoolchildren should not feel embarrassed into avoiding 'local' usages such as 'harmattan' implies that he did – and does – have a local audience in view; and he has subsequently repeatedly insisted on the writer's responsibility to his own society, whatever the difficulties. Further, the situation of the writer in English in Africa has been changing rapidly since the first appearance of *Things Fall Apart* in an expensive hardback abroad: shortly after Nigerian independence in 1960, a cheap paperback edition appeared and then, in 1964, it became the first novel by an African writer to be included in the syllabus for African secondary schools throughout the English-speaking parts of the continent (except South Africa). The following year, Achebe reported proudly that the pattern of sales of the paperback edition (priced at five shillings) in the previous year had been: 'about 800 copies in Britain; 20,000 in Nigeria; and about 2,000 in all other places'.[11]

It is hard to overestimate Achebe's achievement. After instant acclaim at home and abroad, *Things Fall Apart* remains the most important novel in the development of 'new' African writing in English. The book's status has long become assured, it has won its author numerous prizes and awards, it has been translated and read worldwide, and it has become a point of reference for all subsequent novels of Africa, if not also of the English-speaking diaspora. This is not only a function of the way in which it registers the familiar experiences of colonial or ex-colonial societies, although that is central to it; but also of its production and acceptance in the post-independence world. Its initial reception abroad, especially in the UK, was a key contributory factor, despite a condescending emphasis in the early reviews upon its 'simplicity' and documentary or anthropological interest

– an emphasis perhaps encouraged by the author's next, and weaker novel, *No Longer At Ease* (1960), an uneasy satire upon 1950s Nigeria. But the dominant assumption about African writing in English at the time, even in left-wing magazines such as the *New Statesman*, was a condescending amazement that such 'new' writing should be so good.[12]

The word 'new' in this context is somewhat misleading. Achebe's novel was by no means the first African novel in English, much less the first prose by an African about Africa. The first English prose by an African may be found in the *Letters* (1787) of Ignatius Sancho, a former slave and Mayfair grocer who became a friend of Laurence Sterne, David Garrick and Samuel Johnson. More remarkable is the *Interesting Narrative of the Life of Olaudah Equiano* (1789), like Achebe an Igbo from West Africa, who, after buying his freedom, travelled widely as a merchant seaman, gentleman's valet and, finally, surgeon's assistant on an expedition to the Arctic. The first novel by a black African was probably South African Solomon Plaatje's *Mhudi*, written about 1917 and published by the local missionary press in 1930. 'Probably', because there may be other candidates yet unknown, and because, depending on your definition of novel, the first may be *Ethiopia Unbound* (1911), part-autobiography, part-prophecy, part-fiction by the Ghanaian lawyer-statesman E. Casely-Hayford. The first extended prose fiction from West Africa came much later: Nigerian Amos Tutuola's wild allegory, *The Palm-Wine Drinkard* (1952), quickly succeeded by country-man Cyprian Ekwensi's more realistic *People of the City* (1954).

Rummaging in the lumber-rooms of literary history reminds us that works like *Things Fall Apart* do not spring fully fledged out of nowhere, and helps to raise the point that there is a question about what is meant by 'novel' here. The realist novel came into existence at a particular period in Western European history and as such the genre was shaped by the cultural and literary assumptions of that time – which were, of course, not the same as those of African or Asian peoples, then or later. This is certainly not to say that story-telling or narrative is in any sense a European invention, as some Nigerian critics, such as Chinweizu,[13] have been quick to point out. Yet it is clearly one result of colonization – when societies and cultures intermingle – that the literary forms, like the languages, of the colonizers have been adopted. How, precisely, such adoption comes about depends upon the specific situation of particular writers – including, inevitably, their education.

Given the colonial British education system in pre-independence Nigeria, and the lack of interest by the authorities in African writing, Achebe could not have read Plaatje's *Mhudi*, much less Equiano's auto-biography. Indeed, even today these works (both reprinted in recent decades) are only gradually becoming known outside specialist college or university departments. Yet they clearly anticipate some of the concerns of *Things Fall Apart*, especially its emphasis upon the depiction of a traditional society under pressure to change. The title of Achebe's novel comes from Yeats's 'The Second Coming', a poem familiar within the modernist Western literary tradition as a lament for the passing of order and innocence from the world. But Achebe's treatment of the pre-colonial order is more even-handed than this suggests. His novel is set in the forest area of inland south-eastern Nigeria towards the end of the nineteenth century, when Europeans (mainly British) were just beginning to penetrate inland, although they had long occupied the coast. The Igbo-speaking people occupied a large area, organized into groups of related villages in a democratic system based on subsistence farming, and their lives were lived within a highly formal framework of family, social, cultural and religious bonds, of which respect for ancestors played a crucial part.

Part I of the novel shows one community, Umuofia, a group of nine related villages, in the period just before the arrival of the whites. Although the use of firearms and certain crops had preceded the whites inland, none of the villagers had seen a white man – variously alluded to by the villagers as a leper or a man without toes (i.e. wearing shoes). Their society is depicted as stable, governed by traditions and customs such as the settlement of matrimonial disputes by the elders and the *egwugwu* (masked representatives of the ancestral spirits), and Okonkwo is a man who has made himself a success in terms of its values. Thus, when there is a dispute with a neighbouring village, he is sent as ambassador and becomes guardian of the young hostage, Ikemefuna, given to the clan by way of reparation. After Okonkwo accidentally kills a fellow clansman, he is exiled to his mother's village. During his seven years there, he learns that white missionaries have arrived in the district, first converting outcasts and others who, like his estranged son Nwoye, have reason to feel dissatisfied with Igbo society. When at last Okonkwo returns, he finds that a court, mission-school and hospital have been established by a missionary who accepts that a head-on clash with Igbo ways will be fruitless. But this man is replaced by a narrow-minded type, who allows one of his more enthusiastic converts to commit the unpardonable crime of unmasking an *egwugwu* during a traditional ceremony, with inevitably explosive results: the mission-church is burnt down, several leading citizens, including Okonkwo are detained, and the community fined heavily. The citizens are released after being beaten and humiliated by the District Commissioner's men, who are Igbos from distant tribes, speaking a different dialect; they call a great assembly to discuss what is to be done, and when the Commissioner's men arrive to stop the meeting, Okonkwo, who has been advocating violence, kills one of the messengers. The following day, when men arrive to arrest him, they find he has preferred the shameful course of hanging himself, rather than submit to the white man's justice. The novel concludes with the title of the book the Commissioner decides he will write, including 'a reasonable paragraph' about the incident: *The Pacification of the Primitive Tribes of the Lower Niger.*

## Culture and Identity

The main subject of Achebe's novel is less the individual make-up of the Igbo people, although that is important, than the way in which character merges with and is defined by the community, the culture, as it reacts to change. The longest scene in the opening chapter describes how Okonkwo's 'weak', flute-playing father Unoka dealt with a friend he owed money.

> One day a neighbour called Okoye came in to see him. He was reclining on a mud bed in his hut playing on the flute. He immediately rose and shook hands with Okoye, who then unrolled the goatskin which he carried under his arm, and sat down. Unoka went into an inner room and soon returned with a small wooden disc containing kola nut, some alligator pepper and a lump of white chalk.
> 'I have kola,' he announced when he sat down, and passed the disc over to his guest.
> 'Thank you. He who brings kola brings life. But I think you ought to break it,' replied Okoye passing back the disc.
> 'No, it is for you, I think,' and they argued like this for a few moments before Unoka accepted the honour of breaking the kola. Okoye, meanwhile, took the lump of chalk, drew some lines on the floor, and then painted his big toe. As he broke the kola, Unoka prayed to their ancestors for life and health, and for protection against their enemies . . . Okoye was also a musician. He played on the *ogene*. But he was not a failure like Unoka. He had a large barn full of yams and he had three wives. And now he was going to take the Idemili title, the third highest in the land. It was a very expensive ceremony and he was gathering all his resources together. That was in fact the reason why he had come to see Unoka. He cleared his throat and began:
> 'Thank you for the kola. You may have heard of the title I intend to take shortly.'

> Having spoken plainly so far, Okoye said the next half a dozen sentences in proverbs. Among the Ibo the art of conversation is regarded very highly, and proverbs are the palm oil with which words are eaten.[14]

The meticulous, minute account of ceremonies in the first part of the book brings out what is at stake when this society is threatened by change, and could not be further from the dark pagan mysteries, the primitive chaos, of European myth and stereotype concerning Africa – summed up earlier by Conrad's Marlow, who glimpses village life beside the Congo thus:

> a burst of yells, a whirl of black limbs, a mass of hands clapping, of feet stamping, of bodies swaying, of eyes rolling, under the droop of heavy and motionless foliage. The steamer toiled along slowly on the edge of a black and incomprehensible frenzy . . . It was unearthly and the men were – No, they were not inhuman. Well, you know, that was the worst of it – this suspicion of their not being inhuman.[15]

Even if Conrad does not fully endorse this vision, it is striking how the mere possibility of kinship to the howling savages reveals an image of Africa as 'the other world', the 'antithesis of Europe and therefore of civilization', where 'man's vaunted intelligence and refinement are finally mocked by triumphant bestiality', as Achebe put it in a bitter attack.[16] What we are offered instead in *Things Fall Apart* is an image of different, but human beings: engaged in the custom, the 'ceremony of innocence'. Yeats's lines are used ironically, on the assumption that they derive from a European vision of order at home and anarchy abroad, whereas the novel shows Europeans order abroad.

But things are not quite so straightforward - as far as Yeats as well as Achebe are concerned. Critics and reviewers of *Things Fall Apart* have long found it possible to respond favourably to the novel's reversal of cultural stereotyping, and to commend its achievement as an anti-colonial work. Rewriting history involves a more comprehensive, a more objective perspective. This is achieved by presenting not simply the alternative stereotype, of precolonial society as somehow not prey to the usual ills that flesh is heir to. One of the ways Achebe manages this is by the construction of his narrator, whose position is far from easy to determine. 'Among the Ibo the art of conversation is regarded very highly and proverbs are the palm oil with which words are eaten': very neat, using a proverb to explain the proverbial, oral nature of Igbo conversation, summing up a position simultaneously involved with and at a distance from its material, the verb tense implying that this is true in the narrative present as well as in the more distant past of the narrative. Towards the end of the opening chapter, we are informed that when Unoka died he had taken no title and was heavily in debt. 'Any wonder then that his son Okonkwo was ashamed of him? Fortunately, among these people a man was judged according to his worth and not according to the worth of his father. Okonkwo was clearly cut out for great things'.[17] The final sentence is only straightforward on a first reading, as the reader realizes retrospectively when the slowly looming irony of Okonkwo's tragic fate bears down upon us – most notably when, in chapter 7, we learn that his exaggerated masculine strength, developed in compensation for his father's feminine 'weakness', leads to the killing of the boy hostage who has become like a son to him.

### The Gender Agenda

If we have come to accept the clan's rules to the extent that we understand why Ikemefuna has to be sacrificed, we also realize that the situation has been set up to underline the inflexibility, and hence vulnerability, of the masculine clan ethic to which Okonkwo adheres so closely. When a friend brings the Oracle's fateful ruling on the boy's fate, Ikemefuna, Okonkwo, and his elder son Nwoye (whom he has begun to alienate with his fierce ways), are shown in one of their happier moments, crunching locusts. The journey into the forest that follows is represented with haunting power – the elusive sound of a peaceful dance from a distant clan rising and falling with the wind as the little group trudge on in silence. The unexpected deepening of tone is amplified as we enter Ikemefuna's innocent, unsus-pecting consciousness – his initial uneasiness quelled by thinking of his foster father behind him, and happily anticipating return to his original home with a childhood song (given in untranslated Igbo).

> One of the men behind him cleared his throat. Ikemefuna looked back, and the man growled at him to go on and not stand looking back. The way he said it sent cold fear down Ikemefuna's back. His hands trembled vaguely on the black pot he carried. Why had Okonkwo withdrawn to the rear? Ikemefuna felt his legs melting under him. And he was afraid to look back.
> As the man who had cleared his throat drew up and raised his matchet, Okonkwo looked away. He heard the blow. The pot fell and broke in the sand. He heard Ikemefuna cry, 'My father, they have killed me!' as he ran towards him. Dazed with fear, Okonkwo drew

his matchet and cut him down. He was afraid of being thought weak.[18]

This is comparable with the great tragic moments in Sophocles or Shakespeare in its plainness of utterance, and the complex resonances it sets up, marking the beginning of the end for Okonkwo, and for the culture to which he belongs.

It also clarifies the book's resistance towards the masculine ethos with which Okonkwo's act is identified. If it is true that, as Kirsten Holst Petersen has argued, the 'woman's issue' has been ignored in the fight against imperialism, or worse, it has been 'conscripted in the service of dignifying the past and restoring African self-confidence'[19] – a point to which I shall return – is this a fair criticism of works such as Achebe's, which Petersen singles out as an example of such patriarchal nostalgia? *Things Fall Apart* also brings out the appalling consequences of ignoring or devaluing women, and maintaining rigid gender divisions. A less well-known part of the narrative recounts the life-threatening illness of Ezinma, the only child and daughter of Okonkwo's first wife, who married him before his rise in wealth and stature. Her father thinks 'She should have been a boy', in contrast to Nwoye whom he despises as effeminate for preferring the 'women's stories' of skill and endurance, rather than the men's, of war and death. When Ezinma's mother defies the Oracle on behalf of her daughter, in contrast to Okonkwo's zealous acceptance of its ruling on Ikemefuna, the gender dimension of his and the clan's tragedy is clarified. There is more to the structure of this narrative than some feminists have given credit; although the general issue remains. The dominance of the male perspective overall seems to me undeniable.

In this sense, *Things Fall Apart* is of its time: the time of realist legitimation of nationalist, anti-colonial striving. It would be anachronistic to expect it to confront feminist, or gender issues in a sophisticated way; something which Achebe's self-consciously modernist later novel, *Anthills of the Savannah* (1987), does superbly, offering women a role not only as subjects, but as central protagonists, while transforming the given form of fictional narrative he himself established earlier in order to do so. Achebe's continuing concern to respond to his country's present, rather than its past, is ultimately evident as much in the kind of novel he writes, as in his persistent themes, of tradition versus change, of the individual versus the community – above all, in his interest in engaging contemporaries with the complex, shifting inheritance of the post-colonial.

## Summary

Literary texts such as *Things Fall Apart*, which it is a major aim of post-colonial criticism to celebrate, make us aware of how ethnocentric the reader's own position is in the modern world. If readers are to gain an understanding and appreciation of such texts, acknowledging their interest in matters of history, language, identity, race, gender and culture, then, wherever we start from, we may begin to understand our own perspectives and situations better too. The rhetoric of understanding encourages a new sense of what makes literature and its study important today.

### Notes

1  Nayantara Sahgal, 'The schizophrenic imagination', *From Commonwealth to Post-Colonial*, ed. Anna Rutherford (Dangaroo, 1992), p. 30.
2  See Terry Eagleton, *Literary Theory: An Introduction* (Blackwell, 1996), p. 205.
3  See Frantz Fanon, *The Wretched of the Earth*, tr. C. Farrington (Penguin, 1967), p. 31.
4  A. Sivanandan, *A Different Hunger: Writings on Black Resistance* (Penguin, 1982), p. 94.
5  Laura Chrisman and Patrick Williams, *Colonial Discourse and Post-Colonial Theory: A Reader* (Harvester Wheatsheaf, 1993), p. 13.
6  Chinua Achebe, 'Named for Victoria, Queen of England' (1973), in *Morning Yet on Creation Day: Essays* (Heinemann, 1975), p. 70.
7  Ibid., p. 70.
8  Joyce Cary, *Mister Johnson*, first publ. 1939 (Penguin, 1965), p. 13.
9  Chinua Achebe, *Things Fall Apart*, first publ. 1958 (Heinemann, 1986), p. 3.
10  Chinua Achebe, 'The Novelist as Teacher', 1965, in *Morning Yet on Creation Day*, p. 44.
11  Ibid., p. 42.
12  See, for example, Keith Waterhouse, 'New novels', *New Statesman*, 17 September 1960, p. 398, where he remarked that 'simplicity is all we ask for in the African novel'.
13  See Chinweizu et al., *Toward the Decolonization of African Literature: African Fiction and Poetry and Their Critics* (KPI Ltd, 1985).
14  Achebe, *Things Fall Apart*, pp. 4–5.
15  Joseph Conrad, *Heart of Darkness*, first publ. 1899, ed. Joseph Kimborough (New York and Norton, 1988), p. 37.
16  From a 1975 lecture amended and reprinted as Chinua Achebe, 'An image of Africa: racism in Conrad's *Heart of Darkness*', pp. 251–62 (p.252). Achebe there called Conrad 'a thoroughgoing racist', which earned him much critical

opprobium; he subsequently told me 'I could withdraw "thoroughgoing"' (personal interview, London, 28 June 1989).

17 Achebe, *Things Fall Apart*, p. 6.
18 Ibid., pp. 42–3.
19 Kirsten Holst Petersen, 'First things first: problems of a feminist approach to African literature', *Kunapipi* 6, 3 (1984), in *The Post-Colonial Studies Reader*, eds Bill Ashcroft, Gareth Griffiths, Helen Tiffin (Routledge, 1995), p. 253. See also Florence Stratton, *Contemporary African Literature and the Politics of Gender* (Routledge, 1994), chapters 1 and 2.

# Part I

*Studying Post-Colonial Literatures*

# 2

## *History*

The settler makes history; his life is an epoch, an Odyssey
Frantz Fanon, The Wretched of the Earth (1961), 1967

I met History once, but he ain't recognize me,
A parchment Creole
Derek Walcott, 'The Schooner Flight', 1979

But he shall also have
cycles of history
outnumbering the guns of supremacy
Arthur Nortje, 'Native's Letter', 1973

This part is about the basic issues involved in studying post-colonial literatures. Getting to grips with these literatures involves getting to grips with three basic issues: history, language and theory. History has to do with context; language with medium; and theory, with approach. I will devote a chapter to each.

### *Making History*

Let's start with history. There is a well-known rhyme which begins:

> In fourteen-hundred and ninety-two
> Columbus sailed the ocean blue

It was written by the American poetess, Winifred Sackville Stonier Jr, whose name has not survived as well as her little ditty. Generations of schoolchildren have learnt it to help them remember the date. And in 1992, publishers and the media worldwide set themselves up for what was meant to be the largest anniversary splash ever: the 500th anniversary of the arrival of Columbus in the New World. At least ten books came out in the UK alone, and a veritable flood of articles, television series, films, festivals and other celebrations emerged around the globe – including a World Expo event in Spain, whose monarchy funded the Genoese explorer, and a $40million monument in the Dominican Republic, formerly part of Hispaniola, one of the first places he 'discovered'.

We all know Columbus arrived in the Americas when he did. But he wasn't the first European to arrive in the Americas – the Vikings got there before him; and some historians believe others preceded them. Further-more, the indigenous peoples already knew about Turtle Island – they'd been there since 30,000 years BC, if not earlier. Nor had Columbus found what he was sent to find – a new route to Asia, displacing the Portuguese, whose recent voyages round the southern tip of Africa and across the Indian Ocean had already shown the way to get silks and spices and all the other things badly wanted in Europe. To his dying day Columbus insisted that the 'new' continent was India, a belief still commemorated in the name of the West Indies – original home of the Caribs and Arawaks, whose own place names he took to be mispronunciations of place names in the East. When Columbus landed in Guanahani in the Bahamas he thought he had arrived in India, and so, as the novelist V.S. Naipaul has put it, he called the people 'Indians, and Indians they remained, walking Indian file through the Indian corn'.[1]

For someone like Naipaul – the grandson of indentured labourers brought from India to replace freed African slaves on the sugar plantations in Trinidad – Columbus seems at least partially responsible for what he calls his 'improbable', his 'colonial' identity: an 'East Indian' from the West Indies. It is an identity created by others, by Europeans like Columbus. Like those who succeeded him, Columbus was following a European dream, a Christian vision of being the first man, Adam naming the world. On his third voyage, dedicated to the Holy Trinity, he imagined he saw three hills on a new island: he promptly named it Trinidad. As Naipaul reminded readers of *The Loss of El Dorado* (1969) Columbus dreamt also of of gold. He believed he had found the mines of Solomon, the source of all the gold in the world. An indigenous Indian memory or legend added to the temptations for the Spaniards: of a chief who once a year was rolled in turpentine, covered in gold dust and who then dived into a lake – becoming el dorado, the gilded one. The dream of El Dorado, of a people and a place wealthy beyond anything previously experienced, always a step further on into the unknown, continues to grip the Western imagination, not least through its embodiment in Hollywood adventure films. What was being celebrated in 1992 was this complex mixture of imaginings, centred on the opening up of the world to European enterprise. And yet the impact of these imaginings upon those involved was far from imaginary.

Columbus's landfall at Guanahani and his further discoveries before returning triumphantly in 1493 to accept the prize for being first to see land (actually a member of his crew was first) led to a claim upon the peoples and territories of the New World by Europeans which was to end up with the death or enslavement of most of the original inhabitants, and the headlong exploitation of their resources. One in three of the indigenous population of Hispaniola were dead within two years of Columbus's arrival; in thirty years they had all been wiped out. What torture, disease and imprisonment did not achieve, mass suicide completed. Gaps in the local labour force were soon filled by slave labour from Africa; thereby initiating one of the worst aspects of European domination – the Atlantic slave trade.

The greed, violence and brutality of the conquest of Central America by the Spaniards offers another perspective upon the opening up of the world to the Europeans, a perspective which undermines the idea of an achievement deserving celebration. So it isn't too surprising to find that an 'anti-Columbus' campaign sprang up to coincide with the quinqennial celebrations in Europe and the Americas: to register not merely the inevitable disputes among historians about the details of Columbus's voyages and discoveries, but also the possibility of an alternative way of understanding what they mean at the end of the twentieth century. It's not easy to decide what Columbus's arrival in the New World means today: partly because we still live in a world shaped by the long colonial experience that arrival initiated; partly because, even if we understand that there is always more than one history, it is not so easy to enter into a new and unfamiliar one. And if we accept that an account of the colonization of the New World by the Spanish is not the same thing as an account of that process from the perspective of the colonized, there is also the point that it is different from later forms of European colonization in other parts of the world. Beyond dispute, however, is the fact of the spread of European power and culture, languages and literatures over the last five hundred years, and across the whole world; of which Columbus's voyages were the crucial early part.

This is not to ignore the immediately preceding Portuguese push around the Cape of Good Hope in search of spices and Christians on the Calicut coast. Rather, it is to identify the major factor in an unprecedented shift in global history, the results of which are still with us, even after decolonization. The spread of European power is one of the most astonishing features of modern world history – taking 'modern' to mean post-medieval. By 1800, some three hundred years after Columbus, European nations laid claim to more than half the world's land surface and, in varying degree, actually controlled about a third. Settler populations large enough to constitute new centres of civilization had developed in places as far apart as North America and South Africa; and almost everywhere else you could find European traders, merchants and missionaries. Only the interior of Africa was protected by disease and climate, although not for very long. It was during the hundred years after 1800 that Britain became the leading nation among those involved in this dramatic transformation of world relationships – a transformation based upon exploration, enterprise, government patronage and cultural (including technological) advantage.


### *Whose History?*


The other side to this story as it develops from exploration to trade and conquest reflects not only the possession by Europeans – and, increasingly, the British – of powerful motives and overwhelming advantages leading to their domination over the peoples of America, Asia and Africa; it also reflects the limitations of these other civilizations. Yet the limitations were far from obvious at first. The year 1492 also marks the defeat of Islam in Spain, and the dispersal of a culture which, ironically enough, had first brought the astronomy and mathematics upon which European navigational supremacy was based. Like the Arabs, the Mayas, Aztecs and Incas of Central and South America all had mature and complex civilizations – the Aztec capital Tenochtitlan (later Mexico City) was five times larger than Madrid at the time of Spanish conquest. The trading ventures of Akbar, the great Mogul emperor of India, were on a much grander scale than those of his contemporary Elizabeth I of England, who granted a charter to what became known as the English East India Company on 31 December 1600. Indeed, not only was Akbar more powerful than any European monarch of the time; as soldier, politician, hunter, painter and booklover, he was the complete 'renaissance man', his court more splendid than any in the West.

In Africa, a number of rich and ancient societies still flourished when Europeans began to arrive at the coasts; and although non-literate, these societies exhibited great confidence, coherence, moral and artistic vigour. Most of their towns lay beyond the observation of the West until the nineteenth century, when a different attitude towards African peoples prevailed – an attitude evident again in Conrad's *Heart of Darkness* (1899), which, for all its criticism of the Belgian exploitation of the Congo, shudders at every contact with indigenous people, depicted as demonic savages engaged in mysterious and peculiar rites. Yet the impressions of early Portuguese travellers to the Congo were of things strange and puzzling, rather than inviting contempt or any special sense of mystery:

> They ran into many surprising beliefs and superstitions, but few or none that seemed more disconcerting than others they could find at home. Victorious Congolese armies tended to see signs and ghostly symbols in the sky, yet there was nothing out of the way in that. The Portuguese themselves regularly saw angels, and so of course did other Europeans. More often than not they found it easy to accept the peoples of the Congo as natural equals and allies.[2]

The West African city of Benin, whose name belongs to some of the finest surviving sculptural artefacts in the world, was regarded by a Dutch visitor in 1602 as a great city, its dwellings, court and environment quite fairly compared with those of Amsterdam.[3] Viewing the early colonial past through the lens of later, predominantly Western, writings, obscures the existence of those civilizations and empires in South America, Asia, Africa and in the Arab world which flourished and often surpassed Europe in various ways until at least the sixteenth century and sometimes later.

Yet gradually, inevitably (with the inevitability of hindsight), it appears as if the inflexibility, weakness or ossification of these older feudal or slave-based empires, when brought into contact with the dynamic, emergent peoples of the new industrializing nation-states of north-west Europe, led to the spread of European, and especially British hegemony. 'Hegemony', rather than direct control: since, except in the Americas, where Spain and Portugal had established their rule from early on (and then lost it), it was not until the middle of the eighteenth century that European states or their representatives had the will or power to impose colonial rule over the rest of the world. Arab or Asian states continued to be their equals, even their superiors, in many respects, as some Europeans happily acknowledged – those mainly interested in exploiting existing trade links or collaborating with local suppliers, rather than, as happened during the nineteenth century, those who became part of that drive towards conquest and annexation, all too easily justified by contemporary evangelical and evolutionist notions of racial superiority. Even during the greatest spread of direct political control or administration, there was always also an important hinterland under semi-official or indirect European interference, where European manners and beliefs came to hold sway. This is especially important when considering the British Empire, which was always more of a cultural than a constitutional grouping.

The peak or climax of that Empire may be said to have occurred before its greatest extent in territorial terms. Jan (then James) Morris's brilliant if impressionistic three-volume account of the rise and fall of the British Empire (*Heaven's Command, Pax Britannica* and *Farewell the Trumpets*) situates the high-point at Queen Victoria's Diamond Jubilee of 1897, the celebration of which began when the Queen telegraphed this simple message from Buckingham Palace to almost every corner of the world: 'Thank my beloved people. May God bless them.' As Morris points out, the empire 'hitherto seen as a fairly haphazard accretion of possessions', now appeared to the British people to be settling into 'some gigantic pattern', distributing their power and values across the seas and continents, to the extent that 'they felt that their power was self-engendering, that they were riding a wave of destiny, sweeping them on to fulfilment'.[4] The new imperialism, as it is called, was a European phenomenon, the Western powers seeking expansion in the closing years of the nineteenth century to a degree previously unknown, leading to collisions and friction which were part of the slide towards the conflagration of 1914–18. But from the popular music-hall song which brought 'jingoism' into the English language, to the dum-dum bullet, from the Boy Scouts and cricket to sheep and steamships, courts and railways, the spread of British ways across the world seemed to themselves as to others, truly epic, and unique.

Equally unique, and characteristic, appeared to be the lack of uniformity amongst Britain's various possessions, dependencies, protectorates, Crown Colonies and dominions at the peak of Empire. At one end of the spectrum stood the great white self-governing colonies, semi-willingly released into semi-nationhood – Canada, the six Australian colonies, New Zealand, Cape Colony, Natal and Newfoundland. They were not fully independent, and Britain looked after security and foreign affairs. But they had their own parliaments, based on the British model, and could decide for themselves whether or not to go to war for Britain. Then came the Crown Colonies, like Gambia, Jamaica and Barbados, some ruled simply by a governor and his officials, others, with fully elected assemblies, although the governor could veto any legislation. Many territories were officially protectorates, run more or less like the Crown Colonies, but technically foreign countries, their citizens not British subjects. In three territories, including Rhodesia and Nigeria (and North Borneo), chartered companies were all-powerful, just as they had been earlier in by far the largest, and most sui generis of all, a kind of empire of its own: India.

The slow conquest of this, the largest and most important part of the British Empire, had begun as a matter of predatory and private exploitation, followed only gradually by moral and improving zeal, until the mixture of motives of the governing class were impossible to disentangle. D.K. Fieldhouse suggests that Britain's conquest of India changed the nature of the colonial enterprise, from 'the original self-governing settlement empire of America', to the 'polyglot and largely dependent empire of the nineteenth century'.[5] The American colonies were like Ireland, in that the settlers maintained a close and continuous connection with the metropolitan state, a relationship reproduced later by similar colonies in Canada, Australasia and South Africa; but by the nineteenth century the Empire was dominated by British involvement with territories with more resistant, independent or alien peoples than in the Americas. During the first (seventeenth- and eighteenth-century) phase of colonization, the empire included mainly English settlers, Amerindians and African slaves; once the American colonies had become independent, and British naval supremacy ensured the defeat of European competition, the move towards Asia and then Africa became irresistible. By the end of the nineteenth century most of the world belonged to a handful of great European powers, of which Britain was the greatest.

## The 'Other' View

From early on, some Europeans recognized the value of what their civilization was destroying; and some questioned, even opposed, the colonizing process. One of these was the conquistador turned priest, Bartolomé de Las Casas (1484–1576), whose *Short Account of the Destruction of the Indies* (first published in 1552) represented the first of many struggles by Christian missionaries and enlightened Europeans against the behaviour of their compatriots abroad; although Las Casas (who preserved and edited Columbus's diaries) also saw the Spanish conquest as a great opportunity for Christian conversion, and his revelations were later used as much for the purposes of anti-Spanish propaganda as to undermine the achievements of Europe. Even today, in our post-holocaust times, Las Casas makes chilling reading. His task, as he saw it, was to bear witness to the manner in which a trading and evangelizing mission had been transformed into genocide, the predominantly peaceful and friendly indigenous peoples treated worse than wild dogs, in the headlong rush for precious metals, land and power. When Cortés and his men made their way to Tenochtitlan, they were greeted by the great king Montezuma himself on a gold litter, who made the Spaniards welcome, only 'or so I am reliably informed by a number of eye-witnesses' to be imprisoned 'by a trick', while Cortés left to deal with a troublesome inferior. The garrison decided to stage a show of strength in Cortés's absence, 'and thereby boost the fear they inspired in the people', who had meanwhile organized fiestas of traditional dancing throughout the city.

> These dances are called in the local language *mitotes* (those typical of the islands being known as *areitos*), and since these dances are the typical form of entertainment among the people, they deck themselves out in all their best finery. And the entertainments were organised with close attention to rank and station, the noblest of the citizens dancing nearest the building where their lord was being held. Close by this building, then, danced over two thousand youths of quality, the flower of the nobility of Montezuma's whole empire. Thither the Spanish captain made his way, accompanied by a platoon of his men, under pretence of wanting to watch the spectacle but in fact carrying orders to attack the revellers at a prearranged time, further platoons with identical orders having been dispatched to the other squares where entertainments were being staged. The nobles were totally absorbed in what they were doing and had no thought for their own safety when the soldiers drew their swords and shouting: 'For Saint James, and at 'em, men!' proceeded to slice open the lithe and naked bodies of the dancers and to spill their noble blood. Not one dancer was left alive, and the same story was repeated in the other squares throughout the city. This series of events caused horror, anguish and bitterness throughout the land; the whole nation was plunged into mourning and, until the end of time, or at least as long as a few of these people survive, they will not cease to tell and re-tell, in their *areitos* and dances, just as we do at home in Spain with our ballads, this sad story of a massacre which wiped out their entire nobility, beloved and respected by them for generations and generations.[6]

Las Casas wrote to reverse the stereotyping assumption of the colonizers that the indigenous peoples were less than themselves, indeed less than human, and could therefore be maltreated with impunity. His suggestion was that the conquistadores, far from being the Christian heroes of ballad and romance who had defeated the 'Moorish barbarians', were themselves unchristian and barbaric in their relations to the American Indians, whom he characterizes in terms of innocence and purity. Unusually, the Montezuma massacre led to resistance (called 'defensive' and 'just' by Las Casas), and the dispersal of the Spaniards, who later regrouped and submitted the population to atrocities, rendering the province a near wasteland.

Las Casas' testimony is important not only as a record of a blot on

European civilization in its expansive phase, but also as the first of many succeeding attempts to speak out on behalf of those who could not, because they had been murdered, silenced, or simply ignored. Sometimes those who spoke out came themselves from the invaded populations, even if they spoke the language of the invader. Inevitably, the voices of the colonizing, literate community have survived best, and yet it still requires a conscious refocusing of vision, to perceive the uncertainty and criticism which occasionally accompanied the quest for empire. Samuel Daniel's 'Epistle. To Prince Henry', written within a few years of the start of the British colonial enterprise in the Americas, has found space in a revisionist anthology of *Renaissance Verse* which reflects this shift in perspective: it asks the Prince – and, by implication, all his expansionist supporters – to

> Consider whither all the good that came
> From that new world to this, acquits the some
> Of th'ill events, which since hath by the same
> Accrewd to theis our parts of Christendome,
> Or wherein wee are bettred in our state
> By that accession, and the excessive vayne
> Of gould, which hath but here inhanc'd the rate
> Of things that doe, but as they did, conteyne;
> Or whither we, with what we had before
> Produc'd not fairer actions to behold
> Then since we have performd, and had not more
> Of men that time, when wee had less of gold.[7]

Unimpressive as verse, this does register reservations towards the militant colonialism of Drake, Spenser and Walter Raleigh, and the 'ill events' which accompanied their activities in 'that new world'.

More important, notice how it is, of course, *that* New World to the speaker of the poem, and those he addresses. As Tzvetan Todorov argues in *The Conquest of America*, the conquest, colonization, and destruction of the indigenous cultures of the Americas set the pattern for much of the history of Western colonialism thereafter. This was tied up with the creation of the 'Other': that is to say, the creation of the specific social groups who are not 'I' or 'we', in the writings or discourses about those 'other' people, in 'that' (therefore also 'other') place. As Todorov says, 'others' are also 'I's:

> subjects just as I am, whom only my point of view – according to which all of them are *out there* and I alone am *in here*– separates and

authentically distinguishes from myself. I can conceive of these others as an abstraction, as an instance of any individual's psychic configuration, as the Other – other in relation to myself, to *me*; or else as a specific social group to which *we* do not belong. This group in turn can be interior to society: women for men, the rich for the poor, the mad for the 'normal'; or it can be exterior to society, i.e., another society which will be near or far away, depending on the case: beings whom everything links to me on the cultural, moral, historical plane; or else unknown quantities, outsiders whose language and customs I do not understand, so foreign that in extreme instances I am reluctant to admit that they belong to the same species as my own.[8]

Todorov goes on to analyse numerous texts from the colonization of America, including Las Casas' writings, to demonstrate the way in which the indigenous Amerindians were viewed as 'other' to a greater or lesser degree; finally with the aim of ensuring that the story of a Mayan woman who was literally thrown to the dogs by the conquistadores is not forgotten.

The histories of the colonizing process (like all histories) have continually to be rewritten. But at the centre of that rewriting from the post-colonial perspective, is the reclamation of the voice(s) and experiences of the 'other'. Some perhaps can never be reclaimed. Some speak out through surprising channels – such as that of the Tory Dean of St Patrick's in Dublin, Jonathan Swift, mediated by his most well-known work, *Gulliver's Travels* (1746). Towards the end of Gulliver's adventures abroad, our hero hesitates to inform the government of his discoveries, and thereby

> enlarge his Majesty's dominions, because that enlargement typically involves a crew of pirates . . . driven by a storm they know not whither, at length a boy discovers land from the topmast, they go on shore to rob and plunder, they see an harmless people, are entertained with kindness, they give the country a new name, they take formal possession of it for the king, they set up a rotten plank or a stone for a memorial, they murder two or three dozen of the natives, bring away a couple more by force for a sample, return home, and get their pardon. Here commences a new dominion acquired with a title by *divine right*. Ships are sent with the first opportunity, the natives driven out or destroyed, their princes tortured to discover their gold, a free license given to all acts of inhumanity or lust, the earth reeking with the blood of its inhabitants: and this execrable crew of butchers employed in so pious an expedition, is a modern colony sent to convert and civilize an idolatrous and barbarous people.[9]

Swift seems to have the earlier history of the Americas in mind in this astonishing passage – astonishing because of the strength of its opposition to prevailing attitudes and assumptions, although perhaps not so surprising when one recalls his Irish origins. The first colonization of North America by English-speaking settlers in the early seventeenth century was contemporaneous with the far larger settlement of Ireland, mainly by Scottish Presbyterians, with the aim of 'reducing to civility' the indigenous, Gaelic-speaking Catholic people.[10]

Swift's version of the colonial enterprise suggests the later, Enlightenment willingness to admit the shared humanity of those civilizations outside Europe then coming under the sway of the British and the French – the dominant powers of the eighteenth century. On one level, what the representatives of these powers looked for abroad was men that seemed to conform to European ideals: of high-minded, aristocratic scholarship; or, later, of primitive virtue. 'Brahmin' and 'savage' became terms of praise – for a time. And so Sanskrit, the learned language of the Indian subcontinent, was studied and admired, and its affinities with the classical languages of Europe expounded by self-styled 'orientalists'; while a host of literary 'primitives', like black Tarzans, turned up to question by their presence the supposed artificialities of European urban behaviour and belief. None of this halted the spread of colonization and slavery, or the competition between European powers for trade and territory abroad, most obviously in North America and the Indian subcontinent. None of it finally undermined the presumption of 'otherness', as that most representative of Enlightenment figures, David Hume, revealed in 1753, when he argued that 'negroes and in general all the other species of men' were 'naturally inferior to whites', on the grounds that blacks in 'our colonies' and throughout Europe lacked the 'civilised' arts, in particular, of writing.[11] The absence of writing was considered crucial, and their possession of it (at least among the elites) was one reason why Hindu and Muslim cultures were thought superior to slave or oral cultures in the Americas and Africa.

### Slavery and the 'Civilizing Mission'

This also meant, however, that: 'Wherever else the Briton went he felt and spoke as representative of the power at whose feet crouched a hundred million Hindus'.[12] If, by 1800, Britain had lost its American colonies, it had also taken a major stride towards the conquest of its largest and most important colony, India, with Clive's victory at Plassey (1757) and the establishment of East India Company rule over Bengal. British power over the next hundred years radiated from there. Other territories were taken with the help of Indian troops, often at the expense of the Indian tax-payer – in South Africa, for example. By 1900, the time had arrived of the 'sahib's war', in the words of the title of Kipling's Boer War story.

One of the causes of the South African War (1899–1902) was the longstanding tension over slavery between the original, largely Dutch settlers, and the British (to whom the Cape fell in 1806 as one of the prizes of the Napoleonic wars). Much of the historiography of European expansion and American growth has, rightly, been dominated by this subject.

There isn't room to go into it in any detail here. But a few points can be made. To begin with, it was the lucrative prospect of providing the Spanish and Portuguese colonies with African labour to replace the dwindling Amerindian (and 'poor white', often Scots and Irish) supply which led Sir John Hawkins to transport the first 'cargo' of five hundred slaves from West Africa to the New World in 1562. Later, as Britain established its own plantation colonies there, British interest in the slave trade and slavery increased, until by the mid-eighteenth century, it had become the centre of the Triangular Trade, and British ships carried manufactured goods to West Africa, took slaves to the New World plantations, and brought back sugar, tobacco, and cotton – thereby earning gigantic profits. Aboard ship, the Africans were treated as an item of cargo, to be packed (or lost, or even thrown overboard, as in one notorious incident of 1783, depicted by J.M.W. Turner's *Slave Ship*, 1840); on the plantation, they were catalogued with livestock and treated as work-animals; while back in Britain, where thousands of aristocratic or ex-planter households used slaves as domestic servants, they often wore padlocked collars, and were frequently mistreated. To justify all this, the usual arguments were advanced by churchmen, historians and philosophers (like Hume) to establish the inherent inferiority of the black race. And yet there was opposition, too; most notably from evangelicals such as John Newton (a converted slaver), which led Britain to abolish the trade in 1807, and finally slavery itself in 1834; this lead was followed by other European nations.

It is worth saying that there is no historical foundation for the notion that Europeans altogether imposed the slave trade on Africa, any more than there is for the idea that the institution of slavery was peculiar to Africa. Equally, however, Europeans dominated and then vastly enlarged the trade, turning it to their advantage and to Africa's loss, a loss countable in millions of dead; before at last the Europeans themselves, primarily the British, brought the appalling trade to an end. There has been slavery in one form or another before and since, in Africa and elsewhere; nevertheless, apart perhaps from disease, no single factor has been responsible for so much cruelty and misery at the time or later in the history of colonization. The Atlantic slave trade also brought about one of the largest migrations in history, involving during its peak in the eighteenth century, millions of people. Many slaves did not last long on the sugar and tobacco plantations for which they were first brought across the Atlantic, even supposing they survived the notorious 'middle passage'. But they became the main population of the Caribbean, and an important minority in the United States, maintaining fragments of their original customs, traditions and languages, in forms of folklore, music, religion, and speech.

According to the Trinidadian historian, C.L.R. James, in his classic study of *The Black Jacobins: Toussaint L'Ouverture and the San Domingo Revolution* (first published in 1938), one favourite slave song in the Caribbean, was about destroying the whites with all their possessions: the colonists knew it and tried to stamp it out, along with the voodoo cult with which it was associated; 'In vain. For over two hundred years the slaves sang it at their meetings, as the Jews sang of Zion, and the Bantu today sing in secret the national anthem of Africa'.[13] Ironically, the strength of ex-slave resistance to the plantation work was a major factor in one of the first large internal migrations of the British Empire, the hire and shipping of poor Indians and Chinese as indentured labourers to the West Indies – many of whom died on insanitary ships en route, and many more of whom remained when their contracts ran out, to add another strand to the social, racial and cultural mix of the Caribbean.

Behind the abolition of slavery lay the growing European conviction that there ought to be some goal beyond penetration and greed in their overseas expansion, a goal commonly expressed in the phrase 'civilizing mission'. Unfortunately this meant that whatever the whites did could be regarded in some way as 'civilized'; but it also meant accepting a sense of responsibility for what was done, whether as a missionary, civil servant, or 'Company officer'. The last word of Meadows Taylor's *Story of My Life* (1878), the autobiography of one type of British officer in India during the nineteenth century, was 'duty'; his was the liberal, Christian view, in the best sense, according to which the Indians could not in the end be ruled by military or political, but only by moral power. And yet Taylor, who was in the service of a 'native prince' (the Nizam of Hyderabad), married the granddaughter of a begum of Oudh, spoke numerous Indian languages and was a master of the local dialect, and whose 'improving' activities are still remembered with respect and admiration among the people of the Deccan – Taylor himself could be heard echoing the racist ideology which became dominant with the Indian 'mutiny' or 'rising' of 1857, an event which transformed relations between ruler and ruled, ringing the death knell of 'progressive' attitudes towards Empire.

### The 'New Imperialism' and Resistance

The 'new imperialism' was not new except for the increased pace and participation of European powers in Africa, the Far East and the Pacific from the 1880s onwards. Despite corruption and near-bankruptcy, Company rule in India continued long after state intervention became a necessity if the British were to keep this major market and source of raw materials. But after the events of 1857, the East India Company was abolished at last, and Queen Victoria was proclaimed Empress of India. Railways, and a more efficient administration were introduced; while the feudal princes who had supported the status quo during the rising became puppet rulers of 'independent' states – a development that became a hallmark of this phase of British imperialism, especially in tropical Africa where, as 'indirect rule', it allowed a handful of Britons to administer the lives of millions through their traditional chiefs. Lord Lugard, who introduced the system into Africa on the basis of his experience as a soldier in India, saw it as a way of bringing firm and impartial rule while respecting local customs and traditions. At its best, 'indirect rule' minimized the impact of colonial culture; but, as increasing numbers of Western-educated intellectuals later maintained, it also helped to preserve the conservative social order of the past with all its iniquities.

The Indian Mutiny or Rising – both terms are applicable depending on your point of view towards what began as discontent among the sepoy or 'native' soldiery, but then flared up because of wider discontents – this was one of a number of dramatic moments of resistance towards colonial rule from the 1780s onwards. Any history of Ireland will have at least half a dozen risings or rebellions in the index; but one of the most significant was that associated with Wolfe Tone and the United Irishmen, a group of radicals influenced by the American and French Revolutions in their demands, and whom Pitt put down with exceptional ferocity, sowing the seeds for more than a century of struggle between Irish 'patriots' and the British, not yet finally resolved, despite the arrival of the Irish Free State in 1922. Slaves in the Caribbean were among the first and most frequent to rise against their rulers, and in 1804, Haiti became the first independent black country as a result of the successful rebellion against the French led by the 'Black Jacobin', Toussaint L'Ouverture. A groundswell of rebellion continued throughout the region until, in 1865, Paul Bogle led a revolt of ex-slaves in Jamaica, which turned bloody in the face of white intransigence, led by Governor Eyre. Troops were sent in and more than 400 executed without proper trial. A commission of inquiry split public opinion at home, with Huxley, Spencer and J.S. Mill ranged against Dickens, Ruskin and Carlyle, who defended the governor against the 'nigger philanthropists' wanting him recalled (which he was). The South African War is often seen as a moment of resistance to imperial rule with a uniquely local twist: an almost exclusively white man's war; yet it took place within the context of a lengthy series of African risings, none of which, however, deflected the peace agreement by which the defeated Afrikaners became British citizens and their country another white dominion, with the rights of the black inhabitants set aside.

During the first three-quarters of the nineteenth century the British, unlike other European nations, such as the French, lacked any fixed or coherent colonial policy. In historian J.R. Seeley's memorable phrase, 'We seem, as it were, to have conquered and peopled half the world in a fit of absence of mind'.[14] In fact by then the British had conquered a quarter of the world. Yet there was truth in his remark. Until the 1880s, colonial expansion was largely undertaken by commercial companies rather than nation states, and the preceding hundred years had begun with a decrease in European (including British) control abroad, with the loss of the North and South American colonies. It was official British policy from the late eighteenth century onwards to resist further expansion, making an exception only for the acquisition of bases such as Shanghai and Singapore, or, in the 'white dominions' (Australia, New Zealand, Canada) and settler colonies such as the Cape and Natal, for immigration from distressed areas of the home country, on the assumption that these colonies would become self-supporting. An important distinction developed: between *settlement colonies*, established by Europeans who had left (or been sent from) their homes for religious, political or economic reasons; and *commercial colonies* (including military bases), used as sources of raw materials, whose first beneficiaries were private trading companies protected by the state. The discovery of diamonds in the 1860s and gold in the 1880s turned South Africa from the former to the latter, as one of the greatest colonial entrepreneurs of them all, Cecil Rhodes, was quick to realize.

Rhodes had a world outlook which chimed closely with that of a key figure who arrived at the Foreign Office in 1895 – Joseph Chamberlain. Already from the 1880s onwards there had arisen a kind of frenzy among all the major European powers for domination, so that by 1914 they controlled more than three-quarters of the world. The explanations for this 'new imperialism' are many, although one of the most influential remains that of the Liberal John A. Hobson, whose *Imperialism: A Study* (1902), based on a visit to South Africa, fed Lenin's conviction that imperialism was essentially and inevitably a creation of monopoly capitalism. The needs of the growing industrial–financial complex of the West, especially Britain, could only be satisfied through new investment in other parts of the world, with all the inequities and dependence that fostered.

Whatever the reasons for it – including the whole complex of motivating ideas associated with thinkers such as Charles Darwin, whose doctrine of natural selection was developed into a theory of racial superiority by Count de Gobineau (a hero of Hitler's) – the last two decades of the nineteenth century witnessed an unprecedented increase in the aggressive acquisition of territory, later nicknamed the 'scramble for Africa'. The advent of mass electorates and sensational journalism brought new audiences to cheer on the exploits of the 'pioneers' – farmers, missionaries, administrators and, as the popularity of Kipling's *Barrack-Room Ballads* (1890–2) proved, soldiers. This is not to deny the genuine appeal of the sense of duty inherent in Kipling's invocation to 'Take up the White Man's Burden' (in *The Times*, 1898); rather, it is to suggest the complex mingling of material and spiritual factors that underlay the often cruel and violent results, as Ashantis, Afghans, Dervishes, Matabele, Zulu and other indigenous peoples were subjugated.

### From Empire to Commonwealth

The British Empire in its ascendancy before the First World War was a vast mosaic of colonies, states and territories, extending over a quarter of the globe (on which, as it was said, the sun did not set). Thinkers from Ruskin to Seeley saw it as the special genius of the Anglo-Saxon race to rule the world. The racial element in this dominant attitude helped ensure that white settlement colonies such as Australia or South Africa were moving towards forms of self-government, while 'native lands' or Crown Colonies in Africa, the East or the Caribbean remained under indirect, paternalistic rule. By the time Edward VII came to the throne, British prestige and self-confidence was at an all-time high, despite growing anti-imperialist feelings at home and abroad. The Empire stood by 'the mother country' and helped to win the war – India alone supplying 800,000 soldiers, of whom 65,000 died. Ireland, arguably the oldest colony, was split on the issue of whether to fight for the Empire (informally during the First World

War, formally during the Second), although 200,000 Irishmen joined up, of whom 60,000 did not return.

By the mid-1960s, most British-held possessions were independent, the Empire had been dismantled, and in its place, the Commonwealth had come into being, with the Queen as its head. The fratricidal conflicts between the European powers had ensured both a dramatic decline in their ability to hold on to colonial empires, and their displacement by the superpowers. The transition from Empire to Commonwealth during the interwar years meant a continuation of white British hegemony, although nationalist feeling was growing apace, especially in India. The six white dominions (Australia, Canada, the Irish Free State, Newfoundland and New Zealand) had their status confirmed by the Statute of Westminster (1931) in terms which made them equal but autonomous, while united by their allegiance to the Crown. A key moment in the transition took place in April 1919, in the Jallianwallah Bagh at Amritsar in the Punjab, when General Dyer, a British officer in the Indian Army, ordered his soldiers to fire on a crowd of unarmed civilians, after an attack on an English woman, followed by protests in the city: nearly 400 were killed and over 1,000 wounded. The massacre, and the way in which Dyer's action was defended turned Gandhi (not long returned from two decades in South Africa representing Indian indentured labourers) against the British, and led to an upsurge in support for the Indian National Congress (founded 1885, and a model for the African National Congress of South Africa, founded 1912). Gandhi campaigned for an end to British rule; he also campaigned to improve the status of the untouchables, and women. He believed that peoples and nations should be self-sufficient, and he struggled in vain to overcome the growing gap between Hindu and Muslim which led to an explosion of violence coinciding with the granting of Independence in 1947, Partition, and his own assassination.

Indian independence marked the new, post-colonial era. Over the next fifteen years, forty countries with a population of eight hundred million won their independence from European colonizers. 'Never before in the whole of human history had so revolutionary a reversal occurred with such rapidity.'[15] The 1955 Bandung Conference of twenty-nine non-aligned African and Asian nations (often misleadingly called 'Third World') symbolized a new-found solidarity against the former imperialists. The failure of the British and French in their war against Egypt over the Suez Canal the following year clarified the ending of the age of European colonial control. Among the English-speaking diaspora, a second Commonwealth came into existence, which by the 1960s was truly multiracial – a condition signalled most clearly by the departure from it of South Africa, under its white minority government. This was followed by the futile 'declaration of independence' by the settler regime in Rhodesia, which predictably led to a small but bloody guerilla war, before the new, democratic state of Zimbabwe was declared in 1980 – an event which, equally predictably, did not bring the white minority regime further south to its senses, delaying the arrival of multiracial democracies in Namibia and South Africa until 1990 and 1994 respectively. The handing-over of Hong Kong to China in 1997 under a 'one country-two systems' agreement has seen another defining moment in world history, and a new version of the post-colonial moment.[16]

## Summary

The impact of European (not only British) colonialism on the world was always a complex process, taking many forms. The damage to indigenous cultures, the suffering and loss of life, can never be measured; and the smouldering resentment of those formerly colonized for having been instilled with a sense of inferiority based on race is part of the price we all have to pay for the ascendancy enjoyed by the West since Columbus's first voyages. As Fanon described it, colonialism was a denial of all culture, history and value outside the colonizer's frame; in short, 'a systematic negation of the other person'.[17] On the other hand, the constructive, or at least modernizing effects of colonial rule are apparent too – from the introduction of railways to the breaking down of taboos; from the building of schools and hospitals, to the rediscovery and revitalization of cultures. Similarly profound and ambivalent has been the impact of colonization upon Europe, from the arrival of vast quantities of precious metals in the early years, to the effects of slavery and immigration more recently. In the post-colonial era, we cannot expect to agree about the weight or balance of these factors. Where we should be able to agree is that colonization is a process requiring analysis and interpretation. There is much about its histories that remains obscure, unknown, or open to debate.

## Notes

1  V.S. Naipaul, 'East Indian' (1965), in V.S. Naipaul, *The Overcrowded Barracoon* (Penguin, 1976), p. 36.
2  Basil Davidson, *Black Mother: Africa and the Atlantic Slave Trade* (Pelican, 1980), p. 137.

3 Ibid., p. 232.

4 Jan (then James) Morris, *Pax Britannica* (Penguin, 1979), pp. 21–2. See also Denis Judd's chapter on the Diamond Jubilee in his *Empire: The British Imperial Experience from 1765 to the Present* (Fontana, 1997), pp. 130–53.

5 D.K. Fieldhouse, *The Colonial Empires: A Comparative Survey from the Eighteenth Century*, 2nd edn (Macmillan, 1982), pp. 72ff.

6 Bartolomé de Las Casas, *A Short Account of the Destruction of the Indies*, ed. and tr. Nigel Griffin (Penguin, 1992), pp. 50–1.

7 *The Penguin Book of Renaissance Verse 1509-1659*, selection and intro. David Norbrook, ed. H.R. Woudhysen (Penguin, 1993), p. 434.

8 Tzvetan Todorov, *The Conquest of America: The Question of the Other*, first publ. 1982, tr. Richard Howard (HarperPerennial, 1992), p. 3.

9 Jonathan Swift, *Gulliver's Travels and Other Writings*, ed. Louis A. Landa (Oxford University Press, 1976), p. 237.

10 Lawrence James, *The Rise and Fall of the British Empire* (Abacus, 1995), p. 14.

11 David Hume, 'Of national characters' (1748), qtd Henry Louis Gates Jr, *Figures in Black: Words, Signs and the 'Racial' Self* (Oxford University Press, 1989), p. 18.

12 Victor Kiernan, *The Lords of Human Kind: European Attitudes to the Outside World in the Imperial Age* (Pelican, 1972), pp. 25–6.

13 C.L.R. James, *The Black Jacobins* (Allison & Busby, 1991), p. 18.

14 J.R. Seeley, Lecture 1, *The Expansion of England* (1883).

15 Geoffrey Barraclough, *An Introduction to Contemporary History* (Pelican, 1967), p. 153.

16 See, for example, Martin Jacques, 'Sleeping giant wakes to claim the new century', *Observer* (15 June 1997), pp. 8–9.

17 Frantz Fanon, *The Wretched of the Earth* (Penguin 1967), p. 200.

# 3

## Language

You taught me language; and my profit on't
Is, I know how to curse.

The Tempest, 1611

languages are the pedigree of nations

Samuel Johnson, Journal of Tour to the Hebrides, 1785

I have crossed an ocean
I have lost my tongue
from the root of the old
one
a new one has sprung

Grace Nichols, i is a long memoried woman, 1983

### A Language That Is Not One's Own

Culture is entangled with history; so, too, is literature, which is part of
culture. Writers have registered the stirring events of European expansion
from its earliest days, however they have themselves been situated in
relation to it, as ruler or ruled, as Prospero or Caliban. In Shakespeare's *The
Tempest*, partly inspired by the fortunate escape of a group of colonizers
wrecked in the Bermudas two years before, the relationship between
European ruler and native slave is a major theme; and as the 'savage and
deformed' Caliban snarls to Prospero his master, his new language has the
wonderful advantage of allowing him to express how he feels towards him.

In the history of colonialism and decolonization, the literary dimension
is apparent not only in the themes and preoccupations of literary producers,
but also and more profoundly in their chosen medium. Caliban's attitude
prefigures that of many colonial writers who have used the imposed
European tongue to represent their condition; including, in recent years,
versions of *The Tempest* itself (by, for example, Aimé Césaire and George

Lamming) in which Prospero becomes the villain, and Caliban the hero. This is also a way of redefining, rather than simply rejecting, the role imposed upon the colonized by the colonizers' cultural mediation of their position and experience. In this book, I am talking about literatures in English, and so I am talking about a medium which has been imposed by English-speaking colonizers; but even within that limitation, the results are rarely as simple as Caliban's response seems to imply.

In the foreword to one of the first really successful and influential novels in English by an Indian writer, *Kanthapura* (1938), the author Raja Rao defined the problem of his medium thus:

> One has to convey in a language that is not one's own the spirit that is one's own. One has to convey the various shades and omissions of a certain thought-movement that looks maltreated in an alien language. I use the word 'alien', yet English is not really an alien language to us. It is the language of our intellectual make-up – like Sanskrit or Persian was before – but not of our emotional make-up. We are all instinctively bilingual, many of us writing in our own language and in English. We cannot write like the English. We should not. We cannot write only as Indians. We have grown to look at the large world as part of us. Our method of expression therefore has to be a dialect which will some day prove to be as distinctive and colourful as the Irish or the American. Time alone will justify it.

Time alone *has* justified Rao's chosen method of expression, although Indian writers in English may not be as well known worldwide as Irish or American. That says something about the relative brevity of Indian writers' use of English, compared with Irish or American writers; it says nothing about the level or quality of the English that they use. There's little doubt that the success of writers from the former colonies has given their work, and the varieties of English found in it, a large and lasting impact.

The Guyanese poet, Grace Nichols (b. 1950), long settled in England, registers the newness of her 'tongue' precisely in a new form of English. But is 'new' really the word to use here? That depends on what you mean. Indian writing in English as a literary medium is relatively recent, and yet the first stirrings can be located in the early nineteenth century. It was not until the 1930s, and the publication of works like *Kanthapura*, that international recognition came. But this is still well before decolonization. African creative writing in English goes back a long way too, but the appearance of major works is even more recent – hence the Nigerian novelist Chinua Achebe's remark: 'let no one be fooled by the fact that we write in English for we intend to do unheard of things with it'.[1] His tone arises in the context of Eurocentric paternalism towards this body of writing, despite its success. Some writers, such as the East African novelist, Ngugi wa Thiong'o, after using English with great creative force, have decided it is better to return to their own tongue, arguing that accepting a language means accepting its values too.[2]

This is an option for African or Indian writers who have indigenous languages of their own, even if in other respects they face different choices. Yet they have more choice than the writer in English from the Caribbean. Caribbean writers do not in the same sense have their 'own' language. Which language is theirs, then? For V.S. Naipaul, the English language 'was mine; the tradition was not';[3] and what this means for him is that the narrative voice in his fiction and non-fiction is always standard English, although his characters speak in local varieties. But what about a Caribbean poet like David Dabydeen, who, like Grace Nichols, writes much of his poetry (although not his criticism or fiction) in Guyanese Creole? This, he says, is the language of his childhood, the rhythms and accent of which, and the 'various Asian and African words mixed into it, would make it foreign to an Englishman's ear'.[4] A further complication: it was the energy, 'lawlessness' and 'primarily oral form' of medieval alliterative poetry from the north of England which inspired Dabydeen to go back to this language, having found in the north/south divide of England an echo of the divide between 'the so-called Caribbean periphery and the metropolitan centre of London'.[5]

And yet, whatever English now represents, or has represented over centuries of colonization, it belongs to everyone. It is a global language, the first of its kind. The Australian poet Peter Porter satirically emphasized the point in a 'World Conference Welcome Poem' published in the *Times Literary Supplement* (28 February 1992) to the effect that

> Everything will be exposed in English
> So delegates and lovers understand

For a century and a half English has been called a world language, used in different forms for different purposes; and the number of people who now speak some form of it as their 'mother tongue' is estimated at between 300 and 400 million, some seven times the population of modern Britain; and that is still about half the number of those who use it. But as the slightly eccentric usage ('exposed' instead of 'explained' or 'expressed') in Porter's lines implies, there remains the question of what we mean by English in this world context. What kind or kinds of English are we talking about?

## *Pidgins, Creoles and 'Nation Language'*

The answer takes one into linguistics, but it doesn't have to be too technical. Strictly speaking, there are two aspects to answering such questions: one has to do with how the language looks to have changed over time (the 'diachronic' approach), the other has to do with how it looks over space or geography at a particular moment (the 'synchronic' approach). We can combine these approaches, in order to clarify what we mean by the kind or kinds of English now used all over the world. The recognizably 'modern' form of English may be said to have arrived within Britain from the fifteenth century onwards, when the East Midlands dialect became adopted as 'standard' by, for example, Caxton and Wycliffe, for their first printed works. The arrival of printing in any society is always critical for the development of a standard form of the language and for a sense of national identity (as Benedict Anderson has pointed out in his influential book, *Imagined Communities*, 1983, revised 1991). The distinction between the standard form of a national language and local and class variants which are called dialects, should be familiar; although it may be news that the contest between the forces of standardization and localization, on written and spoken levels, goes back such a long time. But it is important to remember that it is a distinction which has been constructed over time, the standard form being traceable back to a dialect which gained prestige and acceptance for sociopolitical and economic reasons – including at times its adoption as a literary medium, for example in the case of the poet Chaucer's use of a southern, London-based version of what was becoming the dominant Midlands dialect towards the end of the fifteenth century.

The north of England dialects found in earlier fourteenth-century poems such as Langland's *Piers Plowman* or the anonymous *Gawain and the Green Knight* (which so impressed Dabydeen) did not prevail, and so their language is quite unfamiliar and remote for modern English readers, compared with that of Chaucer. Chaucer also wrote in Latin and French, the languages of previous invaders of the British Isles and used by them for law, administration, religion, scholarship and literature. These languages were still current when he wrote, as were the dialects of other areas of the islands. But the gradual conquest of Wales, Scotland and Ireland by the English from the sixteenth and seventeenth centuries onwards, as well as the colonization of America, India, Australia, parts of Africa and the Far East by the British over the following centuries, led to the present global pre-eminence of the south-eastern English dialect – or rather, of various related forms of that dialect.

These different forms have to do with the development of the language as the British Empire expanded, from the seventeenth century onwards, within and outside Britain. Eighteenth-century grammars, dictionaries and pronunciation manuals reinforced the value of a standard form of English, with Samuel Johnson's famous *Dictionary of the English Language* (1755) the first of its kind and the model for numerous later attempts to stabilize usage and establish canons of correctness. During the nineteenth century this standard form was what was exported like an item of machinery through the system of education to many areas of the Empire, especially India, where trading had already brought the language into use there. Through trading, employment and slavery, simplified versions of English came to be used in various places penetrated by English speakers, mingled with elements of the first languages of other traders as well as their employees or slaves.

These varieties are known as *pidgins*, simplified mixtures of two or more languages current in trading or 'contact' situations, but without necessarily being anyone's first tongue. *Pidgin English* is when one of the languages (usually that drawn from the socially dominant group) is English. Examples are the forms developed on the plantations in the Caribbean for communication between white overseers and their black, mainly West African slaves, involving English, French and Spanish, as well as Igbo, Yoruba, Fanti and other elements; 'Kisettla', the pidgin Swahili used between the British settlers and indigenous Africans of Kenya; or 'Fanagalo', a pidgin made up of elements of English, Afrikaans and Nguni (the Zulu, Xhosa, Swazi and Ndebele family of languages), used and formerly taught to workers on the South African gold mines, where it came to be condemned as racially offensive by the National Union of Mineworkers. On the other hand, the 'Tok Pisin' ('pidgin talk') of Papua New Guinea has expanded and stabilized to an extent that has made it viable as an established lingua franca with official status.

As David Crystal points out, generations of popular representations of the 'primitive' have promoted a stereotypical 'Me Tarzan – you Jane' image of pidgin, whereas in many parts of the world pidgin languages are used for such daily matters as newspaper reports and safety instructions. The more developed pidgins have been used to translate Shakespeare and the Bible. The Gospel According to St Mark in Tok Pisin begins: 'Dispela em i gutnius bilong Jisas Kraist, Pikinini bilong God' ('The beginning of the gospel of Jesus Christ, the Son of God'). The most well-known speech in Shakespeare in Cameroon Pidgin English begins 'Foh di foh dis graun oh foh no bi sehf – dat na di ting wei i di bring plenti hambag' ('To be or not to be – that is the question'). Pidgin Englishes are found in two main 'families' that have grown up along the world trade routes, one in the Atlantic, one in the Pacific.[6] In Africa, they are widely used in countries like Nigeria (reflected in the speech of some of Achebe's characters, for example); Pacific varieties include, again, the Papua New Guinea form, Tok Pisin, but also, for example, Queensland Kanaka English, descended from an early contact language taken north by explorers, convicts and settlers and spoken in the late nineteenth, early twentieth century. Probably about thirty-five million people today speak or understand one or other varieties of Pidgin English.

It is important to distinguish between pidgins, which have small vocabularies, restricted structures, lack expressive potential and are usually not a first language, and *creoles*, which are distinct varieties of English spoken as their mother tongue by 'native speakers'. (Another use of 'creole' in the West Indies and Latin America applies to native-born people, sometimes of mixed European and African ancestry, like the Cosway family in Jean Rhys's *Wide Sargasso Sea*, 1966, who may also speak creole – or not!) Creole comes about when the children of pidgin speakers acquire it as their first language, not just for specific transactions, but for social and intimate use. It is difficult to hold to any final distinction, since a long-established and expanded pidgin is in effect a creole. The development from pidgin to creole may well go further, as the variety of English moves from being used merely in servile or very limited situations, to a fuller range of human activities, becoming a regional 'standard' of its own – or a 'nation language', as the Barbadian historian and poet, Edward Kamau Brathwaite, refers to the variety of English used in his country (see below, chapter 6).

Brathwaite's usage reflects a polemic designed to improve the status of Caribbean English Creole, which has been inherited by immigrants to Britain who speak a variety called British Black English. Pidgins and creoles have long been neglected, on the grounds that they were not 'real' languages, despite their widespread use and expansion. This is in part a function of their location in the former colonial territories; it is also a result of lack of interest in this dimension of language among linguists. But the situation has changed dramatically, with the appearance of, for example, the *Dictionary of Jamaican English*, edited by F.G. Cassidy and R.B. Le Page (1967, revised 1980). Jamaican Creole in particular has been studied for many years, as a result of the presence in the country since 1948 of a campus of the University of the West Indies. Yet it is still avoided by many educated Jamaicans, who prefer to strive towards standard English. Similar views and practices may be found in countries as far apart as Singapore and South Africa.

## Pomfrets and Patois

What the particular variety of English is called involves the level of recognition or prestige it can claim, as it becomes accepted as a local standard dialect – a dialect, by the way, is a variety of the language involving differences in grammar and vocabulary, not just accent or pronunciation, as in the Scots dialect poems of Hugh MacDiarmid, the Jamaican dialect poems of Louise Bennett, or the South African 'township' dialect poems of Mongane Wally Serote. So a creole may be understood as a kind of dialect which has arisen out of a specific, typically colonial, situation of cultural mixing.

In the more formal transmission of English around the world, education (including missionary work) has been the primary factor. As part of the 'civilizing mission' of the British, the colonial authority took it upon itself to educate local people in English. The Indian experience is particularly revealing. There had already developed an indigenous, modernizing, reform movement within British-held territory (mainly Bengal) during the early decades of the nineteenth century, led by Ram Mohan Roy (1772?– 1833), when Thomas Babington Macaulay arrived. In his famous 'minute' of 1835, Macaulay set out the case 'for the intellectual improvement of the people of this country'; arguing that, while he himself had no knowledge of the indigenous languages, he had never found an orientalist 'who could deny that a single shelf of a good European library was worth the whole native literature of India and Arabia'; and that henceforth available funds should be employed 'in imparting knowledge of English literature and science through the medium of the English language'.[7]

Indian reformers such as Roy, without accepting Macaulay's dismissive attitude, nevertheless agreed with his conclusion: that for the people to enter the modern world, they required English. Roy was one of the first to defy Hindu orthodoxy by 'crossing the water' to England, where he went to argue the case against the traditional practice of sati, or widow-burning. He also started a movement of religious reform, aimed at taking the best out of the huge variety of religions in the subcontinent, and founded several secondary schools to further his modernizing aims. He deserved the title of 'Father of Modern India', given him by his countrymen and women. Not only were schools and colleges set up as a result of Macaulay's initiative, but English replaced Persian (the court language of the Moguls) as the official state language and, more gradually, English procedures and assumptions replaced Indian in law and administration. At the same time, the personnel became more Indian, sustaining and spreading cultural interaction of the kind favoured by reformers.

By the time the Indian National Congress was founded by predominantly Western-educated men in 1885, a system of English-medium schools, colleges and universities existed throughout India as well as the rest of the British Empire, providing the elite which was to dominate the professions, trade and missionary activity, and to spread European values. In India this elite was increasingly drawn from the indigenous population (and similarly in West Africa), but in the settler colonies in the Caribbean or South Africa, it remained predominantly European. Everywhere the standard form of English came increasingly into contact with variant forms which influenced it even as educationists and improvers struggled to maintain its predominance. This is a matter as much of elements such as rhythm, accent and pronunciation, which vary from place to place, even within what may now be a single country, as it is of syntactical or lexical elements, which may appear to vary less, but are sometimes thought of as more fundamental in defining difference.

The way these distinctions count can be illustrated in some of the creative writing from former colonies, perhaps especially in poems, which are generally more linguistically self-consciousness than prose. Keki Daruwalla (b. 1937) says of his 'Mistress' that

> You can make her out the way she speaks;
> her consonants bludgeon you;
> her argot is rococo, her latest 'slang'
> is available in classical dictionaries . . .
> She will not stick to *vindaloo*, but talks
> of roasts, pies, pomfrets grilled
> She speaks of contreau and not cashew
> arrack which her father once distilled.
>
> No, she is not Anglo-Indian . . .
> She is Indian English, the language that I use.[8]

By using terms such as 'vindaloo', the poet legitimizes it for poetic use, even as he makes his audience aware it is the Indian or indigenous part of his language, 'Indian English', while its 'argot' (slang or jargon peculiar to a particular group, formerly thieves) and latest 'slang' (non-standard or informal variety, usually only diction) is from abroad, and from the past – hence 'rococo' and 'classical dictionaries'. And, of course, the male poet imagining his muse as his mistress may come from, although it does not belong exclusively to, the European 'classical' tradition: an example of gender-stereotyping across cultures. How far the poet accepts the implicit values of 'the language that I use' in this respect is open to question.

A further variation on this theme of language variety and usage is provided by Kamau Brathwaite's neat example of his own awareness of the complexity and richness of 'nation language' when he says that 'I got pretty close to Bajan [Barbadian] country speech (free cadence and vocabulary)' in one section of his collection *Rights of Passage* (1967). A woman in Barbados recalls a volcanic eruption in another island:

> Some say
> is in one o' dem islands away
> where they language tie-tongue
> an' to hear them speak so
> in they St Lucia patois
> is as if they cahn unnerstan'
>
> a single word o' English.
> But uh doan really know. All uh know
> is that one day suddenly so
> this mountain leggo one brugg-a-lung-go[9]

That last phrase is a wonderful example of the potential of sheer physical sound-expression present in such variant usages. Try saying it out loud, and you discover why so much of this poetry is written for performance. But Brathwaite's poem also relies on and confirms developing linguistic distinctions, such as what is meant by 'patois'. *Patois* refers to an unwritten regional dialect, considered substandard or of low status; here it is the Barbadian speaker herself of a variety which to the outsider is simply Caribbean Creole, who distinguishes the speech of another small island as merely 'patois' – a variety so 'tie-tongue' it suggests to her something hardly English, although, as we can tell, it is truly expressive. There is a delightful play here on the familiar idea that it is always somebody's else's usage which is a departure from the standard or norm; it also recalls the fact that as a language gets standardized, the vernacular or local, spoken casualties are commonly thought of as inadequate, broken or crippled, despite having their own individual creative potential.

Awareness of these linguistic distinctions is as important as an awareness that such distinctions are always fluid and changing. It all depends on the context in which you are looking at a specific example of language use. This is obviously the case for colonial and post-colonial literatures in English, since these are mediated through varieties of the language which have been, and still are, emerging in the context of colonial and post-colonial history. By 'emerging', I don't only mean that they have been uttered or written in recent times; but also that earlier usages are becoming known about and considered worth knowing about. Thus, in Stephen Gray's groundbreaking introductory study of *Southern African Literature* (1979), despite the manifest limitations of having been produced at a time when much contemporary creative writing, especially by black South Africans, was banned, the author recorded a remarkable find: a popular song-sketch from the 1830s in Cape pidgin-patois, entitled *Kaatje Kekkelbek* or Kate Chatterbox, in which the 'Hottentot' or Khoikhoi woman of the title rebels against her missionary education like this:

> Myn A B C at Ph'lipes school
> I learnt a kleine beetje,
> But left it just as great a fool
> As gekke Tante Meitjie.[10]

Dr John Philips was a prominent missionary from 1819 until his death in 1851, much resented among the settlers for his championing of the rights of black people, especially the so-called Coloureds, which included people of mixed race, especially of San ('Bushman') or Khoikhoi origins; and 'kleine beetje' means 'little bit', while 'gekke Tante Meitjie', 'mad aunt May'. More remarkable is the fact that this song, a testimony to the development and mingling of languages used by people resisting the school-imposed standard, was produced by a Scots immigrant road-builder, Andrew Geddes Bain, in collaboration with the supposed illegitimate grandson of George III, one Frederick Rex. The first book published in this as yet unrecognized language variety appeared in 1856 – a book on the Islamic faith written by 'Cape Coloured' Muslims who used Arabic lettering to convey its sounds.[11]

It was not until nearly a century later (in 1925) that pidgin Dutch, promoted by a group of white self-styled 'Afrikaners' became an official language, Afrikaans; and, ironically, it has only been in recent decades that this kind of mingling of English and Afrikaans has become acceptable in 'literature', in the work of Cape writers such as Athol Fugard and urban 'township' poets such as Mongane Wally Serote, who also bring in African elements.

How, when and where to adopt such usages has been a matter of sharp and continuing debate, fraught with political overtones, within South Africa; and, as we've seen from the words of Rao, Daruwalla, Dabydeen, Achebe and Brathwaite, also in countries as far apart as India, Britain, Nigeria and Barbados. What these debates have in common is an emphasis upon status and use, upon the practice rather than the code, primarily in countries where English was first imposed by some form of colonial regime, although also within the colonizing country itself, by Black American or Black British writers.

### *Decolonizing the Mind*

Achebe explains the overall position well:

> The price a world language must be prepared to pay is submission to many kinds of use. The African writer should aim to use English in a way that brings out his message best without altering the language to the extent that its value as a medium of international exchange will be lost. He should aim at fashioning out an English which is at once universal and able to carry his peculiar experience . . . But it will have to be a new English, still in full communion with its ancestral home but altered to suit its new African surroundings.[12]

This is partly a defence of Achebe's own practice as a writer; and it reflects his assumptions about what the practice of writers in the former British colonies should be. One of these assumptions is that his audience is an international one. The difficulty that arises if you reject this assumption is well illustrated in the career of Ngugi wa Thiong'o, who has written at length on the language issue, most notably in *Decolonising the Mind* (1986), in which he argues the case for refusing to adopt the language of the colonial master: 'What is the difference between a politician who says Africa cannot do without imperialism and the writer who says Africa cannot do without European languages?'[13]

Depending upon your assumptions, there may be a big difference. But it has to be argued through, and Ngugi has taken on the implications in practice. From being a writer of books capturing world renown, he has become a writer known to a much smaller, but more specific, local Kenyan community of Gikuyu speakers who attended his plays and who now read his novels – a small number, since literacy is still low. In Africa, as elsewhere in the former colonial territories, the majority of the population cannot read, and so the writers' choice of language also depends on whether or not they wish to be read, locally or abroad, and what kind of publishing industry, if any, they can rely on. Without some kind of market, literature cannot exist; and many writers have had to address English-speakers and readers rather than 'traditional' indigenous audiences simply in order to get published, and to this extent inevitably become cut off from their own literary and cultural roots.

The strength, even ferocity of division on this issue is widespread in parts of the world where new varieties of English as a second (or third or fourth) language have emerged. It is most acute among literary producers in the most recently independent countries (including South Africa), where English is, naturally enough, considered the language of cultural, if not also other forms of colonial oppression. Among writers of the Asian subcontinent, a more pragmatic approach is common, exemplified in these lines by Kamala Das (b. 1934):

> I am Indian, very brown, born in
> Malabar, I speak three languages, write in
> Two, dream in one. Don't write in English, they said,
> English is not your mother-tongue. Why not leave
> Me alone, critics, friends, visiting cousins,
> Every one of you? Why not let me speak in
> Any language I like? The language I speak
> Becomes mine, its distortions, its queernesses
> All mine, mine alone. It is half English, half
> Indian, funny perhaps, but it is honest,
> It is as human as I am human, don't
> You see? It voices my joys, my longings, my
> Hopes, and it is useful to me as cawing
> Is to crows or roaring to the lions . . .[14]

Das's colloquial ease has been an inspiration to younger Indian women poets in particular, like Eunice de Souza (b. 1940), who shares her directness and sense of freedom. Coming from a Goan Catholic background, de Souza may have a more obvious need for English than Das, who comes from the rich Malayalam poetic background of her home state Kerala. Yet both have found it possible to write about themselves and their concerns at a profound and stirring level in English, the colonizer's tongue.

What we have to remember is that the large issue, of which language to use, involves a number of smaller, but no less important issues for particular writers in particular countries or language communities. Another option for Ngugi might have been kiSwahili, the official language of Kenya and Tanzania, and a language that has developed out of Arabic and several Bantu languages used along the coast of east Africa over many centuries. But, like Hindi, the Indian government's chosen national language, despite the millions who speak or know it, many other millions do not, or do not

wish to. And so some writers opt for their own, local languages, even as –
in Ngugi's case as in others – they translate what they write or say back into
English for their wider local, and the international audience! One reason
for the difference in approach of two major twentieth-century African
writers, Achebe and Ngugi, to the use of English, lies in their peoples'
different experience of colonization and decolonization. Nigeria, like
other West African territories, was governed by the British under the
system of indirect rule which, as I have already pointed out, minimized the
impact upon local cultures. East Africa, and in particular the area which
became Ngugi's Kenya, saw the introduction of an East African Protector-
ate, empowered to sell land to white settlers, who came to feel that the land
was 'theirs', including the 'natives' they found living on it. This in turn led
to the special viciousness of the Mau Mau rebellion and its suppression,
which took the country into independence and an uncertain future.
Further, as Angela Smith points out, 'it is easy to understand the lack of
cultural confidence' a writer such as Ngugi might feel in the face of the
West and South Africans, who had long periods of writing in English
behind them. 'Though there was a substantial amount of writing in
Kiswahili in the colonial period in Tanzania, East Africa produced very
little in English apart from autobiographies and Kenyatta's *Facing Mount
Kenya*.'[15] In Ngugi's view language was 'the most important vehicle
through which [colonial] power fascinated and held the soul prisoner. The
bullet was the means of physical subjugation. Language was the means of
spiritual subjugation.'[16]

   The difficulties of language choice do sometimes seem intractable,
precisely because they are so bound up with historical and cultural
pressures. In South Africa, the African National Congress, founded in 1912
to resist the racial basis to the new, British-created dominion or 'Union of
South Africa' and finally come into power, has said that in the 'new South
Africa', there are eleven official languages: the two European (is Afrikaans
'European'?) ones, the seven major (there are numerous minor) African
languages, and the two Asian languages current there. Is this possible? Is it
desirable? What will the effect be on literary production? That remains to
be seen. An already complex literary situation looks to become more
complex still.

## Summary

The most important point to emerge from any discussion of the language
issue as an aspect of post-colonial literatures is this: whatever the generali-

zations, suspicions and admonitions of critics, politicians, theorists and legislators, the writers are eager to go on writing, whether in their new, 'borrowed' tongue, or in the old original. Their specific histories decide their position for them, as much as they themselves feel they have done. Yet the forms of language, of English, adopted are very varied, and are best thought of in terms of a continuum, upon which different positions are defined in terms of usage and status – themselves varying over time and space. To understand the debates further, to adopt one's own approach, requires a sense of what approaches have already developed, and where they seem to be going. Which is the subject of my next chapter.

## Notes

1 Chinua Achebe, 'Colonialist criticism', *Morning Yet on Creation Day* (Heinemann, 1975), p. 7.
2 See especially, Ngugi wa Thiong'o, 'The language of African literature', in Ngugi wa Thiong'o, *Decolonising the Mind: The Politics of Language in African Literature* (James Currey, 1986), pp. 4–33.
3 V.S. Naipaul, 'Jasmine' (1964), in *The Overcrowded Barracoon* (Penguin, 1976).
4 David Dabydeen, Introduction, *Slave Song* (Dangaroo, 1984), p. 13.
5 David Dabydeen, 'On not being Milton', in *The State of the Language*, eds Christopher Ricks and Leonard Michaels (Faber & Faber, 1990), p. 4.
6 David Crystal, *The English Language* (Penguin, 1990), pp. 12–15.
7 The complete text of this important document may be found in *Imperialism: the Documentary History of Western Civilization*, ed. Philip Curtin (Walker & Co., 1971), pp. 178–91.
8 Keki Daruwalla, *The Keeper of the Dead* (Oxford University Press, 1982), pp. 22–3.
9 This was in Brathwaite's influential lecture-essay, *History of the Voice: The Development of Nation Language in Anglophone Caribbean Poetry* (New Beacon, 1984), pp. 35–6.
10 *Journals of Andrew Geddes Bain*, ed. Margaret Lister, qtd Gray, *Southern African Literature: An Introduction* (David Philip/Rex Collings, 1979), p. 54.
11 See Allister Sparks, *The Mind of South Africa* (Heinemann, 1990), p. 80.
12 Chinua Achebe, 'The African writer and the English language' (1964), in *Morning Yet on Creation Day*, pp 61–2.
13 Ngugi wa Thiong'o, 'The language of African literature', *Decolonising the Mind*, p. 26.
14 Kamala Das, 'An Introduction', reptd in *The Arnold Anthology of Post-Colonial Literatures in English*, ed. John Thieme (Arnold, 1996), p. 717.
15 Angela Smith, *East African Writing in English* (Macmillan, 1989), p. 7.
16 Ngugi wa Thiong'o, *Decolonising the Mind*, p. 9.

# 4

## Theory

Wits, like physicians, never can agree,
When of a different society

Aphra Behn, Prologue, *The Rover* (1677)

### *Why Theory?*

The importance of 'theory' for an understanding of post-colonial literatures can be easily and dramatically demonstrated. In one of the lectures on
which his book *Decolonising the Mind* was based, Ngugi urged his Kenyan
student audience to read two books, without which, he said, 'it is
impossible to understand what informs African writing, particularly novels
written by Africans': V.I. Lenin's *Imperialism, the Highest Stage of Capitalism*
(1916) and Frantz Fanon's *The Wretched of the Earth*.[1] Five days later, on 31
December 1977, Ngugi was detained. While in prison, writing on toilet
paper, he began his first novel in his own language, Gikuyu, called *Caitaani
Mutharaba-ini*, translated two years later as *Devil on the Cross* (1982).
According to Fanon's *Wretched of the Earth*, anti-colonial movements
would fail unless they addressed the issue of the survival after decolonization
of the international power of the departed colonizers. This was a development of Lenin's classic account of the endless need of industrial capitalism
to invest overseas, hence to exert a 'neo-imperial' economic power after
the formal decolonization of a country, with the collaboration of a
privileged class created by the colonizers to take over after them.

The national elite of post-colonial Kenya were unlikely to approve of
these views, much less their open recommendation by the then Chairman
of the Literature Department at the University of Nairobi, formerly a
college of the University of London. Moreover, Ngugi was at the same
time running drama workshops on resistance among the rural Gikuyu in
their own language – an activity precisely embodying what Fanon had

gone on to call for from the 'native' writer as the final stage of liberation: militant identification with the 'wretched of the earth', that is, the have-nots of the countryside.

Ngugi's position as a Kenyan dissident writer/teacher, a position bound up with a set of ideas derived from Lenin and Fanon, is just one, perhaps extreme, example of the importance works of theory can have. Lenin's book has long been part of a debate among historians about the nature and impact of colonialism which can be pursued in such places as D.K. Fieldhouse's *Colonialism 1870–1945* (1981). Fanon's *The Wretched of the Earth* remains more important for post-colonial thinking. Why? In the first place because Fanon wrote from the perspective of a colonial subject in the thick of an independence struggle, addressing other colonial subjects. Second, because he placed the cultural (including literary) aspect of colonial and post-colonial history at the centre of his discussion. Lenin's *Imperialism* and other Marxist anti-colonial critical texts have been influential among oppressed peoples in the so-called Third World and elsewhere (for example, among Americans of colour). But the *Wretched of the Earth* has spoken more directly, profoundly, and lastingly than any other single anti-colonial work on behalf of and to the colonized. Many writers and critics (whether or not they agree with Fanon's assumptions) consider that this book raised most of the fundamental issues concerning post-colonial writings. As I have already said (in chapter 1), I derive my own position to some extent from his. So I will devote some space to his views in what follows.

First, however, I would like to make some general points about theory in relation to literary studies; and then say something about how we have got to where we are now in post-colonial theory – which will bring me back to Fanon.

## The Arrival of Theory

During the 1970s, traditional methods of Anglophone literary study were challenged by the appearance of new ideas arriving in bundles labelled 'theory'. 'Theory' nowadays means something more than the analysis of texts and the discourses associated with them. Since the late 1960s, and the cultural and intellectual turmoil surrounding the strikes, student revolts and anti-Vietnam War protests in the US and Europe, traditional literary criticism in English and the associated 'canon' of texts came to be attacked as part of a critique of the whole complex of conservative if not authoritarian attitudes supposedly buttressing the liberal-democratic ('bourgeois') states of the West. The thinking of Marx and Freud was reinterpreted and reapplied, especially by radical French intellectuals such as Althusser and Lacan, so as to undermine the received notion of the individual as an autonomous self whose actions were in some sense free. The familiar division between text and context in literary studies was redefined to suggest that the meaning of the text could not be found in itself, but only in relation to its context, i.e., in relation to those forces of history, society, language or the unconscious which are beyond the individual's control or even knowledge.

Language was a key feature of the new 'theorizing' of literary study – or rather, a particular set of ideas about language, which chimed in with the general suspicion of familiar 'liberal humanist' conceptions of the individual and society. According to the 'structuralist' tradition, inaugurated by the Swiss linguist Ferdinand de Saussure (1857–1913) in a lecture-series delivered before the First World War, language is not directly connected with the reality outside itself, but refers to it according to a set of rules; which was interpreted to mean that what was called the signifier is crucially separable from the signified. This may not seem much of a discovery (a Frenchwoman will call what I call a dog by a different word in her signifying system), but what the later structuralists made of it is what counts here. Language, according to them, was the means by which reality was constructed, rather than some passive medium through which we could perceive things. Literary works came to be seen as texts referring to each other, rather than to some external reality; and the point of criticism was to find the more general rules according to which language issued in texts, literary or not, so as to question the received ways of thinking which became visible in particular uses of language.

A good example may be found in the widely influential 1968 essay on 'The death of the author', by the witty Parisian writer and cultural critic Roland Barthes (1915–80). Here the literary text is released from the intentions of some godlike guarantor of meaning, into revealing the myriad possibilities of language by a rhetorical ploy of the author Barthes pretending (before collecting a cheque in his name as author, perhaps) that he is not subject to his own questioning of the author's role. Barthes characteristically offered entertaining subversion, anticipating the post-structuralist or 'deconstructionist' turn which subsequently broadened the attack upon Western norms of thought. Important from our point of view was the idea that these norms enshrined a presumption of centredness focused upon white or at least European, bourgeois, male attitudes and behaviour, while marginalizing black, non-European, working-class, female attitudes and behaviour.

Barthes' celebration of the demise of the author was just one instance of the unsettling universe in which 'everyone' now lived, and in which everything was relative, and nobody could claim authority. For the literary work, this meant that the organic unity formerly found and praised when found, was an illusion; instead, the work became a text which, like any other, was torn with the gaps and contradictions of an unstable linguistic entity, the so-called 'site of struggle'.

The interest of 'theory' as a set of critical approaches was never the concern of more than an active and voluble minority within the academic institutions of the West, approaches which have nonetheless continued to have an impact abroad, especially in those places where the colonial system of education was deeply rooted, as in India or Australia, and where the various 'isms' – from structuralism to post-structuralism, from feminism to new historicism – may now be found in sometimes strange and attenuated forms. Nevertheless, the arrival of new, or newly formulated ideas about literature, language, history, culture and society has had a profound effect upon literary studies generally, and has helped pave the way for the specific ideas associated with post-colonial writings and their mediation. The reversal of perspective which has undermined universalist claims about the centrality of the accepted canon of great works around which criticism and teaching has circulated, has opened up the possibility of attending more closely to the alternative claims of the neglected or marginalized works which promote a sense of difference, of the 'other'. Tzvetan Todorov's account (referred to in chapter 2) of the voices submerged by traditional versions of the 'discovery' of the Americas, is an instance of the effect upon literary–cultural studies of this reversal of perspective.

### Why Post-Colonial Theory?

Post-colonial theory is an area of literary and cultural study that has come into being as part of the decentring tendency of post-1960s thought in the West. But it was also part of a metropolitan, left-wing response to the increasingly visible and successful struggles for independence of colonized peoples worldwide from the 1950s onwards. Fanon's voice in *The Wretched of the Earth* and his earlier *Black Skin, White Masks* (1952, first translated 1967) spoke in the terms and language of French radical thought of the time, and indeed was mediated by, for example, the Marxist philosopher Jean-Paul Sartre, whose introduction to *The Wretched of the Earth* is itself a key document in the development of European awareness of the condition of the colonized as decolonization proceeded. This European, rather than merely Anglophone, dimension of the development of post-colonial theory has been largely neglected or ignored, especially and perhaps unsurprisingly by those English-speakers outside the so-called metropolitan centres such as Ashcroft, Griffiths and Tiffin, whose influential notion of 'writing back' to those centres has been widely accepted.

One important effect of their book *The Empire Writes Back* has been the recognition of the role of literary creativity in the former colonies. As theorists, they might be slow to acknowledge the role of specific literary works such as V.S. Naipaul's *The Mimic Men* (1967) and R.K. Narayan's *The Vendor of Sweets* (1967) in dislodging received notions of what counts as works worth attending to, but as experienced teachers, they do provide some account of these and other texts in the course of their discussions of the various 'models' of post-colonial theory. The remarkable upsurge of writings in countries involved in the decolonization process since the Second World War, from Nigeria to South Africa, from Jamaica to India, has led readers (if not publishers, critics or 'theorists') worldwide to see that their own communities could produce writings of great power and relevance, if in the language of the former colonizers. Yet there remain vast areas of outstanding literary endeavour which, if they have been heard of outside the countries of their production, have yet to be considered worthy of inclusion in the standard English literary histories, except in off-hand or marginalizing terms.

Andrew Sanders's popular and widely recommended *Short Oxford History of English Literature* (1994), for instance, is apparently too short to mention the Nobel Prizewinners Soyinka, Gordimer or Walcott, although a one-sentence gesture is made towards the 'destabilizing' and 'decentralizing' effect upon 'the canon' of the 'distinctive English-language literatures of Canada, Australia, New Zealand, Africa and the Caribbean'; and a small clutch of ex-colonial writers who have settled in Britain, such as Salman Rushdie and Timothy Mo, are said to represent the impact of 'writers and subjects from the old colonial Empire'.[2]

Post-colonial theory is needed because it has a subversive posture towards the canon, in celebrating the neglected or marginalized, bringing with it a particular politics, history and geography. It is anti-colonial; so it may look back as far as the first moment of colonization by the West, and cover all parts of the world touched by Empire, which means it may well also take the classics of the literary canon from Shakespeare onwards as grist to its mill. But to keep within the limits of our times, that is, the times of twentieth-century decolonizing processes – primarily post-war – is to keep within a manageable and coherent period, even if it is absurd to pretend that this is hermetically sealed off from the earlier histories and their writings.

Post-colonial theory does not confine itself to written materials: oral and performance media, art and film, are also fit areas for study. I am mainly concerned with literary texts here, and I confine my account to the writings that have attended literary production in varieties of English, although when I talk about drama, I will of necessity take into account the means and timing of its performance; and in my concluding chapter, I take up some implications of the film versioning of post-colonial texts.

## The Commonwealth Project

If post-colonial theory seems to have a rationale, then, how has it arisen within the groves of Anglophone academe? There is a suggestive mini-history which helps clarify where we are now. Inevitably the focus was for a long time predominantly UK based. First, there was Commonwealth Literature. Sometime during the 1950s, what was called English Literature ceased to be a unitary subject – in certain quarters. Before then, most writers who lived outside the UK but who wrote in English – such as the South African Olive Schreiner (1855–1920) or the Indian Rabindranath Tagore (1861–1941) – were either ignored or assimilated. Literature from the USA was not normally studied outside North America. Then things changed. Courses in American, Commonwealth, Irish and African Literature began to emerge in a few provincial UK universities, while little clusters of 'local' texts were admitted into the syllabuses of English Departments in former colonial countries, often with patronizing disclaimers, as I recall from my own experience at the relatively advanced University of Cape Town where the Department was run by an urbane Oxford-trained Australian, R.G. Howarth.

The newly independent nations, such as Nigeria and Kenya, and the older dominions of settlement, such as South Africa and Australia, were producing new literary works that began to seem important outside their countries of origin. It was probably no coincidence that this happened as British power and influence went into decline. A major effect of the Second World War had been to weaken British prestige, while stimulating local economies and the demand for independence. The granting of independence to India, the largest country of the British Empire, in 1947, was, as we've seen, a critical moment; another was the Suez crisis of 1956, which marked the permanent demotion of the imperial power in the face of nationalist strivings. The literary and cultural expression of these strivings during the (often lengthy) process of decolonization produced some of the first writings in English to have a major impact abroad – from the novels of Mulk Raj Anand and Raja Rao in India during the 1930s, to the fiction, drama and poetry of Kenyan Ngugi wa Thiong'o (James Ngugi at the time), Nigerians Wole Soyinka and Chris Okigbo, and Ghanaian Kofi Awoonor in the 1950s. Summing up what these writers were trying to do was – as we have seen – Achebe's hugely successful *Things Fall Apart*, published two years before Nigerian independence, and setting out to tell his people's own story in their own way.

The first school of Commonwealth Literature was founded at Leeds University in 1964. By then, works such as Anand's and Achebe's had come to be recognized by wide readerships, and some of the best found their way onto the Leeds syllabus. The first Commonwealth Literature Conference was simultaneously organized by the Leeds enthusiasts, with the resulting papers published as *Commonwealth Literature: Unity and Diversity in a Common Culture*, edited by John Press (from the British Council) and brought out by Heinemann Educational in 1965: Heinemann, whose African Writers Series was launched with the paperback of *Things Fall Apart* in 1962, took an initiative in the field from then on. One of the authors discussed in Press's book, V.S. Naipaul, commented fretfully:

> Things move so fast nowadays, even in the Literature Schools. Commonwealth writing as we understand it is so new, and it is already being picked to pieces . . . there is the West Indian writer with his search for identity . . . a phrase that has gone deep. Students, already – how disquieting! – preparing theses, write or even telephone to say they get the impression from my books that I am engaged in a search for identity. How is it going? At times like this I am glad to be only a name.[3]

The speed with which this new category of literary study emerged and became institutionalized despite the objections of writers such as Naipaul (Achebe was another) was striking. By 1970, William Walsh, enthusiastic Leavisite and Professor of Education and Commonwealth Literature Fellow at Leeds, had produced *A Manifold Voice: Studies in Commonwealth Literature* (Chatto), to show which of the authors 'writing in English outside Britain and the United States' had made a significant contribution to 'the canon of Literature in English' (Preface). The book included persuasive studies of such (even then) well-known authors as Naipaul, Narayan, Patrick White and Katherine Mansfield, as well as the less familiar Nirad Chaudhuri, A.D. Hope and Chinua Achebe.

In the following year, the first volume of a new series of Penguin Companions to Literature appeared, edited by David Daiches of Sussex

University, covering *British & Commonwealth Literature*. And by 1973 Walsh, now the first full Professor of Commonwealth Literature, produced his

> personal chart of writing in the English language outside the traditions of Britain and the United States – essentially writing within those areas of the world loosely gathered together into the British Commonwealth. Not that I have any structural theory of the nature of this institution. I take it to mean what most people do, and while I recognize that the writers I speak of see themselves as Africans or Canadians, and not as contributors to some nebulous organization, the term is at least a useful category of denotation grounded in history and making a point of substance about those it is applied to.[4]

*Commonwealth Literature* identified 'six major divisions' of writing – Indian, African, West Indian, Canadian, New Zealand and Australian. The arbitrary mix of continents and countries betrayed the difficulties into which the Commonwealth label was leading Walsh.

Yet his emphasis upon the importance of national identity, or how the writers saw themselves, was vital – as was his insistence that the label carried a certain history with it. But he thereby implied a wider reach than the book was able to deliver, which threw into question the whole enterprise of defining from within the UK the worthwhile writers to add to the canon of what was now routinely called 'Literature in English'. Walsh omitted writers from South Africa and Pakistan (neither then in the Commonwealth), while confessing that they had certainly produced work 'deserving of attention'. The critical discriminations he aimed to provide were soon lost in a bog of familiar names going back to the early nineteenth century. Despite the claim that these writings were grounded in history, no serious atempt was made to contextualize them.

During the next ten years the whole project became somewhat undermined, although the term 'Commonwealth' continues in play. The challenge to it was in part the result of the general debate within English Studies centring on the notion of the 'canon', with its tendency to set up a small cast of writers as the central (or notoriously, in F.R. Leavis's word 'great') tradition, harking back to the standards of the mainstream. It was also the result of a growing concern to include the wider range of what was coming to be called 'Literatures of the World in English'.

## New Writings

*Literatures of the World in English* (Routledge & Kegan Paul, 1974), was in fact the title of a book edited by Bruce King, a US Professor of English with experience of teaching in Africa and elsewhere in the English-speaking world, who pulled together a multinational group of critics to introduce the important authors, themes and works. Ironically, William Walsh was given the job of surveying the literature of England, while another Leeds enthusiast (and King's doctoral supervisor), A.N. Jeffares, wrote about Ireland – which had some justification because the former was English and the latter Irish. (Nobody wrote about Scotland or Wales.) For the first time, it seemed important to attend to those who could claim more than outside knowledge of a given field of writing. Thus King himself covered the US, Brian Elliott from Adelaide introduced Australian writing, and the Trinidadian Kenneth Ramchand discussed the literature of the West Indies.

This was in line also with King's emphasis upon the importance of cultural differences, as well as similarities. Moving outside the Commonwealth frame – which, according to a contradiction inherent in the way it was used, often did not include the writings of its leading member, the UK – meant acknowledging range and variety, not only of theme and genre, but also of criteria of evaluation. Nor did King ignore history. As he pointed out

> Colonialism is as responsible in North America and Australia as in Africa and Asia for the development of national literatures around the world. Colonialism, whether as indirect rule or the exploration and settlement of continents, brought with it the English language, English literary forms, and English cultural assumptions. Colonization also brought the possibility of a new literature emerging once English becomes a vehicle for the expression of local culture. A new English literature may express a culture which has grown up with the settler communities, it may be a continuation of indigenous cultural traditions, or it may be some mixture of the effects of colonization, including the bringing together of various races into one nation.[5]

This emphasis upon the newness and national identity of the literatures emerging outside the UK and USA, which in effect meant concentrating upon the writings of the postwar period of decolonization, was more fully developed in King's *The New English Literatures – Cultural Nationalism in a*

*Changing World*, published by Macmillan in 1980 as part of a series on the 'major "new" literatures', edited by A.N. Jeffares. In this usefully wide-ranging 'handbook', King paid special attention to six so-called new literatures – those of Nigeria, India, Australia, Canada, New Zealand and the West Indies – and the work of several of its 'major' writers, such as Achebe, Soyinka, Patrick White, V.S. Naipaul, R.K. Narayan, Wilson Harris and Derek Walcott.

The formation of a Commonwealth or (as it was increasingly called) New Literatures canon was implicit in the way certain authors, and countries or areas were repeatedly being introduced or surveyed. By the time of the appearance of *The New English Literatures*, critical and scholarly periodicals were taking up the job of asserting the importance of the field, while redefining it in the same terms or framework. Thus the rather staid *Journal of Commonwealth Literature* was started at Leeds in 1965, edited by the expatriate South African Arthur Ravenscroft; to be later taken over by Alastair Niven, another member of the Jeffares–Leeds stable who returned from teaching in Ghana to set up a course in Commonwealth Literature at the then new Stirling University; and the present editor is John Thieme, formerly Professor of New Literatures in English at Hull. (Meanwhile the Leeds chair, finally occupied by someone actually from a former colonial territory, Singaporean Shirley Chew, has been renamed 'Commonwealth and Post-Colonial'.) New university departments of the 1960s played a role in the development of interest in the whole area; for example at Kent Lyn Innes and Louis James (both with expatriate colonial backgrounds) helped promote the much livelier journals *Okike* and then *Wasafiri* (now edited by Susheila Nasta). The trend towards indigenous journal titles ('Wasifiri' is from the Swahili for travellers) was exhibited also in the appearance of *Kunapipi* (an Australian Aborigine rainbow serpent), originating in Aarhus, Denmark, and the baby of Australian Anna Rutherford, an active promoter throughout Europe of writing from the former colonies. I will return to the North American aspect of these developments, but it is worth noting here that at the same time as these journals appeared in Western Europe, *Ariel: A Review of International English Literature* emerged from the University of Calgary, and *WLWE* (*World Literature Written in English*), was first published in the USA, then Canada and is now edited in Singapore. *Commonwealth*, a periodical originating in Dijon, reflects the more recent sharp growth of interest in continental Europe, especially in the large English departments of French and German universities. The editors, Jean-Pierre and Carole Durix of the Université de Bourgogne, went on to produce *The New Literatures in English*, a title claiming to offer 'a valid alternative for a body of writing which has emerged mostly in the last hundred years and which now stands on a par with the older British, Irish and American literatures'.[6] The popularity of the New Writings label in Europe (where 'Commonwealth Literature' also remains in play) may be gauged from its deployment by Hena Maes-Jelinek at the University of Liège, where she initiated the study of the subject as long ago as 1969; and by Dieter Riemenschneider of Frankfurt, whose collection of papers from the 10th Annual Conference of Commonwealth Literature and Language Studies at Koenigstein in 1987 was published as *Critical Approaches to the New Literatures in English* two years later.

Meanwhile, the terrain had for some time become more intensively if sporadically covered by the first appearance of monographs on individual authors, such as G.D. Killam's *The Novels of Chinua Achebe* (Heinemann, 1960), group studies such as Gerald Moore's influential *Seven African Writers* (Hutchinson, 1962), revised to *Twelve* in 1980; or Louis James's *The Islands in Between: Essays in West Indian Literature* (Oxford University Press, 1968), and Kenneth Ramchand's groundbreaking *The West Indian Novel and its Background* (Faber, 1970). As this suggests, area studies had begun to appear, as had descriptive bibliographies, such as Hans Zell's *Reader's Guide to African Literature* (Heinemann, 1971, rev edn, 1983) – all adding to the momentum, which was to increase manyfold during the next decade.

In the 1970s African and Caribbean writers in English were as much (if not more) written about by Western expatriates as by indigenous critics, causing some resentment at 'metropolitan bias'. On the other hand Australasian writers tended to find themselves scrutinized by home-based critics, in now-classic, locally published works such as K.R. Srinivasa Iyengar's *Indian Writing in English* (Asia Publishing House, 1962, rev edn, 1973), C. Nair's *Singapore Writing* (Woodrose, 1977), or Tom Moore's *Social Patterns in Australian Literature* (Angus & Robertson, 1971).

## The Arrival of the Post-Colonial

Tensions between the former imperial centre or the 'metropolis', and the former colonies or 'periphery', became the central metaphor for the first book claiming to offer post-colonial literary theory as such – *The Empire Writes Back: Theory and Practice in Post-Colonial Literatures* (1989). The authors had already published literary criticism or scholarship under the Commonwealth and New Writings banners. But this book represented a new generation entering the field of Anglophone literary studies, as its appearance in the brash 'New Accents' series of paperbacks implied. New Accents was edited by Terence Hawkes, whose *Structuralism and Semiotics* came out in 1977 as the first in the series, with the overall aim 'to encourage rather than resist the process of change' in literary studies. Structuralism, deconstruction, reception theory, cultural politics, narrative poetics, semiotics: all the trends that had come to affect familiar or traditional notions of English studies since the late 1960s were represented, and so it was inevitable that 'post-colonialism' should join them – if a little late.

A major difficulty for Ashcroft, Griffiths and Tiffin was that by trying to open up the debates about the writings of India, Australia, the Caribbean and so on, they were simultaneously trying to reflect the impact of the theorization of English studies since the 1960s – no mean task, while most writing about Commonwealth or New Literatures remained blissfully unaware of this development. This was partly because the main academic players, such as Walsh, Jeffares and King (and their protégés) preferred on the whole to resist change and keep to the established methods and arguments, merely extending them to include (not always with conviction) writings from outside the UK or the USA. It was also because much of the best criticism and commentary came from the producers of those writings themselves, who did not know or did not care to know what was going on in the increasingly rarefied atmosphere of the academy. Novelists, poets, and playwrights such as Raja Rao, Chinua Achebe, Ngugi wa Thiong'o, Wole Soyinka, Derek Walcott, Edward Kamau Brathwaite, Edwin Thumboo, Margaret Atwood and Stephen Gray had all published introductions, essays, surveys, even books upon the literature of their countries – documents still of prime importance. For example, Ngugi's collections of essays on African literatures, culture and politics, from *Homecoming* (1972) to *Decolonising the Mind* (1986) remain widely influential; Gray's *Southern African Literature: An Introduction* (1979), though written in the apartheid years when many local authors could not be referred to or quoted, remains the standard (and until 1996, was the only) work on its subject.

The question that seemed to require answering was of the form: 'What's Canadian about Canadian literature?', as Margaret Atwood put it at the outset of her *Survival: A Thematic Guide to Canadian Literature* (Anansi Press, 1972). These works were consciously written from their places of origin, addressing their own (English-speaking) constituencies; and with national identity firmly on the agenda. They represented a step forward from writing for the 'metropolis' or former imperial centre; but that is far from saying that they have been overtaken by more recent critical writing 'against' the metropolis, as is claimed by the authors of *The Empire Writes Back*, which reads as if written from a specifically white Australian, academic version of the metropolitan viewpoint. This much is evident in its title, ironically alluding to the second film in the *Star Wars* trilogy (in which the rebellion of the guerillas is checked by the Empire), an allusion in turn derived from Salman Rushdie's article in *The Times* of London (3 July 1980), attacking 'collaborators' among the colonized who migrated to the West. It was to prove a doubly ironic reference, since Rushdie was to become the victim of Islamic fundamentalist condemnation precisely on the grounds of his supposed complicity with the West in *The Satanic Verses* (1988). These complexities are hardly likely to be familiar outside the groves of academe, whether in the so-called metropolis or the self-styled 'periphery' of the Universities of New South Wales, Queensland or Western Australia.

The main point to be taken from *The Empire Writes Back* is that there is no escape from global power-structures, because there is no escape from writing, discourse or language. This is true historically: the colonized have been part of the processes of subjugation accompanying European advance around the world, from the moment of its inception. So the term post-colonial is used 'to cover all the culture affected by the imperial process from the moment of colonization to the present day'. What each and every national literature has in common 'beyond their special and distinctive regional characteristics' is their emergence out of this process, and their assertion of 'differences from the assumptions of the imperial centre. It is this which makes them distinctively post-colonial'. 'Writing back' is the key motive for this approach to post-colonial writings. The authors go on to identify four 'major models' supposed to have emerged as writers and critics became 'aware of the special character of post-colonial texts': 'national' or regional models (first, American literature, then much later Nigerian and West Indian literatures, for example); second, the 'Black Writing' model (from writers of the African diaspora, in the US, Afro-Caribbeans); third, simple 'comparative' models (such as Commonwealth or Third World approaches); and finally, more complex comparative models (involving 'hybridity' or 'syncretism'). Their own approach emerges as a development within the third major grouping of theory, of a 'dominated–dominating' model, emphasizing the 'inevitable tendency towards subversion' of 'dominated' literatures, so that, as they put it,

> Directly and indirectly, in Salman Rushdie's phrase, the 'Empire writes back' to the imperial 'centre', not only through nationalist assertion, proclaiming itself central and self-determining, but even more radically by questioning the bases of European and British metaphysics, challenging the world-view that can polarize centre and periphery in the first place . . . Writers such as J.M. Coetzee, Wilson

Harris, V.S. Naipaul, George Lamming, Patrick White, Chinua Achebe, Margaret Atwood, and Jean Rhys have all rewritten particular works from the English 'canon' with a view to restructuring 'realities' in post-colonial terms, not simply by reversing the hierarchical order, but by interrogating the philosophical assumptions on which that order was based.[7]

This promotion of a disparate gaggle of writers on the grounds that they all 'interrogate' the 'metaphysics' of the West by rewriting versions of the English 'canon', thereby 'inevitably' offering a more radical 'writing back' than mere 'nationalist assertion', reveals the potential for rigidity and contradiction in the 'writing back' model. The specific histories and politics of the individual writers are ignored so as to propose an all-inclusive, flattening perspective upon their works; the polarization between centre and periphery claimed as central to their own approach is blamed upon a colonizer–colonized dichotomy apparently derived from that very 'European and British metaphysics' (hard to understand what 'metaphysics' means here, perhaps 'value-systems'?) which it is, apparently, the function of these writings to undermine; most alarming of all, the richness and complexity of the debates which the use of the term 'post-colonial' is meant to arouse, are lost.

Ashcroft et al. do offer specific examples of post-colonial texts, but understood as 'always a complex and hybridised formation'– that 'always' a give-away, reflecting the dominating, essentializing method which the authors presume to locate within the metropolis, while unaware of their own mimicry of the position, to the degree that they resist even their own sense of the potential of specific texts to question the monolithic conception of their subject. 'Texts such as Nkosi's *Mating Birds* and Naipaul's *The Mimic Men* articulate the impossibility of evading the destructive and marginalizing power of the dominant centre and the need for its abrogation' (abrogation = refusing the categories of imperial power).[8] These remarks bear little resemblance to the reading experience of the novels to which they refer: Nkosi's 1986 South African novella about the rape of a white woman, told by the black perpetrator from his prison cell, and Naipaul's 1967 Trinidadian story of political change in the island colony, told by an exiled politician in London. Of course, these two works do have something in common – a concern with the realities of colonial power in two contrasting, and only very distantly related situations, as they impinge upon individuals. But as Vijay Mishra and Bob Hodge have well demonstrated, the concern in *The Empire Writes Back* with 'textuality' as an abstraction 'tends to function at the expense of specific histories and power-relations in different parts of the world'.[9] *The Empire Writes Back* moreover conflates the distinct but related kinds of colonial and post-colonial writings or 'sets of discourses', while pinpointing certain recent literary texts (from India, Canada and Australia as well as South Africa and the Caribbean) for offering a 'radical critique' towards 'Eurocentric' assumptions about race, nationality, language and literature. Mishra and Hodge sum up the danger of this kind of operation well: it is that 'the post-colonial is reduced to a purely textual phenomenon, as if power is simply a matter of discourse and it is only through discourse that counter-claims might be made'. This is, in the end, 'a move clearly aimed at making the diverse forms of the post-colonial available as a single object on the curriculum of the centre', and so difference 'is recognized but contained'.

### The Said Enterprise: Reading the Other

The publication of *The Empire Writes Back* coincided with the twenty-fifth anniversary conference of the Association for Commonwealth Literature and Language Studies (ACLALS) at the University of Kent. The keynote speaker was Edward Said (b. 1935), who has been described as the founder of Anglophone post-colonial theory. Said, a Christian Arab raised in the Middle East and based for many years at Columbia University in New York, showed in his book *Orientalism* (1978) how the Western image of the Orient has been constructed by generations of writers and scholars, who thereby legitimated imperial penetration and control. By training a comparativist in the European high cultural tradition of Erich Auerbach (*Mimesis*, 1946), Said studied English and History at Princeton and Harvard, completing a doctorate on Conrad, a figure for whom he continues to show great respect, as he does for most of the major figures in the familiar canon of English literature. The most important influences upon Said's *Orientalism* were the Italian Marxist cultural critic Antonio Gramsci (1891–1937), and the French post-structuralist Michel Foucault (1926–84). Both crucially theorized the way power is internalized by those it disempowers through ideology, discourse or language.

> My contention is that without examining Orientalism as a discourse one cannot possibly understand the enormously systematic discipline by which European culture was able to manage – and even produce – the Orient politically, sociologically, militarily, ideologically, scientifically and imaginatively during the post-Enlightenment period . . . How this happened is what this book tries to demonstrate.

It also tries to show that European culture gained in strength and identity by setting itself off against the Orient as a sort of surrogate and even underground self.[10]

Said's focus was on English and French scholarly texts from the end of the eighteenth century, showing their construction of the 'East' by the 'West' as inferior and 'other'. If, as he argues, the languages of communication are subject to prevailing power structures, they inevitably reinforce control. However, as he seems unaware, they may also generate resistance, shown by the many 'oppositional' writings of the colonized, from the time of the earliest imposition of imperial control onwards.

Yet Said's explicit aim at the time of the 1989 Kent conference, was to continue to undermine the 'humanist' overtones of Commonwealth literary study, by arguing that the literatures it took as its subject should be reinterpreted in terms of the 'revolutionary realities' of the world today, in which post-colonial societies were embattled and marginalized. Criticism should, according to Said, 'situate' literature in terms of emerging connections across national boundaries and other 'coercive' global power-structures.[11] In this international context, Commonwealth was not much more than a temporary label of convenience, carrying besides unfortunate overtones of neo-imperial control. How might such situating criticism work in practice? Far from granting attention to the literary products of the colonized, as one might have expected from this stance, Said looked for support from the traditional monuments of the English literary canon, especially the nineteenth-century realist novel and its modernist successors. Thus, in his next book, *Culture and Imperialism* (1993), it is in the 'great canonical texts' – by Defoe, Jane Austen, Dickens and, again, Conrad – that he finds 'what is silent or marginally present', reading them afresh in the context of imperial histories.[12]

Nevertheless, the results are provocative, suggestive and reveal how new perceptions may be gained from well-known texts by adopting a post-colonial perspective, which in Said's hands (he avoids the term for his own work), means offering 'contrapuntal' readings so as 'to formulate an alternative both to a politics of blame and to the even more destructive politics of confrontation and hostility'. This is evident, for example, in Said's reading of Kipling's well-known but undervalued or patronized novel *Kim* (1901). Said says we must keep two factors in mind as we interpret this text. 'One is that, whether we like it or not, its author is writing not just from the dominating viewpoint of a white man in a colonial possession but from the perspective of a massive colonial system whose economy, functioning and history had acquired the status of a virtual fact of nature.' The second is that *Kim* was written at a specific moment in the changing relationship between the British and the Indian peoples, when, 'even though Kipling resisted this reality, India was already well on its way towards a dynamic of outright opposition'. The result is that *Kim* provides a 'very illuminating part' of the interdependent history of colonizer and colonized.[13]

Said's influence can hardly be underestimated, despite serious worries about his method and conclusions. More recent critics, while acknowledging his importance in drawing attention to, if not always persuasively illuminating the ways in which the processes of imperialism and colonization are represented, have come to see him as fatally resembling the figure he most claims to undermine – the globalizing, humanist and (by virtue of his position if not his language) Western intellectual. This is what his most forceful critic, Aijaz Ahmad, claims in his chapter on 'Orientalism and after'.[14] Ahmad, who shares Said's basic anti-colonial stance while differing from him on almost every other point, is a post-colonial critic who avoids the label precisely because of its global reach. An explicitly socialist academic in New Delhi, he argues that what we now need to recognize is that Western 'Third Worldism' and 'post-structuralism' have succeeded each other in misrepresenting the many different (and especially indigenous) literatures and cultures flourishing in Africa and Asia. Where, then, to turn?

### Back to Fanon: Recovering the Material from the Textual

Ahmad, who disparages the whole discourse-oriented, Foucauldian trend of post-colonial theory as a Western imposition, reminds us of the distinct and varied traditions of resistance to colonial ways of thought developed by the colonized themselves. As another forceful (ex-colonial) critic, Benita Parry, has pointed out, the ideas of Frantz Fanon should not be overlooked or forgotten. This view, like Ahmad's, is part of what I would call the *materialist* wing of post-colonial theory, as opposed to the *textualist* – although I do not wish to parody what are quite complex, interconnected sets of ideas. But the broad distinction has some use, if only to suggest the importance of not allowing the notion that ideology is structured like a language to push away entirely the social and historical realities which interweave, if not determine, both language and ideology. As Parry argued in a cogent and influential account of some 'Problems in current theories of colonial discourse', these theories tend to find what they look for in the colonial encounter, that is, underlying them lies a privileged or ethnocentric assumption that it is the colonizer's voice that counts, since that is the dominant or dominating discourse; which means erasing the 'voice of the native', or limiting resistance to a mere dodging around colonial authority, rather than actively challenging if not simply ignoring that authority.[15] Parry's emphasis upon opposition, even conflict, between colonizer and colonized, as the defining characteristic of the colonial encounter, is derived from the stark vision most powerfully adumbrated by Fanon in *The Wretched of the Earth*.

As a psychiatrist based in Algeria during the independence struggle of the 1950s, Fanon wrote from the perspective of a colonial subject in the thick of decolonization, addressing other colonial subjects. He placed the cultural (including literary) aspect of colonial and post-colonial history at the centre of his discussion. Various anti-colonial critical theories have been influential among the oppressed peoples of the world; but *The Wretched of the Earth* has spoken more directly, profoundly and lastingly than any other single anti-colonial work on behalf of and to the colonized, with the result that many writers and critics, whether or not they agree with Fanon's assumptions or conclusions, consider that his work deserves repeated rereading. During the late 1950s and 1960s, Fanon shaped an increasingly influential account of the consequences of colonization, which developed both Marxist and psychoanalytic strands of Western thought, primarily in two books – *Black Skin, White Masks* (originally *Peau noir, masques blancs*, Paris, 1952) and *The Wretched of the Earth* (*Les damnés de la terre*, Paris, 1961) – but also in two collections of essays, *Studies in a Dying Colonialism* (*L'an cinq de la révolution algérienne*, Paris, 1959) and *Toward the African Revolution* (*Pour la révolution africaine*, Paris, 1964). Fanon also drew on the earlier theorization of modern black writing by the 'Négritude' movement. This was conceived in Paris during the 1930s by a group of Francophone writers, including Aimé Césaire of Martinique, Leopold Senghor of Senegal and Léon Damas of French Guiana, who attempted to identify and affirm a whole ensemble of black cultural and literary attitudes, ranging from protest and anger at white brutality to a celebration of the 'primitive', instinctual black 'soul'. The basic problem with this movement, which has its parallels elsewhere (in Hindu revivalism, for instance), and which continues to prove convincing among Black American as well as Francophone Caribbean and African writers, is its dependence upon the categories of the colonizing culture itself, in the sense that its language and conceptual apparatus is derived from the West.

But then the most potent influences detectable in Fanon's writing are also Western, especially French. Yet, paradoxically, the main drive of his thought is towards revealing the crippling effect of Western colonial attitudes on the colonized, in particular the colonized intellectual elite – like himself. This paradox is not as disabling as it may seem: the origins of a theory don't necesarily determine its validity; and, arguably, it is almost impossible to find some notionally pure, authentic, indigenous discourse – although some critics, for example in India, have tried to do so. But there are immensely ancient, unbroken traditions of criticism going back centuries in the indigenous languages of the Indian subcontinent, which is not the case for the cultures Fanon knew.

As a French-trained psychiatrist on the staff of a hospital in Algeria, Fanon observed at close quarters the psychological effects of the colonial situation on the brink of decolonization. He noted that the majority of the victims of violence (rape, torture, shootings) were Arabs, although sympathetic Europeans were not immune; further, that all efforts to bring those responsible to justice seemed worse than useless. He became convinced that the atrocities could only be explained as a symptom of sadistic, racist anger, basic to the colonial system, and yet which European intellectuals at home, from left to right, persistently refused to acknowledge. In 1956 he resigned his hospital post to devote himself full-time to the revolutionary movement, and in 1960 he was sent to newly independent Ghana as Ambassador for the Algerian Provisional Government. That year he was found to be suffering from leukaemia, and he died in the USA shortly after the publication of *The Wretched of the Earth*, aged thirty-six.

*Black Skin, White Masks* was a powerful polemic invoking a large range of thinkers, from Marx to Jean-Paul Sartre (who became an important mediator of his views), from Freud to Lacan (then relatively unknown in the Anglophone intellectual world). The aim was to articulate the colonial situation from the perspective of the Black man, undermining the whole arsenal of attitudes enforced by colonization. At its centre was a fierce critique of the French psychologist Oscar Mannoni's *Prospero and Caliban: The Psychology of Colonization* (*Psychologie de la colonisation*, Paris, 1950), a study of relations between colonizer and colonized in Madagascar, written by a colonial administrator during and just after the 1947 revolt which was so brutally put down by the French it resulted in nearly 100,000 deaths. Mannoni (whose originality deserves respect) sought to explain the instability and extremism of the colonial situation in terms of a 'dependency complex' among the colonized, and a 'Prospero complex' among the colonizers. Acknowledging Mannoni's contribution towards understanding the inner, subjective conditions of colonialism, and the guilt and violence it produced, Fanon went on to try and show how Mannoni's theory ended up justifying the status quo and white superiority. *Black Skin, White Masks* was written in a fragmentary, aphoristic style which, as Homi Bhabha pointed out in a Foreword to the 1986 edition, reveals Fanon's desperate sense of the extreme alienation of the colonial subject, driving him from one conceptual scheme to another, from psychology to sociology, from phenomenology to existentialism, without finding a 'dialectic of deliverance' (neither does Bhabha himself, of course).

*The Wretched of the Earth* is altogether more coherent and thoroughgoing, as Fanon brings together psychoanalytic notions of the alienation of the colonized, with Marxist notions of the economic and historical forces which have brought about that alienation. With the Algerian revolution as the model for succesful independence struggles, Fanon commits himself to the violent overthrow of colonial regimes as the only solution to the problem he identifes of the continued existence of exploitative structures in the post-colonial situation. This is really the major problem we live with today, in the decolonized world: of the expansion of neo-colonial, global interventionary structures, beside the absence of more than a handful of states that have managed to overcome the tensions inherited from the colonial situation to create relatively stable, liberal democracies – as in India or Singapore. The problem was lyrically articulated in the time of transition by Okot p'Bitek (1931–82) from Uganda, whose *Song of Lawino* (1966), translated into English from his own Acholi, drew on the myths, proverbs and rhythms of traditional indigenous oral techniques to question 'Uhuru' in the voice of a woman:

> Someone said
> Independence falls like a bull buffalo
> And the hunters
> Rush to it with drawn knives,
> Sharp shining knives
> For carving the carcass.
> And if your chest
> Is small, bony and weak
> They push you off,
> And if your knife is blunt
> You get the dung on your elbow,
> You come home empty-handed
> And the dogs bark at you![16]

Who, then, will overthrow the new rulers? Not the urban proletariat of traditional Marxist thinking; according to Fanon, Western workers were both the beneficiaries and the accomplices of latter-day colonialism; and the native proletariat, like the colonial bourgeoisie, remained tied to the privileges they had enjoyed under foreign rule – hence their support for the corrupt national elites governing so many post-independence countries. Only the veritable 'wretched of the earth' (the phrase comes from the first line of 'The Internationale'), wielders of the sickle not the hammer, retained sufficient sense of community and self-value to reclaim their country and their dignity, by violence. Ultimately, this was the only way out of the so-called 'Manichean delirium' created by colonialism – a phrase coined by Fanon to suggest the absolute dichotomy between the world experiences of colonizer and colonized, most strikingly demonstrated, he said, by apartheid South Africa.

Fanon offered a vision, not a programme; and whether or not readers were taken along by his rhetoric, he provided subversive insights into the cultural aspect of the post-colonial condition, which he repeatedly redefined. According to Fanon, 'native' cultural producers would go through three phases in relations with the dominant, colonial culture:

> In the first phase, the native intellectual gives proof that he has assimilated the culture of the occupying power. His writings correspond point by point with those of his opposite numbers in the mother country. His inspiration is European and we can easily link up these works with definite trends in the literature of the mother country. This is the period of unqualified assimilation . . .
>
> In the second phase we find the native is disturbed; he decides to remember what he is. This period of creative work approximately corresponds to that immersion which we have just described. But since the native is not a part of his people, he is content to recall their life only. Past happenings of the bygone days of his childhood will be brought up out of the depths of this memory: old legends will be reinterpreted in the light of a borrowed aestheticism and of a conception of the world which was discovered under other skies . . .
>
> Finally, in the third phase, which is called the fighting phase, the native, after having tried to lose himself in the people and with the people, will on the contrary shake the people . . . hence comes a fighting literature, a revolutionary literature, and a national literature. During this phase a great many men and women who up till then would never have thought of producing a literary work, now that they find themselves in exceptional circumstances – in prison, with the Maquis or on the eve of their execution – feel the need to speak to their nation, to compose the sentence which expresses the heart

of the people and to become the mouthpiece of a new reality in action.[17]

What Fanon means by this last phase is not too clear, although the earlier phases are well enough represented by many works, from the 'assimilationist' writings of the Francophone Négritude poets such as Senghor, to the early autobiographical writings of authors as disparate as Ngugi wa Thiong'o and the Trinidadian Michael Anthony.

The career of Jamaican performance poet Louise Bennett suggests how Fanon's paradigm may be constructed in practice. At the beginning of her career in the 1940s 'what I knew most about were the English poets of the time', but then as a drama teacher trained in London, conveying to Jamaicans the 'borrowed' view of life 'discovered under other skies', she came to reinterpret her world by responding to local speech forms, 'and writing in this medium of dialect instead of writing in the same old English way about Autumn and things like that',[18] she produced her 'Miss Lou' poems. By drawing on folklore and proverb, an act of cultural retrieval reinforcing nationalist self-assertion, she became a household name and won acceptance in her own community. This popular support enabled her to develop the subversive-assertive writing Fanon finally calls for, as in anti-establishment poems like 'Independence':

> Independence wid a vengeance!
> Independence raisin Cain!
> Jamaica start grow beard, ah hope
> We chin can stan de strain!

Or 'Census':

> But Government fas, eeh mah? Lawd!
> Me laugh so tell me cry,
> Me dis done tell de census man
> A whole ton-load a lie[19]

If the schematizing application of Fanon's three-phase model appears a little too pat, at least it engenders a sense of the comparable shape of individual literary outputs. In Bennett's case, it helps highlight the importance of humour as an undermining force, potentially fracturing more than one cultural monolith, the nationalist as well as the colonial, as when, for example, she advances the claims of women in the post-independence dispensation:

Jamaica oman cunny, sah!
Is how dem jinnal so?
Look how long dem liberated
An de man dem never know! . . .
An long before Oman Lib bruck out
Over foreign lan
Jamaica femala wasa work
Her liberated plan![20]

Fanon's cultural paradigm has been more persuasive among writers and critics in the newly decolonized nations of the Caribbean, and Africa, than in Asia, where the 'assimilation' consequent upon colonization was never so complete, nor were indigenous cultures so thoroughly or consistently penetrated. Even so, what we are talking about here is a range of possibilities, rather than any notional easy fit between the Fanon model and actual cultural practices. Fanon drew attention to the salient issues; although, as the example of Louise Bennett immediately demonstrates, his work needs also to be viewed historically, and critically, for instance in a feminist perspective.

### Nervous Conditions: From Fanon to Bhabha and Spivak

The importance of Fanon's thought in post-colonial theory is often unacknowledged, which is why I have dwelt upon it at some length. If it was true that, as Jean-Paul Sartre's influential Preface to *Wretched of the Earth* announced, here the 'Third World finds itself and speaks to itself through his voice', Sartre's own words made it clear that this voice was also addressed to the European reader, specifically the liberal humanist reader who could 'pretend to forget that you own colonies and that in them men are massacred in your name'. But: 'Have the courage to read this book', for 'it will make you ashamed, and shame, as Marx said, is a revolutionary senti-ment'. 'We in Europe too', Sartre declared, 'are being decolonized: that is to say that the settler which is in every one of us is being savagely rooted out. Let us look at ourselves, if we can bear to, and see what is becoming of us . . . in the past we made history and now it is being made of us'. Crucially, 'the status of "native"' was defined as a 'nervous condition introduced and maintained by the settler among colonized people *with their consent*'.[21] This condition has been concretely imagined by the Zimbabwean novelist, Tsitsi Dangarembga (b. 1959), taking Sartre's phrase for the title of her account of the vio-lence and loss involved in the colonizing process, *Nervous Conditions* (1988).

Dangarembga's text, an autobiographical account of two generations of women living in the Rhodesia of the 1950s, also suggests how far black women's alienation under colonial rule may reflect a continuation of traditional oppressions. The whole question of the role of women, which cuts across, although it implies parallels with, the issues of post-colonial theory, has only recently come to be acknowledged and developed. As Jane Miller has forcefully demonstrated, Fanon, like Said after him (although with more justification), seems to have elided women from his theorization of the colonial process – or rather, both men allow women to become a form of coinage, 'exchange value offered or stolen or forbidden, tokens of men's power and wealth or lack of them'.[22] Apart from his chapter 'Algeria unveiled' in *Studies in a Dying Colonialism*, Fanon barely addresses the potential of women as agents of change; and Said's *Culture and Imperialism* provides little if any advance upon the silence of *Orientalism* as a critique involving women as well as men as agents of resistance, not merely the passive subjects of Western possession. This silencing tendency is evident among other influential voices, such as that of the US-based Abdul JanMohamed, whose *Manichean Aesthetics: The Politics of Literature in Colonial Africa* (1983) is explicitly Fanonist in inspiration.

If (as noted in chapter 1), Fanon argues that Marxist analysis should be 'slightly stretched every time we have to do with the colonial problem', then this is also true of Freudian or Lacanian analysis, although he does not say so, any more than that other dazzling migrant theorist, Homi Bhabha, who operates initially from within Fanon's overlapping frames of reference. Bhabha, formerly of Bombay, Oxford and Sussex, and now based in the USA, writes to unsettle, to break the grip of 'universalist' or 'essentialist' ways of thinking, by means of a characteristically subtle, dense and metaphorically slippery rhetoric which, however, puts off many interested parties. While works such as *The Location of Culture* (1994) excite fellow-academics in literary and cultural studies, usually of the post-structuralist persuasion, many others see it as a way of denying their experience, so contributing to a reaction against theory as an elitist, Eurocentric (although increasingly American) activity.

This is unfortunate, since the purpose of post-colonial theory, whatever its origins, is to aid, not hinder critical understanding of a proliferating area of literary creativity, as well as the reinterpretation of texts from a newly aware position – as Edward Said acknowledged in the 1994 afterword to *Orientalism*, where it is also pointed out that a leading motif of more recent and proliferating 'post-colonial work' has been 'the consistent critique of Eurocentrism and patriarchy'. In Bhabha's words, 'Postcolonial criticism bears witness to the unequal and uneven forces of cultural representation involved in the contest for political and social authority within the modern world order'.[23] Like other theorists since the 1980s, he has increasingly become aware of two constituencies neglected by the major early players in the field – women and migrants. But the 'double colonization' experienced by women in the former colonized societies has been explored mainly and most effectively by women writers and critics themselves – such as Trinh T. Minh-Ha, Sara Suleri and Gayatri Spivak in the USA, Dorothy Driver in South Africa, Vrinda Nabar in India, and Jane Miller and Sara Mills in the UK, to name only a few of those whose concern is to develop a critique involving gender, as well as race or ethnicity, class and nation. Meanwhile the growing sense of the world as a network of patterns of migration, largely from parts of the old empires towards the metropolitan centres of power, registered by writers as diverse as V.S. Naipaul and Bharati Mukherjee, Jamaica Kincaid and Lauretta Ngcobo, has produced a growing body of writing emphasizing 'hybridity' as the characteristic feature of post-colonial histories, cultures and literatures, and not only in varieties of English.

The theoretical perspective on this is well summed up by Spivak's remark 'one is always on the move', glossed as 'always citational in one way or another';[24] which reveals just how closely allied this position is with the textualist, postmodern wing of theory – not surprising, from a group of well-paid, literally high-flying academics, whose celebration of their own multiple pasts and identities too easily becomes a self-regarding expression of their own, rather than others' lives. Spivak, a post-structuralist Marxist who calls herself a 'bricoleur' (i.e. someone who uses whatever is to hand), writes in an often fragmentary, elusive and allusive manner derived from a strategy which, in marked contrast to that of Said, Bhabha and other totalizing theorists, is designed to expose the unsettling heterogeneity of texts and cultures. Her greatest strength is her insistence on the particular problem, the local issue, as it can be drawn out of her chosen text or given moment of utterance; her greatest weakness is her obscurity, and the gadfly logic encouraged by her long commitment to deconstruction (her first claim to fame was as a translator and mediator of the work of Jacques Derrida).

Either way, Spivak's voice is unmistakable, and unignorable: lively, articulate if only intermittently compelling; she addresses a vast range of issues not easily corralled within the post-colonial (such as feminism), despite allowing herself to be presented as *The Post-Colonial Critic* on the occasion of the collection of 'interviews, strategies, dialogues' with that title (1990); while her criticism of Western academic theory for its lack of radical self-awareness is balanced by a deep analysis of the problems of such oppositional intellectual projects as the Indian Subaltern Studies group. The responsibilities of academics in India as in America (her two main points of reference and experience) remain a central concern, as she tries to resist the rush to the margins evident among many recent followers of academic fashion, the over-hasty identification of writers, texts or places as 'Third World' or 'other' without sufficient or sufficiently complex cause. One of her more persuasive interests has been the question of 'voice', of who speaks – through, for, or on behalf of the lost, disenfranchised or otherwise silenced. In 'Can the subaltern speak?' (1988), an essay to which I shall return in the next chapter, she worried fruitfully about the problem of representing some of the most marginalized people – rural Indian women subject to sati – although her critics argue that she ended up not allowing them any voice at all, since that voice is on her terms always mediated, if only by her own attention to it.

Who in the end can escape being caught by the nets of language and position? Rather than sit this problem out in a state of static self-analysis, let us return to some obvious realities – especially that of migrants. Most migrants are not academics, but illiterate refugees pushed about the world by material forces beyond their comprehension and control. Theirs is truly a 'nervous condition'. Yet ideas of cross-fertilization, of the potential richness of traffic between and across boundaries – racial, national or international – can return post-colonial theorizing to a more celebratory, even (to use an old-fashioned word) liberatory mode, as a way simultaneously to acknowledge *while continuing to resist* the oppressions of past *and* present.

## Summary

The literary writings in English of the former colonized peoples have become more prolific and more noticeable since at least the 1940s, the time of the most important successful independence movements. A series of subsequent attempts to incorporate or at least include these writings within the defined parameters of English literary studies as Commonwealth or New Writings has since the 1960s been overtaken by the radical theorization of the subject in terms of the destabilizing influences of Marxism, structuralism, post-structuralism, psychoanalysis and other recent intellectual developments. The writings of Fanon have proved hugely influential (especially as mediated by Sartre), upon both the textualist (or Foucauldian) and materialist (or neo-Marxist) wings of post-colonial theory, and they continue to remind us of the challenge to Western assumptions about history, race and identity – although Fanon's views were limited in respect of the increasingly powerful feminist critique of patriarchal formations which were, and still are, complicit with the colonial. Agency and resistance are key areas of continuing concern, while the element of 'hybridity' involved in a new sense of the world as crisscrossed by migrants, including many writers, has captured the imagination of the most recent theorists – not always persuasively.

Post-colonial then, has to do with the past, but is being reinterpreted towards the future: 'post' does not, cannot shut off historical process. We can see how, for example, from the writings of the Indian subcontinent, a selection of which are discussed in my next chapter.

## Notes

1 Ngugi wa Thiong'o, *Decolonising the Mind:* The Politics of Language in African Literature (James Currey, 1986), p. 63.
2 Andrew Sanders, *The Short Oxford History of English Literature* (Oxford, 1994), p. 636.
3 V.S. Naipaul, 'Images', *New Statesman*, 24 September 1965, reptd in *Critical Perspectives on V.S. Naipaul*, ed. Robert D. Hamner (Heinemann, 1979), pp. 26–7.
4 William Walsh, Preface, *Commonwealth Literature* (Oxford University Press, 1973), p. v.
5 Bruce King, *Literatures of the World in English* (Routledge & Kegan Paul, 1974), p. 2.
6 Jean Pierre and Carol Durix (eds), *The New Literatures in English* (Longman France, 1993), p. 5.
7 Bill Ashcroft, Gareth Griffiths and Helen Tiffin, *The Empire Writes Back*, pp. 2, 33.
8 Ibid., pp. 110, 115.
9 See Vijay Mishra and Bob Hodge, 'What is post(-)colonialism?', *Textual Practice*, 5, 3 (1991), 399–414, reptd in *Colonial Discourse and Post-Colonial Theory: A Reader*, eds Patrick Williams and Laura Chrisman (Harvester Wheatsheaf, 1993), pp. 276–90.
10 Edward Said, *Orientalism: Western Conceptions of the Orient* (Penguin, 1995), p. 3. This edition is unchanged from earlier editions, save for the addition of an 'Afterword'.
11 See Edward Said, 'Figures, configurations, transfigurations', in *From Commonwealth to Post-Colonial*, ed. Anna Rutherford (Dangaroo, 1992), pp. 3–17.
12 Edward Said, *Culture and Imperialism* (Vintage, 1994 edn), p. 78.
13 Ibid., pp. 19, 162ff.

14 Aijaz Ahmad, *In Theory: Classes, Nations, Literatures* (Verso, 1992), pp. 159–220.

15 See Benita Parry, 'Problems in current theories of colonial discourse', *Oxford Literary Review*, 1, 1–2 (1987), pp. 27–58.

16 Okot p'Bitek, *Song of Lawino & Song of Ocol* (Heinemann, 1984), p. 107.

17 Frantz Fanon, *The Wretched of the Earth* (Penguin, 1967), pp. 178–9.

18 Louise Bennett, 'Interview with Dennis Scott', in *Hinterland: Caribbean Poetry from the West Indies and Britain*, ed. E.A. Markham (Bloodaxe, 1989), p. 47.

19 Ibid., pp. 51, 55.

20 Ibid., pp. 53–4.

21 Fanon, *Wretched of the Earth*, pp. 12, 21, 23, 17.

22 Jane Miller, *Seductions: Studies in Reading and Culture* (Virago, 1990), p. 122.

23 Said, *Orientalism* (1995), pp. 352–3; Homi Bhabha, 'Postcolonial criticism', in *Redrawing the Boundaries: The Transformation of English and American Literary Studies*, eds Stephen Greenblatt and Giles Gunn (Modern Languages Association, 1992), p. 437.

24 Gayatri Spivak, *The Post-Colonial Critic: Interviews, Strategies, Dialogues*, ed. Sarah Harasym (Routledge, 1990), p. 38. See also Trinh T. Minh-Ha, *Woman, Native, Other: Writing, Postcoloniality and Feminism* (Indiana University Press, 1989); Sara Suleri, 'Woman skin deep: feminism and the postcolonial condition', *Critical Inquiry* 18 (Summer 1992), pp. 756–69; Dorothy Driver, 'M'a-Ngoana O Tsoare Thipa ka Bohaleng – The child's mother grabs the sharp end of the knife: Women as mothers, women as writers', in *Rendering Things Visible: Essays on South African Literary Culture*, ed. Martin Trump (Ravan, 1990), pp. 225–55; Vrinda Nabar, *Caste as Woman* (Penguin India, 1995); Sara Mills, *Discourses of Difference: An Analysis of Women's Travel Writing and Colonialism* (Routledge, 1993).

# Part II

*Case Studies*

# 5

## Indo-Anglian Fiction: Narayan and Sahgal

To the Indo-British Experience and what its sharers have learned
from each other
> Nayantara Sahgal, dedication to *Rich Like Us*, 1983

It is actually a slender new twig of that giant Banyan tree called Indian
literature
> M.K. Naik, *Studies in Indian English Literature*, 1987

Sky is the same everywhere, and literature is like that . . . there are
certain local colourings, that's all
> R.K. Narayan interview, Open University BBC TV
> *Born Into Two Cultures*, 1989

### *Authority and Creativity*

There is a strong case for considering the writings of the Indian subcontinent first in any account of post-colonial literatures in English, if only because of the scale of the achievement of its writers, from before as well as after 1947, when Independence and Partition initiated that wave of decolonization which was to overwhelm the European empires during the years which followed. Ignorance of Indo-Anglian writing is not as common as it used to be, but if anything should long ago have jolted readers of literatures in English worldwide into a recognition of the range and quality of writing from outside the canonical Anglo-American providers, it is texts by writers from the oldest of the 'new' literatures, most prominent of which have been novelists, including R.K. Narayan (b. 1906) or, more recently (and less well known), Nayantara Sahgal (b. 1927), both of whom I draw on for this case study. Despite the fact that for most Indian observers, writing in English occupies a relatively small part of the literary terrain in the subcontinent, it has for so long featured so much and so varied a body of texts that it has generated a well-established body of criticism and literary histories – the first of which, K.R. Srinivasa Iyengar's pioneering *Indian Writing in English* (New Delhi, 1962, 5th rev. edn, 1985), began as a series of lectures at Leeds University at the invitation of A.N. Jeffares. It would be foolish to pretend to offer a map, much less any kind of comprehensive account here. But the point about my use of 'case study' is that it implies quite severe selectivity of area, genre or text, and a consciously limited approach. Not only for obvious, practical reasons, but because I wish to avoid the tendency to abstraction and (hegemonic) generalization common among post-colonial studies, and to clarify at least some of the terms upon which fruitful debate and understanding may proceed. But if I pursue a small handful of specific texts, I do so within the context of relevant history, language and theory.

The specific texts I focus on are two novels which exemplify the challenge to presumptions about post-colonial writing in English in terms of their creative force and independence: Narayan's *The Painter of Signs* (1976), and Sahgal's *Rich Like Us* (1983). Novels such as these insist upon their own perspective, legitimating an alternative range of views from those still familiar in the West, where the Indian subcontinent tends to remain a vision constructed out of an imaginary amalgam of the (very different) writings of Kipling, E.M. Forster, Paul Scott and J.G. Farrell – not to mention the idealized, nostalgic imagery of Richard Attenborough's film *Gandhi* (1983).

Instead, what we have here are two radically contrasting prose fictions which emerged out of the same moment of crisis during the mid-1970s, when the Indian government faced the most serious challenge to its authority in the post-colonial era. 'The decision to have emergency is not one that could be taken lightly or easily', Prime Minister Indira Gandhi remarked a month after the proclamation of a state of national emergency in June 1975, 'but there comes a time in the life of the nation when hard decisions have to be taken. When there is an atmosphere of violence and indiscipline and one can visibly see the nation going down, then the time has come to stop this process'.[1] India, the largest liberal democracy in the world, has been the jewel in the crown of nations liberated after the Second World War, preserving its unity, parliamentary structure and the rule of law while other post-colonial countries around the world displayed worrying signs of instability, corruption and even disintegration. So when the emergency broke out, and civil rights were suspended, it seemed as if the country would become yet another authoritarian state – ' the world's largest democracy was looking like nothing so much as one of those two-bit dictatorships we had loftily looked down upon'.[2]

But after less than two years, in March 1977, free elections took place, the Prime Minister was defeated and a new government installed. The trauma of that time is not forgotten; nor should it be. It is one indication of the strong socio-historical awareness of the continent's novelists that they should revisit it – for instance, more recently, by Rohinton Mistry's prize-winning novel, *A Fine Balance* (1996). A surprising number of novelists have been women, most of whom – from Kamala Markandaya to Anita Desai, from Ruth Prawer Jhabvala to Bapsi Sidhwa (from Pakistan) – have had some connection (by birth, education or travel) with foreign countries, which helps explain their achievement, despite the 'prison-house' for women in India.[3] It is partly to highlight the remarkable contribution of women writers that I have selected a text by Sahgal, although it is also true that the situation of women as an issue in post-colonial fiction is so obvious and central that it is something to draw out, not only in novels by women writers, but also in works such as Narayan's.

The main issues foregrounded by these two novels as I read them here are: the importance of place (especially in Narayan); and of history (especially Sahgal). Both writers also concern themselves profoundly with questions of identity and gender. Underlying these issues, there is another, which pervades the work of Indo-Anglian writers: it is the question of authority. The word 'authority' implies the notion of authoring, or writing; as well as control and power, or 'agency'. The question of who writes, is also the question of who is permitted to write, and in what genre and language. This requires some explanation.

## The Right to Write: The Language of Indo-Anglian Literature

Traditions of writing in Indian languages go back a very long way – over two millennia if we count the earliest Sanskrit texts; and these traditions, preserved by elites, still speak to many today, to the extent that the literatures of the subcontinent in major languages such as Hindi, Tamil, Marathi, Malayalam or Urdu (each of which has more than ten million speakers), carry an authority which weighs far more in their societies than the analogous indigenous African languages such as Yoruba or Zulu, whose distant traditions are mainly oral, or than the Creoles of the Caribbean, which lost earlier traditions and languages through genocide and slavery. Ngugi's argument that to take up the colonizer's language was to take up his culture – or rather, to be taken up by it, thereby continuing the sense of cultural inferiority engendered by the colonial experience, has had its echoes among writers in India, but in a muted strain. In very large, multilingual and multicultural nations like India (or Nigeria), English, though spoken by a minority, and written by proportionately fewer, still involves millions of people – it has been said that in a country of some 840 million, 'more Indians speak English and write English than in England itself'.[4]

Despite the decision at the moment of independence in 1947 to declare English an 'associate' official language, with the expectation that it would die out within two decades, and although the constitution recognizes fifteen state languages (used in schools and official transactions), the power of English in the life of the subcontinent has not merely survived, it has grown – as a means of keeping people together (tensions between the predominantly Hindi-speaking north and the rest have, if anything, increased), and as a vital medium of communication, between lovers as well as scientists and civil servants. The demands of global economics and technology have proved irresistible – at least, to the middle classes. So, too, has the credibility of English as a literary medium. But not necessarily in its standard form, as a group of poems by one of India's leading English language writers, Nissim Ezekiel (b. 1924), demonstrates. One of them, 'Goodbye Party for Miss Pushpa T.S.', begins

> Friends,
> our dear sister
> is departing for foreign
> in two three days,
> and
> we are meeting today
> to wish her bon voyage.
>
> You are all knowing, friends,
> what sweetness is in Miss Pushpa.
> I don't mean only external sweetness
> but internal sweetness.
> Miss Pushpa is smiling and smiling
> even for no reason
> but simply because she is feeling.

The question is: is this patronizing? or merely comic?

> Coming back to Miss Pushpa
> she is most popular lady
> with men also and ladies also.

> Whenever I asked her to do anything,
> she was saying, 'Just now only
> I will do it.' That is showing
> good spirit. I am always
> appreciating the good spirit.[5]

My first encounter with Miss Pushpa was hearing the poet reading to a large gathering in the Indian Embassy, London. There were chuckles and laughter, followed by loud applause. A questioner then raised his hand: 'Aren't you being insulting to Indian people who speak like this?' The poet's answer was: 'Whenever I read the poem in India, first it gets applause, everyone enjoys it, and then somebody asks that question.'

In short, class, status and authority are as much tied up with this variety of English as with any other. The poem's comic effect is as much if not more at the expense of the speaker's narrowly patriarchal viewpoint as it is at the expense of those for whom it is their natural speech-form. You don't have to be familiar with Browning's dramatic monologue, 'My Last Duchess', to recognize the cleverly deliberate, undermining effect of 'Miss Pushpa is smiling and smiling / even for no reason', and the representation of a silent or silenced woman through the self-regarding speech of the men who have silenced her – although the phrases do offer an ironic contemporary echo of the much earlier, canonical English poem, as well as its of its representation of the sixteenth-century Italian Duke who has destroyed his wife for her gentleness, innocence and pliability. Creating a less exalted, different kind of 'other' to undermine himself, this monologue neatly shifts the cultural-historical ground, reinforcing the continuing authority of the English literary tradition, while at the same time challenging it.

That authority has been most recently analysed by Gauri Viswanathan's *Masks of Conquest: Literary Study and British Rule in India* (1989), which sets out to show how education in English under British colonial rule came to be an effective form of control and containment, encouraging the cultural assimilation of an elite of native-born educators, officials, administrators and politicians. A protégé of Edward Said at Columbia, Viswanathan traces the history of English studies from the passing of the Charter Act of 1813, which brought the assumption of a new responsibility for native education on the part of the East India Company, alongside the relaxation of controls over missionary activity; to 1857, when the Crown took over from the company, and the Indian university system was formally instituted on the pattern of London University. The English curriculum as it exists today was developed as a result of a potent mix of moral, functional and political motives, summed up early on in Macaulay's famously dismissive Minute of 1835, followed immediately by Bentinck's English Education Act, which officially required the natives of India to submit to the study of English literature. As we've seen, even before then, reformers such as Ram Mohan Roy were encouraging the study of English as a language and a culture. The result was that by 1941 the great Bengali writer and Nobel Prizewinner, Rabindranath Tagore (1861–1941) could look back and say: 'Our direct contact with the larger world was linked up with the contemporary history of the English people . . . It was mainly through their mighty literature that we formed our ideas'; as it 'nourished our minds in the past' so does it continue 'even now to convey its deep resonance to the recesses of our heart'.[6]

Over fifty years later, Harish Trivedi, Professor of English at the University of Delhi, asserts that: 'Even as the English literature which has been taught in India has remained substantially the same over the decades . . . so has the regard in which we hold this literature.' Yet, as Trivedi also points out, Viswanathan's book reveals a common paradox: her critique of the Anglicization of India is not just expressed in the sophisticated transatlantic English of the academe, but she considers it irrelevant even to consider how the colonized received and responded to the British hegemonic thrust. The way writers in, for example, Hindi, reacted, points towards their slow liberation from the 'historically necessary but now also historically exhausted stimulus' of English literary studies. Trivedi is sceptical of the achievements of 'so-called Indo-Anglian literature, itself a "half-caste" offspring of English literature' now taught at Indian universities, alongside the Anglo-American canon. His preference is for a fully-fledged comparative literature programme, involving the study of several literatures together, 'in relation to each other, and in interpenetration with each other', including 'English Literature', and 'English Literature from Elsewhere', as well as 'Literature in a Modern Indian Language', according to a range of approaches, including 'Indigenous' and 'Post-Colonial, favouring both Local and International Literatures'. Certainly in a multilingual, multicultural country with a colonial heritage, it seems important to include the literatures of indigenous as well as international spread; and, yet, it is precisely in varieties of 'Indian English' writing that the 'interpenetration' Trivedi seeks to examine has most obviously taken place over the last half-century.[7] He does not ignore it nor, indeed, do many prominent Indian academics, critics and scholars – not to mention readers at home and abroad. The point is: writing in English (standard or dialectal) is only one of many forms of writing in different languages available in the subcontinent.

Nissim Ezekiel is considered 'the first modern poet' in the literature of

English in India.[8] The value of his work does not appear to need any further validation; yet, in its range, its formal and linguistic subtlety and variety, Ezekiel's work registers the strength of the long (and, despite Trivedi's view, still growing) Indo-Anglian tradition. The enthusiasm of outsiders like Bruce King and William Walsh, both of whom have written forcefully on the achievement of Indian poetry in English, is no longer needed (if it ever was) to acknowledge the vitality of what is there, or to look for the work of the newer generation, such as Eunice de Souza (b. 1940) – who says

> No matter that
> my name is Greek
> my surname Portuguese
> my language alien.
>
> There are ways
> of belonging.[9]

One of those ways is the way of R.K. Narayan, who has observed of 'Indian English' that it is 'often mentioned with some amount of contempt and patronage, but is a legitimate development and needs no apology'. Narayan's defence of his position as an Indian writing in English is salutary. 'We have fostered the language for over a century', he says, 'and we are entitled to bring it in line with our own thought and idiom. Americans have adapted the English language to suit their native mood and speech without feeling apologetic, and have achieved directness and unambiguity in expression'.[10] Narayan has expressed mixed feelings about the effect of the rise of English upon Indian languages, literatures and cultures. In *The English Teacher* (1945), published just before Independence, the English headteacher (one of the very few non-Indian characters in his fiction) is keen to preserve the 'purity' of the language, much to the anger of the protagonist Krishna, who abandons his teaching career, and repudiates the education which 'has reduced us to a nation of morons; we were strangers to our own culture and camp followers of another culture, feeding on leavings and garbage'.[11]

This hostility may have something to do with the fact that Narayan's father was a headteacher. Nevertheless, the English language itself he later imagines arguing, 'I will stay here, whatever may be the rank and status you may assign me – as the first language or the second language or the thousandth. You may banish me from the classrooms, but I can always find other places where I can stay . . . I am more Indian than you can ever be.

You are probably fifty, sixty, or seventy years of age, but I've actually been in this land for two hundred years'.[12] So for Narayan, English is as Indian as any other language used in the subcontinent. Hence he has remained committed to writing his novels in standard English, if with a local habitation and a name. That name is Malgudi.

### Imagining Place: The Making of Malgudi

The novel is pre-eminently the Anglophone literary form which has been adopted with enthusiasm by writers of the subcontinent – in indigenous languages (especially Hindi) as well as in English. Precisely how this came about during the nineteenth century is matter for continuing debate, although on one level it is obviously the product of cultural interaction resulting from the imperial education policy. The first novelists in English in India were Bengalis like B.C. Chatterjee (1838–94) and R.C. Dutt (1848–1909), and it was in Bengal that the impact of British cultural policies was earliest and most profound. In *Indian Writing in English* Iyengar noted that while the 'literary renaissance' first manifested itself in the novels of Bengal, signs of 'new life' were almost immediately 'to be seen in Madras, Bombay and other parts of India as well'. According to him, the novel in Bengal, and generally in India, has passed through three stages: restoring national self-respect; bridging East and West; and identifying with 'the common people'. But, he adds, the 'post-Independence age' has 'witnessed the crash of all our hopes and . . . deepening despair'[13]. The novelists who have written themselves through his three stages are (again – triads are popular among post-colonial critics) three: Mulk Raj Anand, Raja Rao and Narayan.

Of these, it is Narayan who has proved most lasting, highly rated, and widely accessible, while his writing is the most consciously rooted in local circumstances, traditions and values. Anand and Rao are best known for their earlier novels, *Untouchable* (Anand, 1935) and *Kanthapura* (Rao, 1938), which established the centrality of the rural theme, although by differing means and with different motives: Anand, the social realist, to expose the sham of caste; and Rao, the mythmaker, to assert an indigenous 'idea' of India. Both belong to the earlier, pre-Independence world (although Rao wrote two more novels in the 1960s, another in 1988) to which Narayan, too, belongs, but which, by sheer staying-power, as well as a constant widening and deepening of interest in novel after novel, he has also gone beyond. The first cluster of novels belong to the turbulent pre-Independence period, and focus upon the growth of a young Indian to adulthood; thereafter, the novels grow darker, and focus more upon corruption and disillusion.

What is most remarkable is that his fourteen novels and nine volumes of short stories are centred almost exclusively upon the small fictional town of Malgudi in Mysore. Highly localized and particular, distinctively Indian, even at times pre-colonial, the town's details emerge gradually in and between the events of his narratives, giving it an identity which has even been illustrated (like Hardy's Wessex) in a map, published with one of his books – the collection of short stories, *Malgudi Days* (1941). This has led to a tendency to read his work as charming and quaint, if not naively straightforward – which allows it to be too easily incorporated within a familiar Western paradigm, and perhaps equally easily rejected by the postmodernist branch of post-colonial studies, at home and abroad. For Iyengar, Narayan 'is of India, even of South India: he uses the English language much as we used to wear dhoties manufactured in Lancashire – but the thoughts and feelings, the stirrings of the soul, the wayward movements of the consciousness, are all of the soil of India, recognizably autochthonous'.[14] This complex sense of the relative autonomy of his work is crucial for an understanding of what it's about.

Born 1906 in Madras the son of a headmaster, but educated by his grandmother in his mother-tongue Tamil, Narayan settled in Mysore, where the regional language is Kannada, and he writes almost exclusively in standard English, with occasional local variations. After a brief spell as a teacher at his school, the Maharajah's College in Mysore, some hand-to-mouth journalism (both the subject of some hilarious pages in *My Days: A Memoir*, 1975), and rejection by local publishers, his first novel, *Swami and Friends*, was published in 1935, after a friend in far-away Oxford took it to Graham Greene, who recommended it to Hamish Hamilton. The beginning of the novel was inseparable from the fictional terrain Narayan was to make his own:

> On a certain day in September [1930], selected by my grandmother for its auspiciousness, I bought an exercise book and wrote the first line of a novel; as I sat in a room nibbling my pen and wondering what to write, Malgudi with its railway station swam into view, all ready-made, with a character called Swaminathan running down the platform peering into the faces of passengers, and grimacing at a bearded face.

Some three decades later, when Narayan's work had won high literary honours, a large readership worldwide, and had been translated into several

European and Indian languages, there came the (perhaps inevitable) film-project:

> At the beginning, before starting the picture, they went to great
> trouble to seek my advice, and I had spent a whole day taking them
> round Mysore to show the riverside, forest, village, and crowds,
> granite steps and the crumbling walls of an ancient shrine which
> combined to make up the Malgudi of my story [*The Guide*, 1958];
> they went away promising to return later with crew and equipment,
> but never came back. I learnt subsequently that they had shifted the
> venue of *The Guide* to Jaipur and had already shot several scenes on
> a location as distant from Malgudi as perhaps Iceland. When I
> protested, they declared, 'Where is Malgudi, anyway? There is no
> such place. It is abolished from this moment . . .' By abolishing
> Malgudi, they had discarded my own values in milieu and human
> characteristics.[15]

Precisely. On one level, the authority and conviction of Narayan's work is derived from this sense of place, as a realizable, detailed, fictional milieu thoroughly imbued with his own values, themes and issues.

According to Said, one thing which links writings out of the 'moment' of 'anti-imperialist nationalism', is a desire to create distance from the 'British, French or (later) American master' – a distance which is achieved in part by imagining place. 'For the native', Said argues, 'the history of his/her colonial servitude is inaugurated by the loss to an outsider of the local place, whose concrete geographical identity must thereafter be searched for and somehow restored'.[16] This sounds more persuasive as an explanation of the writing trajectory of someone like Achebe, whose *Things Fall Apart* represents a search for lost roots, and a recreation of identity out of the recreation of a specific place and culture. Yet Narayan, beginning to write during the period of strong nationalist assertion leading to Independence, initially proclaims a sense of the local which can be understood as a response to the (declining) power of the Raj. More positively, however, it can also be seen as the developed vision of a writer brought up with a sense of the continuity of his roots within the specific, South Indian Tamil culture. The writer's project is less a reaction to the colonizer (*pace* Said and Viswanathan), than a gradual and profound working out of a cultural situation or 'moment' which includes, amongst other histories, the colonizing history. In this sense, the very specificity of Narayan's writing restores 'agency'.

Malgudi includes representations of the British presence – the Mission College, the courts, the railway and the police station – but it is evidently run by and for the local people who, like Narayan himself, bear the marks of cultural traditions which predate the British by more than a thousand years. His characters are almost entirely local, and although everything is given in English, with hints of local inflection in syntax and style, the reader easily accepts the convention by which we assume characters to be speaking in their own languages. Some of the novels include a glossary, but the ordinariness or apparent transparency of Narayan's chosen idiom – including some few untranslated terms such as *idli* (steamed rice cake: given thus in italics) or usages of Asian origin such as 'bandicoot', in *The Painter of Signs* – acts as a naturalizing agent, like Achebe's practice in *Things Fall Apart*, bridging the gaps between his own and other cultures. The social transactions of Narayan's characters are rendered with so unsurprised a tone that we, too, are not surprised – even when, for example, at the conclusion of his eighth novel, *The Man-Eater of Malgudi* (1961), the eponymous, pugnacious taxidermist Vasu kills himself by bringing his palms down upon his forehead. 'Every demon carries within him, unknown to himself, a tiny seed of self-destruction, and goes up in thin air at the most unexpected moment', remarks Sastri, the elderly Sanskrit scholar, who proceeds to remind the narrator of 'the story of Bhasmasura the unconquerable, who scorched everything he touched, and finally reduced himself to ashes by placing the tips of his fingers on his own head'.[17] This suggests that the parameters of Narayan's realism are more extensive than might appear from the limitations of his chosen place. As he has observed, 'for any story writer the prototype still inevitably remains our own epics and mythological stories, though they might not be in a subtle psychological manner'.[18]

### Signs of the Times: Myth and Modernity

The subtlety of Narayan's fiction resides in the way it uses myth, not in the myths themselves. That way involves little inner analysis of character, more an interweaving of inner and outer voices, mediated by means of a wry, humorously disarming tone. The deliberately narrow focus upon the small town of Malgudi is because there, unlike the big city, 'you see more concentrated life and you can see the types and forces of human relationships, activities, aspirations in greater detail'.[19] What, then, are the types and forces of human relationships, the activities and aspirations signified by *The Painter of Signs*? The novel tells of the failed relationship between an ineffectual Brahmin signpainter and a Westernized, casteless birth control specialist, Daisy. This story has its mythical analogue in the legend from the Mahbharata (referred to in the novel) of King Santhanu and his goddess

wife – who kills her own children.[20] But it also connects with contemporary preoccupations, especially with cultural authority.

The novel begins as it proceeds, with the calm certainty of familiar realist
narrative, offering readers an apparently recognizable place: 'Raman's was
the last house in Ellaman Street; a little door on the back wall opened,
beyond a stretch of sand, to the river . . .'. We are introduced to the trivia
of Raman's life, as he recalls an encounter with one of his clients, a lawyer
'who had ordered his nameboard to be delivered on a certain auspicious
day'. A conflict of potentially profound dimensions soon emerges, however: between the self-proclaimed rationalist Raman, who won't do
anything unless I see some logic in it' (p. 8), and the ritual-preserving
lawyer, who engages the chief priest to ensure that his new sign-board is
properly blessed. It is not easy to say which type seems vested with more
authority. Raman, the central, focalizing character, is a creator of signs
himself, the meanings of which are dependent upon relations between
surrounding circumstances and his own interests. The lawyer, hoarse with
reciting holy verse all morning, is a somewhat ridiculous representative of
the power of tradition; yet Raman's commitment to the modern, 'scien-
tific' approach Indira Gandhi's national government was promoting at the
time itself appears less than secure:

> 'I go by what my astrologer says,' said the lawyer . . .
>   'I prefer to think for myself,' Raman said before turning his cycle
> round homeward. 'All our great minds, from Valluvar down to
> Bernard Shaw and Einstein, say . . .'
>   'Say what? asked the lawyer, pausing.
>   'I couldn't quote,' Raman said, 'even if I were the author of those
> sentiments, but I'll copy them down for you some day.' (p. 9)

Raman's 'sense of fair play' persists, as he promises to replace the lawyer's
sand-splattered sign-board: but the familiar English catch-phrase quickly
expands in implication, towards an awareness of national corruption,
evident even in Malgudi – 'American milk powder meant for the orphans
of India and sold on the black market'; 'the government hospital surgeon
who flourished his knife like an assassin and made money and acquired the
much-coveted building sites beyond the railway crossing'; the 'wholesale
grain-merchant who cornered all the rationed articles and ran the co-
operative stores meant for the poor . . . Raman would expose them all to
the world' (p. 14). His idealism is closely linked with a dreamy passivity,
however, the kind of thing V.S. Naipaul once claimed was sui generis to
India and which, he argued, Narayan's work too well represented: 'an

Indian truth. Too much that is overwhelming has been left out; too much has been taken for granted'.[21]

The tranquil, unhurried texture of life in Malgudi, including the unforced presence of Hindu myth and ritual, may seem to confirm this judgement, which touches on a common response to Narayan – especially from critics within the Anglo-American tradition (Naipaul's own position within that tradition is, however, uneasy), who tend to deal with his work pre- and post-Independence as if it were a seamless whole. But far from taking everything for granted, *The Painter of Signs* expresses uncertainty and anxiety, as it negotiates the clash of different world-views within its small, apparently self-contained place and space. In one of few explicit asides, the narrator briefly reminds the reader that Raman 'would not recognize it, but Malgudi was changing in 1972' (p. 13), alluding to the country-wide process of increasingly violent attempts to enforce reform – including, of course, the ill-fated sterilization programme which has brought Daisy to the town. The serious point is left to us: Raman's conscious mind is engaged with the language of modernity, but he cannot act upon its values, his instincts run contrary to it.

He stands, as Homi Bhabha has put it, 'on the borders of myth and modernity'.[22] The comedy emerges from the reader's more knowledgeable position, a position implicitly negotiating the boundaries between tradition and reform, between local and national, even international, value systems. Overheard at The Boardless Hotel where Raman lunches with his opinionated friend Gupta: ' "Indira Gandhi is dynamic, no doubt, but I do not approve of – " it could be nationalization of banks, export policy, or anything' (p. 16); but Raman's mind is on a woman he has glimpsed washing at the river, suggesting the susceptibility which prevents him from developing any sense of the world beyond Malgudi, much less furthering his self-proclaimed 'Age of Reason'. The contradictory movements of Raman's mind signal the contradictions of the time, which were undermining the plans and authority of the Gandhi government. After telling himself that he must 'design and finish that piece of work for the Family Planning', Raman's thoughts wander:

> Population! Population! What a worry! Why not offer a bonus for those who remain single – like himself? No marriage means no children – no, not necessarily no children! The town hall veranda and the pavements around the market, the no-man's lands of Malgudi, swarmed with children of all sizes, from toddlers to four-footers, dust-covered, ragged – a visible development in five years. At this rate, they would overrun the globe – no harm; though they looked

famished . . . Raman's thoughts went on to the production of food, lands lying fallow, and so forth. He told himself: I am not doing the right thing in carrying on with this sign-board painting. I took it up because I loved calligraphy; loved letters, their shape and stance and shade. But no one cares for it, no one notices these values. Like that bangle-seller and the lawyer and the other, who demand their own style and won't pay otherwise. Compromise, compromise; and now this family planner wants – God knows what – black and white, or white and black, shaded or plain? (p. 27)

Daisy, the family planner, whose thoughts we are not privileged to enter, and who has rejected her Hindu identity, is a person of extremes; Raman is a person of compromise, partly because his desires conflict with his will, partly because he relies on his aunt and her traditional (Hindu) values, although he also wants to go with the times. He is unsure of himself because, as a kind of artist, he is a dealer in signs, in meanings, which refuse certainty. When he laughs at Daisy's proposed campaign message, she grows 'slightly red in the face . . . Such missionary zeal! . . . As far as he was concerned, it was purely professional – his duty being to inscribe whatever he was ordered – and he could not share anyone's passion for the cause' (pp. 46–7). This pliability contrasts with her reforming zeal, derived in part from her missionary upbringing, in part from the idea of civilization she has learnt. Yet there may also be an element of Hindu asceticism about her, echoing her mythical antecedents.

The conflicts and divisions which pervade post-independence Malgudi do not emerge as matters of stark opposition; rather, mediated by the shifting narrative voice, they emerge as a series of provisional positions, searching in vain for closure. The novel's structure is open-ended, as Narayan's narrative strategy itself resists imposed solutions, and the authoritarianism brought on by a range of issues facing the Indira Gandhi government – including, of course, the population explosion, which reached a crisis in the early 1970s, when campaigns urging rural populations to limit their fertility evoked widespread protest, on the grounds that the poor were being compelled to accept a solution to their problems which ignored the complexity of their situation and its causes. These were turbulent times: in 1972 India was at war with Pakistan over the founding of Bangladesh; in 1974 it exploded its first atomic device; by 1975 the State of Emergency, ostensibly to defeat corruption and control inflation, was declared. Daisy evidently represents one aspect of the government, personified in the Prime Minister herself during the crisis years, when reform became a juggernaut which eventually crushed her as well. By the end of 1976, the target of 7.5 million vasectomies was reached, but so, too was the peak of Indira Gandhi's unpopularity, and 'Madam's Dictatorship' faced defeat a few months later, in the first election after she ended the emergency. *The Painter of Signs* can be read as a prophecy of that defeat.

Yet Daisy's single-minded drive to sort out the problems of the poor with the panacea of birth-control ('Hum Do Hamare Do', 'we two, our two' was the government slogan) is depicted with some sympathy.

> Daisy remained inside the hut for some time, conversing in a low voice, came out, and said to the villager, 'Ten childbirths in twelve years of married life: don't you see that it will kill your wife?'
>
> 'True. She is very sickly,' admitted the man. 'I have to spend so much on medicines for her, but nothing helps.'
>
> 'And the children?' she inquired.
>
> 'Six died,' he added sorrowfully. 'God gives and he takes away . . .'
>
> (pp. 50–1)

If anybody supports the authority of reason and reform in this novel, it is the woman, not the man – a reversal of stereotype which is characteristic of Narayan, whose deep compassion for the position of rural women is plain. No wonder Daisy finally refuses marriage; although she is always a step ahead of Raman, for example when she anticipates and so avoids his attempt on her one night on the road, when his mind is occupied by the image of 'Rudolph Valentino in *The Sheik*' and passion overcomes him to the point where he heaves himself 'blindly' into her waggon – to find it empty, except for an undergarment. 'Where is she gone? Eloped with someone for the night, without impediments! . . . Or could it be she was Mohini, who tempted men and fooled them?' He quietly returns to his carpet under the cart (pp. 74–5). Daisy (who spends the night in a tree) despises Western notions of romance as much as its materialism – an unexpected link with Raman's equally self-disciplined aunt, who is so horrifed by the rootless young woman ('*That* girl! What is her caste? Who is she?', p. 115), that she, like Daisy, finally leaves both him and Malgudi behind.

It has been pointed out[23] that one of the most striking facts about *The Painter of Signs* is that it tests the competing ideologies of its time in a space just beyond the boundaries of Malgudi – 'this conservative town unused to modern life', as Raman calls it (p. 115). Perhaps the most striking moment of revelation, in which the competing forms of cultural authority are shown to be comically insecure, takes place in an encounter with a priest in the hills – a distant echo, perhaps, of Forster's Malabar Caves, also a site of ambivalent desire and clashing views. Raman asks the fertility goddess to give him Daisy – another indication of the failure of his commitment to rationality; but, of course, she doesn't. On the other hand, Daisy's determination to disparage traditional belief is also shaken, when the priest tells her about her past (p. 59). The priest remains a figure of enigmatic force, and alongside the favourable impression of traditional Hindu faith provided by Raman's aunt, suggests how far Narayan is prepared to underwrite its authority. The evocation of place is inseparable from his evocation of its cultural milieu, which includes the varying strands of (often conflicting) ancient and modern sets of belief.

The extraordinary vividness and conviction with which Malgudi and its surroundings are depicted in Narayan's work suggests to William Walsh a 'charm and authenticity' which belongs to 'human nature'. To Walsh as to many critics, in India and abroad, the struggles of his characters express a timeless struggle. Even the editor of the most recent collection of 'Contemporary critical essays' on Narayan, argues that

> we should not come to R.K. Narayan in search of a literature that delves into and exposes cultural ailments in topical narratives; rather, we should anticipate light and subtly ironic tales of provincial middle-class individuals who often delight because of their naivete and fallibility and who, despite their local immediacy, remind all readers of our limited capacity for gaining and maintaining control of all that affects us.[24]

*Despite* 'their local immediacy'? This ahistorical, universalizing tendency robs Narayan's writing of its bite. In the post-colonial perspective, a novel like *The Painter of Signs* helps us to understand that at the centre of concern lies a complex shifting of allegiances ultimately connected with the peculiar pressures of its time – a time of sharpened conflict over government, which touched every town and village in the country. If, as the authors of *The Empire Writes Back* rightly claim, in Narayan we find 'the expression of a society no longer conceived as Other',[25] we also find the expression of a society no longer conceived as placeless, or timeless. The disturbing historicity of his work in the post-colonial context should be retrieved from the common, accepted readings which have for so long accompanied it.

### Reclaiming the Flow of History

Nayantara Sahgal's *Rich Like Us* is more obviously amenable to post-colonial readings, because, unlike Narayan's novel, it deals explicitly with historical and political realities on a larger national, even international level. Lacking Narayan's sense of local detail, operating at the level of upper-class, modernized urban India, Sahgal nonetheless shows a powerful awareness of the ties of family, caste and religion, stretching back to the earlier colonial and even precolonial eras. Above all, her work displays the complex determining force of history – imagined as a range of discourses from different sources and traditions, rather than any one, monolithic version of reality. Sahgal's most acclaimed novel (she has written seven others) *Rich Like Us* tries to reclaim the nation at a time when corruption and intrigue have precipitated a crisis, by reclaiming its multiple histories.

One of the most striking trends in the Indian novel in English has been its tendency to reclaim the nation's histories. Benedict Anderson has argued persuasively that the development of the idea of nation has itself been tied to the development of the novel, as a means of stabilizing a people's sense of identity through the use of a single language narrative in widely available printed books.[26] Arguments about the nature of the novel in India have swung to and fro, exploiting a wide range of socio-cultural and historic factors, although there appears to be general agreement that, as Makarand Paranjape puts it, just as the English language 'undergoes nativization in, say, India, before it can carry the burden of Indian experience, the form of the novel also undergoes its peculiar processes of nativization and acculturation'.[27] Whether or not this means that the influence of the powerful ancient narratives of the subcontinent should be identified as its most significant feature (and we have seen how there is a mythical subtext in Narayan's writing), or whether the realist tradition of the English novel (even more strongly evident in Narayan), is more significant, remains a moot point. Discussion tends to be based on reductive versions of these different traditions anyway: neither the original Sanskrit narratives in their complex multitude of surviving forms, nor the varying realist and non-realist strands which interweave within the English (not to mention American or European) novel tradition can be so simply identified, much less the myriad ways in which they might interact within even one writer's strategic development.

These complexities notwithstanding, it remains the case that, from Khushwant Singh's *Train to Pakistan* (1956) and Attia Hosein's *Sunlight on a Broken Column* (1961), from Anita Desai's *Clear Light of Day* (1980) to Bapsi Sidhwa's *Ice-Candy-Man* (1988), from Shashi Tharoor's *The Great Indian Novel* (1989) to Rohinton Mistry's *Such a Long Journey* (1991), novels in English from Pakistan, Bangladesh and India, written at home or abroad, have attached a definable historical weight to their narratives. Perhaps the most well-known and influential example, Salman Rushdie's *Midnight's*

*Children* (1980), while evidently nourished on the indigenous oral traditions which incorporate one tale within another in an ever-increasing
multiplicity of digressions and episodes, nevertheless engages with the
histories of the subcontinent by creating a series of intricate parallels
between the lives of its characters and the broad sweep of events initiated
by that midnight moment of India's 'tryst with destiny' (Nehru's famous
phrase), on 15 August 1947, when independent India and Pakistan came
into existence. As Rushdie's narrator-hero Saleem Sinai recalls his past, he
recalls the nation's past (going back to the defining moment of the
Jallianwallah Bagh/Amritsar massacre of 1919); when he anticipates its
future, he anticipates the mid-1970s emergency (again); thereby covering
some six decades, and three nominally decolonized nations. The crises of
national identity are imagined as the crises of personal identity, by means
of a kaleidoscopic, (on the analogy with Latin American writings) 'magic
realist' structure. Expressing the hybridity of its cultural origins, Rushdie's
work challenges us to develop a critical approach which responds fully to
its stunning range and fluidity of reference. Who, apart from Rushdie
himself, can recognize them all? Perhaps the best any reader can manage
is to be aware not just of our own particular perspective and that of 'the
other', but of the limitations inherent in 'binary' approaches when
confronted by such works.

As Sahgal puts it: 'Not only is it time for interpretation to flow many
ways instead of only west to east, but the question of direction is itself no
longer relevant when the migration of cultures is leaving cultures open-
ended, and when migration can take place without ever leaving one's soil'.
Hers is a state of mind and feeling that is 'firmly rooted in a particular
subsoil, but above ground has a more fluid identity', an identity she
characterizes as a 'schizophrenic imagination', grappling with a sense of self
produced by 'the divisions which history and circumstance have imposed
on the complex creatures we already are'.[28] This complexity is engaged by
focusing upon the shifting network of relationships within a few families
belonging to the Delhi ruling elite at the time of the emergency, within an
almost epic range of historic reference including the Persians, the Mogul
and British Empires, the rise of Indian nationalism and the demand for a
Muslim state, to the events leading up to June 1975. Sahgal's inside
knowledge, as a member of the elite – niece of Jawaharlal Nehru, cousin
of Indira Gandhi – allows her to question and expose the decay of the
democratic ideal in the post-Independence dispensation.

A political journalist and civil rights activist, whose parents were
imprisoned for their involvement in Mahatma Gandhi's 1930 Civil
Disobedience Movement, Sahgal has a sharply satirical and knowing eye.

She protested openly against the emergency herself, while in the novel she creates an alter ego in the figure of Oxford-educated senior civil servant Sonali, whose first-person account weaves within an omniscient narrative detailing the fractures and continuities of present and past for those around her – from Rose, her somewhat stereotyped Cockney English mother-figure, to Dev, her spoilt and brutal brother-in-law, whose rise from feckless entrepreneur to corrupt Minister is guaranteed by 'Madam's' authoritarian regime. Ironically (the novel is replete with such ironies), Dev in effect replaces one indulgent mother with another – an irresistible and doubtless intended reminder to the reader of the indulgence Indira Gandhi displayed to her playboy-entrepreneur son Sanjay, who emerged during the emergency as leader of India's youthful new, Western-oriented business elite, and whose words and actions were reported 'almost as extensively as those of his mother in the carefully controlled and censored press'.[29]

Although the emergency frames the action (which ends before it does), the narrative imagines it as a moment within an immense and varied history, by manipulating anachrony through repeated, abrupt and multiple internal and external analepses, as well as (fewer) prolepses. The circling, digressive structure, within which stories are folded within stories, suggests indigenous narrative traditions; although Sahgal's skilful deployment of free indirect speech and stream of consciousness techniques may derive from modernist Western traditions too – exemplifying on the formal level the cultural 'sharing' she wishes to promote. At times, the narrative sabotages temporal reference entirely, to suggest the immense, unchanging authority of Hindu civilization – although its resistance to change is evidently responsible for many of the social ills the novel displays, from caste and race prejudice to the marginalization of women. Dev's orthodox Hindu mother Mona tells Rose that 'among us questions aren't answered quick quick quick because time is not only clock time'; she proceeds to tell the story of a teacher who asked his disciple to fetch a glass of water,

> and the young man went off to get it, but on the way he met a beautiful girl whom he fell in love with and married. They lived happily together, had three children and cultivated their fields. Before long floods came, and later drought, and they had to work very hard to recover from these calamities, but finally all was well again. Their children were growing fast and in good health, and the whole family was prospering when one day the teacher arrived in the village, looking for his disciple, and said to him, 'Where is that glass of water, my son? I have been waiting half an hour for it.'[30]

Rose represents one aspect of the attempt to 'share' the Indo-British experience in the novel, and her dual perspective as the outsider-become-insider takes up much of the omniscient narrative. Courted and won by Mona's husband Ram in London in 1935, she arrived in India to find Mona with her new son, Dev – who, when his father is paralysed by a stroke and his mother is dying of cancer, uses the opportunity the emergency offers to destroy her, so as to get for himself the legacy she would (under a new law for widows) have received. Rose's sympathetic involvement in the life of the family to which she has committed herself may not leave her with more than a glimpse of understanding, but her struggle to understand is plain – as when she asks Mona for the meaning of her little story. But Mona declines to provide it. The narrative within the narrative *is* the meaning at that point.

The meanings of *Rich Like Us* are mediated by a disconcerting heterogeneity of narratives, to counter, but not completely displace, the monolithic, linear Christian, European chronology. To introduce us to this complexity, Sahgal's narrative cleverly begins by positioning its readers as complete outsiders – like the detached and superior Neuman whose viewpoint we meet in the opening lines.

> The richer the host, the later dinner was served. Dining late was a status symbol, like Scotch whisky, five times the price of the Indian, and the imported car, a particularly costly luxury, that had brought him here from his hotel. 'The first thing those local elites do – not to mention their presidents or generals or whoever's at the top – is to get themselves the biggest, latest model foreign cars,' he had been told in his briefing before this trip, 'and why not? We like the way we live. We can't blame them for wanting to live like us. Besides, it's what makes them ready to buy what we have to sell.'
>
> 'Won't you have another drink, Mr Neuman?' his hostess offered.
>
> 'I still have some, thank you.'
>
> 'It's Scotch.'
>
> He raised his hand in polite refusal. The room was remarkable for its total anonymity. No echo of time past or things to come. Roses stood stiff and upright on display in a blinding array of surgically cut, bulk-bought crystal, to judge by the profusion of vases, ashtrays and bowls all over the room. His host, who had left the room to answer the telephone, returned, a cherubic face on a prematurely elderly frame.

Interpretation has been flowing from West to East, the orientalizing, 'othering' strategy implicit in the language of Neuman's briefing makes abundantly clear – it even uses the stereotyping 'them' and 'us', which underlies the novel title – 'We can't blame them for wanting to live like us', is reinforced by 'If they'd do like we do, they'd be rich like us' (p. 16) – that is, the capitalist West. For Neuman, and those he represents, changes in government simply mean a change in 'whoever's at the top' in the dependent country, wherever that happens to be. The subtly ironic inter-textual echo of T.S. Eliot ('no echo of time past or things to come') empha-sizes the cultural poverty of the encounter between West and East here.

At first 'the top' people seem as anonymous as their *nouveaux riches* furnishings. Later we discover the host is Dev, whose soft-drink factory Neuman has come to invest in, the hostess, languorous Nishi, Sonali's sister – the same Sonali who is sacked from her position in the civil service for questioning the legality of the arrangement between Neuman and Dev. The national 'self-reliance' campaigns of earlier years have been replaced by an urgent desire to collaborate with foreign investment which – with the suspension of trade unions and other measures brought in under the emergency – is made all the easier now. As Neuman reflects upon the declaration of the emergency a month earlier, we're told it made 'no impression' upon him, sitting in the 'cool, controlled climate' of his hotel room. 'If the bosses, whoever they were, made their shambling bureauc-racies easier to handle, it was all he asked' (10). This detached perspective upon the 'other' countries of the world once used to be interrupted by some 'fragment of the past', a 'jewel of a temple'. 'His knowledge of history and archaeology, once his great fascination, had fallen into disuse', because it did not contribute to 'the financial basis of his happiness'. An ironic prolepsis across the entire narrative, which ends with Sonali deciding to take up historical research as the sole remaining worthwhile activity for her in her corrupt and corrupting society – a response urged by Naipaul, whose *India: A Wounded Civilization* (1977) concluded that the emergency could only be countered by such historical 'inquiry and scholarship', by 'intellec-tual rather than spiritual discipline'.[31]

The time-span of the novel's surface-narrative is a mere four months, from July 1975 until the first Divali of the emergency; although flash-backs take us to the 1820s and, if we include the brief account of the medieval tomb across the way from Dev and Nishi's house, the twelfth century. The pervasively pessimistic tone is at least partly explicable in terms of the deliberate limitation of the surface story to the time of the emergency – so that when, towards the end, another outsider, upper-class English Marcella, refers gaily to 'when the emergency is over', Sonali reflects that 'Until she said it I hadn't realized the emergency could ever be over' (p. 264). But this is also a reflection of Sahgal's underlying view of history as a kind of permanent subsoil beneath the present – that 'huger, older universe of which school taught me only a meagre slice' – that is, the brief history of the British imposition, the 'little scrap which filled the textbooks and ruled the world'.[32] Throughout the narrative, historical–ideological perspectives are played off against another. Sonali's implicit acceptance of the liberal view of history-as-progress which she has inherited from her British education, collapses under the impact of the present, authoritarian rule. Until her dismissal, she has been a dedicated member of her professional class, the class created by the colonial regime to take over on its departure. 'We were successors to the ICS, the "steel frame" the British had ruled India with, but with more on our hands since independence than the steel frame had had in two hundred years. And we had a new tradition to create, our own independent worth to prove' (p. 28). Insulated, even complacent, the civil service elite have – if unknowingly – helped sustain a system which has finally begun to crack, as once again idealists like Kishori Lal (flogged by the British in 1919 for refusing to crawl after Jallianwalla Bagh) are imprisoned and beaten by the present regime.

The loss of her post brings depression and cynicism, but it also brings Sonali the opportunity to reclaim her divided past, and begin to reflect upon it. Chapter 9 retrieves her time in Oxford with Ravi Kachru, another Kashmiri Hindu who therefore can share her *thali* (foodplate): arriving 'truly Victorian in our belief in India's inevitable progress, in peaceful change, in democracy everlasting', they hear and respond to 'the siren song of Marxism' (p. 109), which he wants to follow, but which she resists as yet another 'Western concept'; one moreover which is for men who, like him, can afford to believe in doctrines.

> He had never fought a battle for freedom, never been patted down firmly when his sap was rising, never had a sari throttling his legs, making walking in the wind and running to catch a bus a threat to life and limb, never had his mother set up a howl when he went and got a haircut. He had no idea what the simplest subjugations were about. I, who did, had no intention of chaining myself to any doctrine when I had just lost some of my chains . . . I don't like dictatorships, not even of the proletariat, not even as a passing phase because who knows the phase might get stuck and never pass. You are grossly muddled, Ravi told me . . . Naturally I was muddled. So was he. Why wouldn't we be? We had had the West coming at us since our great grandfathers' time, while all we knew of our own culture were the droplets that had managed to seep in through osmosis. (p. 112)

The multiple awarenesses conveyed by such passages reveal a complex project: to reclaim many pasts, to resist simplified explanations, and to present a gendered search for freedom. The reference to dictatorships reminds us of the present emergency, and Sonali's anxiety that it will not cease; it also alludes to the possibility of time 'getting stuck', through intellectual acquiescence – which, for Sahgal, represents part of the debate about the dominant religion of her society, and its view of history, which the novel engages.

### Can the Subaltern Speak?

Not for Sahgal (any more than V.S. Naipaul) the generally accepting posture of Narayan towards Hinduism: 'I have to ask', she said in 1989, 'as I did in my novel *Rich like Us*, whether Hinduism inclines a whole society to the status quo? Does it put out the fires of rebellion? Does it incline women to victimization, to individual and mass acts of horrifying self-sacrifice?'[33] Sahgal's great-grandmother committed the ritual self-sacrifice of a widow on her husband's funeral pyre – sati, the fearful image of which reappears as a pivotal presence in this novel.

> When I got to the river bank where we had cremated my father a new pyre was blazing where the old one had been. I saw her fling her arms wildly in the air, then wrap them about her breasts before she sub-sided like a wax doll into the flames (p. 149).

Reclaiming history involves addressing the significance of such personal histories within the larger histories of the nation. Sonali's discovery in chapter 11 (the structural centre of the novel) of a manuscript belonging to her paternal grandfather puts her in touch not only with the making of British India, but with the painful memory of her great-grandmother's sati; thereby bringing one of the most troubling aspects of her own and her country's past into the present – a present in which, for example, Mona reiterates that past by an attempt at self-immolation only prevented by Rose.

Rose's intervention provides another ironic echo of past histories, as it reminds us of British intervention going back to Governor William Bentinck, who first prohibited sati by law in Bengal in 1829. In the documents Sonali discovers we are also reminded of the support such reformers had from indigenous Hindu men like her grandfather and his father. For her grandfather, writing during the First World War, 'some changes are expected in India', and he believes in 'a gradual progress towards self-government. But underneath there will be the subterranean layers of ourselves we cannot escape' (p. 151). One of those subterranean layers appears to be sati, a matter which has continued to concern the Indian state sufficiently for there to be new legislation outlawing the practice as recently as 1987. According to Rajeswari Rajan, in post-Independence India only 'stray cases have been reported, about forty in all, chiefly in some northern states'; what worries women's groups in the country is 'the more recent phenomenon of the glorification of sati through temples and annual fairs'. As she points out, 'the ban on sati and its celebration pits the state against the community, the colonial or westernized rulers and elites against the "native" Indian subject'.[34] This makes it an intensely difficult and yet crucial site of contestation, a matter of strategic and discursive, as well as moral positions.

For Sonali, and the Westernized elite to which she belongs, the position seems clear enough: her father's struggle with the men who put his mother on the funeral pyre shows that not everyone is 'passive before cruelty and depravity'; she links his struggle with a student she has seen resisting arrest under the emergency regulations, and with 'Rose's beggar', who, having lost his arms trying to save his wife from rape and death, remains 'undaunted by his armlessness', and slips from his tormentor's grasp (p. 152). Yet in the novel as a whole the representation of sati and associated 'sensational' acts against women − Rose is herself murdered in the end − raises a complex of feelings and attitudes which render such acts of resistance opaque in their implications. This opacity surrounds the figure of Indira Gandhi herself, the absent authority whose presence dominates the surface narrative of the novel and who occupied a more ambivalent position than the novel appears to admit. We are invited to resist her emergency, and, for example, to share the satiric response to her 'Twenty Point Programme' which Nishi and the 'other New Entrepreneur wives' support: 'There was so much they could do, take groups to congratulate the Prime Minister, plant trees and prevent their servants from having children' (p. 86). Yet, as Wolpert points out, the Twenty Points had to do with the economy, which was in a bad way, and, assisted by a bumper crop in 1975, the government won a victory over inflation almost unique in the world, while increasing industrial productivity by over 6 per cent in 1975 and 10 per cent in 1976–7. Gandhi even addressed the issue of bonded labour. If not a democratic Raj, 'As long as prices stayed under control, investment continued high, and the monsoon was reasonably kind, it could also be a very popular Raj.[35] Problematizing authority − that authority which, arguably, the population accepted as part of the divine order or *dharma* − or, indeed, questioning the position of women on the subcontinent, was never likely to be high on the agenda, and a feminist critique needs to take this into account.

*Rich Like Us* is not an easy novel to sum up, or even to find one's way around. But it raises important issues in a powerful and persuasive way. Sati, which has often functioned as part of the exoticizing of India, proof of the people's continuing backwardness if not barbarism, of what makes 'them' so different from 'us', is placed at the heart of its many narratives. It is an issue which recent critical and scholarly work has highlighted as part of a wider exploration of the connections between feminist and post-colonial theory. One of the most influential explorers has been Gayatri Spivak, who has taken up the history of sati as an instance of the difficulty of recovering the silenced voice of women by migrant intellectuals like herself. When, as Sahgal's novel demonstrates, almost all accounts of the colonial past are written by the colonizers or the indigenous elites – when, in short, the Other has been 'orientalized' away, the question is: 'Can the subaltern speak?' as Spivak put it in one of her most influential essays. 'Subaltern' is a term derived from the work of Gramsci and adopted by a well-known group of Indian historians seeking to recover the voices of the suppressed or silenced peasantry, of people like Sahgal's armless beggar – or Narayan's fecund villagers, in *A Painter of Signs*. Spivak, while critical of the Subaltern Studies project, turned to its methods to test what might be recovered from the extant accounts around sati.

> As one goes down the grotesquely mistranscribed names of these women [she writes], the sacrificed widows, in the police reports included in the records of the East India Company, one cannot put together a 'voice'. The most one can sense is the immense hetero-geneity breaking through even such a skeletal and ignorant account (castes, for example, are regularly described as tribes). Faced with the dialectically interlocking sentences that are constructible as 'White men are saving brown women from brown men' and 'The women wanted to die', the postcolonial woman intellectual asks the question of simple semiosis – What does this mean? – and begins to plot a history.[36]

Such a history as sketched by Spivak is riddled with present appropriations of the voices of the Other. Her conclusion is that 'the subaltern cannot speak'. Given Spivak's deconstructive approach, this may seem inevitable, since it assumes that everything is mediated by somebody else in an infinite regress of mediating positions.

More recently, in an attempt to apply Spivak's theories to Anita Desai's

*Clear Light of Day* (1980) and Sahgal's *Rich Like Us,* Shirley Chew argues
that Sonali's great grandmother, stereotypically silent and ghostlike, *does*
speak – if only for one moment, when she is heard rather than seen. As the
relatives gather and the widow tells her son of her fears that he would be
disinherited, 'What shall we do?' she asks (p. 146). According to Chew, the
question, hovering as it does 'between helplessness and decision-making,
the weighing of choices and the weight of resignation . . . carries a
distinctive resonance that springs from its applicability to the situation in
1975 as in 1905'; and it is associated in Sonali's mind with other examples
of 'resistance and engagement . . . suggesting broad lines of continuity as
well as the possibility of change'.[37]

  Chew's reading of *Rich Like Us* discovers a positive potential, in the
associative links mediated by Sonali's narrative; a potential perhaps borne
out by our concluding image of her, 'immersed in the past' of her own and
Rose's Western myths, yet 'preparing all the while for the future . . .
waiting to be lived'( p. 266). It is difficult to accept Chew's reading of
Rose's death in the omniscient narrative, however: where Rose's suffoca-
tion by a young thug is an act which echoes another way of ritual, secret
death from the past (thuggee), although perhaps we are to read it in the first
place as wife-killing and final assimilation within that particular, patriarchal
thread of the indigenous culture she has tried over a lifetime to come to
terms with. As her last moment is described, Rose has been reflecting upon
her many pasts in the silence of the old tomb, until the 'last resistance' of
her 'English legs eased and she found herself as relaxed as a yogi in her cross-
legged posture, her thoughts beautifully clear': one of those thoughts is
Mona's voice, telling her 'it wasn't too late to tackle Dev, to cry for justice
. . . She was on her knees in the act of getting up when a cloth came down
over her head, arms pinned hers down, and she heard a thick satisfied grunt
as she lost consciousness' (p. 249). Does this, as Chew asserts, suggest that
Rose, like Sonali, is about to engage in resistance? If so, it also unfortunately
links her with all those women in the novel who are destroyed before they
can do anything about their lot – whether by sati or less ritually sanctioned
deaths, thrown down wells or immured in the brick-kilns beside the
Ganges after they have been used by men (p. 75).

  In short, if Sahgal's novel reclaims some of the many histories of its
people and nation at a time of crisis, addressing the present through the past,
it also carries a troubling air of acceptance, even fatalism. And the
perspective of the poorest, that of the handless beggar, is it addressed? –
beyond the exposure of 'them, the ruling class on one side, the ruled on
the other. Power had changed hands but what else had changed, where he

lived?' (p. 258). Perhaps: unlike his wife, or Sonali's great grandmother, he gets to tell his story in his own words, although in surprisingly 'correct' English (pp. 257–9). Is it, then, some kind of achievement to have gained a listener in Sonali, member of the former governing elite (earlier the 'memsahib' Rose listened to him, we gather)? The very complexity and multilayeredness of the narrative itself, while resisting simplistic or stereotyping impositions upon the nation it narrates, and forcefully reversing the historic flow of interpretation, brings us back to a kind of stasis. The ambivalences seem to cancel each other out, so that we lose the sense of testimony which is one of the most important functions of literary artefacts. The subaltern cannot speak. No wonder, perhaps, that the future seems at times an 'impossible dream', like the image of the Watteau painting, *L'Embarquement pour l'île de Cythère*, which Rose picks up (p. 203) and Sonali keeps, showing the aristocrats of an earlier time, before they lost their heads to the guillotine. Nevertheless, as Spivak repeatedly asserts, there remains a responsibility for the intellectual/teacher/reader: to arouse and sustain an awareness of the mutiple, intersecting factors of race, class, language, gender and identity – within oneself first. Sahgal's 'schizophrenic imagination' may seem symptomatic of the gloomier aspects of a postcolonial perspective; but her novel promotes a critically historicizing view of the national project.

## Summary

This case study of two different kinds of prose fiction, R.K. Narayan's apparently traditional-realist *Painter of Signs* and Sahgal's radically modernist *Rich Like Us*, from the same period of mounting crisis in a post-independence nation, shows the vitality and contemporary relevance of Indo-Anglian writing. Post-colonial readings of such work highlight the importance of place, history and gender, as well as an underlying concern with the question of authority. The credibility of English as a literary medium – mainly though not exclusively in its standard form – is clear, as is the lasting quality of writing in English, which retains its strength as a minority form within a very large, mutilingual and multicultural nation. The origin of its authority has been analysed by Gauri Viswanathan, whose own approach is questioned by Trivedi for metropolitan bias. He favours a more broadly comparative approach. As Iyengar suggests, the novel is the pre-eminent Anglophone literary form. Narayan's comedy subtly demonstrates the continuing sway of local tradition and myth, while engaging readers with the challenge posed by change and modernity. The disturbing historicity of his work needs bringing out, whereas in Sahgal's fiction a multitude of viewpoints are deployed to reclaim the histories of family and nation. *Rich Like Us* deals with the new urban elite, while *A Painter of Signs* details the lives of rural townsfolk. Although there is only a hint of the testimony of the most oppressed, both novels help defeat the monolithic, one-way Western narratives of cultural domination.

## Notes

1 Indira Gandhi, qtd Stanley Wolpert, *A New History of India*, 5th edn (Oxford University Press, 1997), pp. 397–8.

2 Nayantara Sahgal, *Rich Like Us*, first publ. 1983 (Sceptre, 1987), p. 31. Subsequent references will be given in parentheses in the main text.

3 Anita Desai, 'A secret connivance', *Times Literary Supplement* (14–20 September 1990), p. 973.

4 P. Lal, qtd Robert McCrum, William Cran and Robert MacNeil, *The Story of English*, new and rev. edn (Faber & Faber, 1992), p. 33.

5 Nissim Ezekiel, *Collected Poems 1952–1988* (Oxford India Paperbacks, 1992), pp. 190–1.

6 Rabindranath Tagore, qtd Jawaharlal Nehru, *The Discovery of India* (Bombay, 1969), p. 321.

7 See Harish Trivedi, *Colonial Transactions: English Literature and India* (Manchester University Press, 1995), pp. 176–7, 195, 210–16.

8 A.K. Mehrotra, *Twelve Modern Indian Poets* (Oxford University Press, 1992), p. 9. Numerous other anthologizers in India anticipated this judgement over the preceding thirty years.

9 Eunice De Souza, 'De Souza Prabhu', in ibid., p. 119.

10 R.K. Narayan, 'Indian English', *A Writer's Nightmare: Selected Essays 1958–1988* (Penguin, 1988), p. 197.

11 R.K. Narayan, *The English Teacher*, chapter 8 (Indian Thought Publs., 1955), p. 220.

12 R.K. Narayan, *Selected Essays*, p. 15.

13 K.R. Srinivasa Iyengar, *Indian Writing in English*, rev. edn (Sterling Publishers, 1990), pp. 315, 317.

14 Ibid., p. 359.

15 R.K. Narayan, *My Days* (Penguin, 1989), pp. 76, 171.

16 Edward Said, *Nationalism, Colonialism and Literature*, Field Day Pamphlet no.15 (1988), reptd in *Literature in the Modern World*, ed. Dennis Walder (Oxford University Press, 1990), p. 36.

17 R.K. Narayan, *The Man-Eater of Malgudi* (Penguin, 1983), pp. 173–4.

18 R.K. Narayan, interview in *Indian Writers at Work*, ed. D. Kohli (B.R. Publishing, 1991), p. 16.

19 Ibid., p. 16.

20 R.K. Narayan, *The Painter of Signs*, first publ. 1976 (Penguin, 1982), p. 125. All further references in this chapter given parenthetically to this edition.
21 V.S. Naipaul, *An Area of Darkness*, first publ. 1964 (Penguin, 1968), p. 216.
22 Homi Bhabha, 'A Brahmin in the bazaar', *Times Literary Supplement* (8 April 1977), p. 421.
23 By Sadhana Puranik, '*The Painter of Signs*: breaking the frontier', in *R.K. Narayan: Contemporary Critical Practices*, ed. Geoffrey Kain (Michigan State University Press, 1993), pp. 125–39.
24 See William Walsh, *Indian Literature in English* (Longman, 1990), pp. 74–5; Geoffrey Kain, Introduction, *R.K. Narayan*, p. 5.
25 Bill Ashcroft, Gareth Griffiths and Helen Tiffin, *The Empire Writes Back* (Routledge, 1989), p. 115.
26 Benedict Anderson, *Imagined Communities: Reflections on the Origin and Spread of Nationalism* (Verso, 1991), pp. 24ff.
27 Makarand Paranjape, 'The ideology of form: notes on the Third World novel', *Journal of Commonwealth Literature*, 26,1 (1991), pp. 19–32 (p. 26).
28 Nayantara Sahgal, 'The schizophrenic imagination', in *From Commonwealth to Post-Colonial*, ed. Anna Rutherford (Dangaroo, 1992), pp. 36, 30.
29 Wolpert, *A New History of India*, 5th edn, p. 401.
30 Sahgal, *Rich Like Us* (1987), pp. 236–7. All quotations from this edition given in parentheses in text.
31 V.S. Naipaul, *India: A Wounded Civilization* (Penguin, 1979), p. 174.
32 Sahgal, 'The schizophrenic imagination', p. 33.
33 Ibid., p. 34.
34 Rajeswari Sunder Rajan, *Real and Imagined Women: gender, culture and postcolonialism* (Routledge, 1993), p. 17.
35 Wolpert, *A New History of India*, p. 403.
36 Gayatri Spivak, 'Can the subaltern speak?'(1988), reptd Williams and Chrisman, eds (1993), pp. 66–111 (p. 93).
37 Shirley Chew, 'Searching Voices: Anita Desai's *Clear Light of Day* and Nayantara Sahgal's *Rich Like Us*', in *Motherlands: Black Women's Writing from Africa, the Caribbean and South Asia*, ed. Susheila Nasta (Women's Press, 1991), pp. 56–7.

# 6

## Caribbean and Black British Poetry

Ah wonderin how dem gwine stan
Colonizin in reverse
Louise Bennett, 'Colonisation in Reverse', 1966

that's all them bastards have left us: words
Derek Walcott, 'The Schooner Flight', 1979

Shakespeare
Milton
Keats
Shelley

Walcott
Brathwaite
Miss Lou
Berry
Grace Nichols 'High-Tea', Sunris, 1996

### A Diaspora Aesthetic

Historical recuperation seems a legitimate, indeed pressing need for writers in the Indian subcontinent. For writers from the Caribbean, a more radically disturbing view of the past has arisen out of their experience of colonization – which involved the virtual extinction of the local indigenous population, and its replacement by slaves and indentured labourers from Africa and Asia. With the extinction of the indigenous people went the extinction of indigenous languages – apart from a few surviving words like 'hurricane' – and their replacement by imported varieties. Out of the interaction of these imports, spoken by slaver and slave, governor and clerk, plantation manager and indentured labourer, emerged the creole languages of today. Whether or how to use these relatively new 'nation languages' is a question which dominates Caribbean and Black British writing of the post-colonial era. The 'choice' between standard English and creole varieties becomes more, rather than less important as the colonial experience recedes, while migration and the growth of a global economy and communications network proceeds.

As C.L.R. James pointed out in 1962:

> The West Indies has never been a traditional colonial territory with clearly distinguished economic and political relations between two different cultures. Native culture there was none. The aboriginal Amerindian civilisation had been destroyed. Every succeeding year, therefore, saw the labouring population, slave or free, incorporating into itself more and more of the language, customs, aims and outlook of its masters. It steadily grew in numbers until it became a terrifying majority of the total population. The ruling minority therefore was in the position of the father who produced children and had to guard against being supplemented by them. There was only one way out, to seek strength abroad. This beginning has lasted unchanged to this very day.[1]

No surprise, then, that so many writers from the Caribbean have chosen to live abroad, often in the former colonial centres of power, in Britain, France or, since it has become a massive force in the area, the United States: writers such as Edgar Mittelholzer, Samuel Selvon, George Lamming, Wilson Harris and, of course, V.S. Naipaul – all novelists, all having felt what Naipaul called the 'threat of failure, the need to escape . . . Living in a borrowed culture, the West Indian, more than most, needs writers to tell him who he is, where he stands'.[2] James himself sailed to England at the age of thirty-one with the aim of becoming a novelist. After one novel, he became a Trotskyist historian, going on to produce his classic account of slave resistance, *The Black Jacobins* (1938). As war in Europe approached, he moved to the United States, where he extended his range to include a critique of American society and culture – a culture he admired for its art, but which rejected him for his politics. James's final theme, as he went on to become a world figure based in London, was the black diaspora as a central fact of the post-colonial order.

Any study of writing in and from the Caribbean has to acknowledge this basic sense of its diasporic nature – both in terms of its roots in Africa and Asia, and its generation in the wider world. Uncertainty of identity reflects an uncertainty about the past, and the isolation typical of small nations like those of the Caribbean. Mostly densely populated islands, with closely knit but severely stratified societies, the West Indian countries have resisted attempts to found regional identities (such as the West Indies Federation, 1958–62), just as they have resisted attempts to create a unified or common culture. Instead, situating themselves within modernity, writers from the Caribbean have concentrated upon the power of language itself to create a sense of who they are, and where they come from – countering, while inevitably incorporating, imposed colonial identities. Their first significant creative achievement was in prose fiction – an achievement well described by Kenneth Ramchand's pioneering work *The West Indian Novel and Its Background* (Faber, 1970). But since poetry as a genre represents the most conscious use of language, it is appropriate to consider the poetry in English of the Caribbean – including its migrant, diasporic relation in Britain where, as a variously labelled phenomenon, it has come to play an important role for 'Black' communities as well as to challenge monolithic conceptions of British identities. As Stuart Hall remarks, 'Young black cultural practitioners and critics in Britain are increasingly coming to acknowledge and explore in their work this "diaspora aesthetic" and its formations in the post-colonial experience'.[3]

There are interesting and important parallels with 'Afro-American' writing and the way 'Black English' has developed and been defined in the United States – where, for example, the leading African–American scholar Henry Louis Gates, Jr, has argued that because of the traditional oral nature of 'black poetic expression', the Black poet is ' a point of consciousness of the community' and, moreover, 'a point of consciousness of the language', so that ultimately, 'it must be to the poetry that we turn' despite the problem of 'translating' poetry based on the dialect of 'black speech and black music'.[4] This difficulty is particularly acute when we come to look closely at the work of poets such as Kamau Brathwaite, who incorporate the rhythms as well as the metaphors of folklore, spirituals, songs and proverbial speech as a formulation of double or multiple identities in their work.

The Montserrat poet and anthologist E.A. Markham (b. 1939) has articulated the situation of the Caribbean poet in clear and positive terms:

> Few West Indians are so self-contained as to regard the island/ territory of birth as fulfilling the sum total of their aspirations . . . Simply to go to school or to work elsewhere constitutes leaving some of your emotional credit in that place – which you will call on from time to time. We must stop being on the defensive about this, and learn to exploit its possibilities. After all, the geography of most Caribbean poets' lives suggests dual or mutliple citizenship . . . We are multi-national; cosmopolitan – some of us multi-lingual in ways that encompass and extend beyond the standard-English nation-

language debate and have residences on earth that defy the makers of treaties and the laws of immigration.[5]

The anthology, *Hinterland*, from which this comes, offers a celebration of the West Indian multiple and shifting sense of identity, through a large selection of work by fourteen poets (significantly, four of them women), accompanied by substantial interview and essay material. There are other, differently arranged but equally viable anthologies on the market, such as Paula Burnett's *Penguin Book of Caribbean Verse in English* (1986), or Stewart Brown, Mervyn Morris and Gordon Rohlehr's *Voiceprint: An Anthology of Oral and Related Poetry from the Caribbean* (Longman, 1989) which, as its title suggests, promotes the oral subgenres. Yet Markham's affiliation with the written as well as the oral forms from the English-speaking territories of the Caribbean makes his one of the most useful to draw on here, where I focus upon two contrasting giants of the current generation of Caribbean poets – (Edward) Kamau Brathwaite and Derek Walcott – and three self-confessedly 'Black British' poets, Linton Kwesi Johnson, James Berry and Grace Nichols. Brathwaite was born in Barbados in 1930, educated at Cambridge and Sussex Universities, and worked as an Education Officer in Ghana for eight years, before becoming a Professor of History at the University of the West Indies in Jamaica (he moved to New York in 1990). Walcott, born in St Lucia in 1930 and educated at the University College of the West Indies (as it then was), worked as a journalist in Trinidad, where he founded the Theatre Workshop, before taking on a succession of visiting professorships in America, where he now teaches 'creative writing' for half the year, returning to his home island the other half. James Berry was born in 1924 in Jamaica, and arrived in Britain in 1948, becoming a full-time writer after more than two decades as a telegraphist. Like Nichols, who was born in Guyana in 1950, where she was educated at the University and worked as a schoolteacher and journalist before emigrating in 1977, and Johnson, who was born in Jamaica in 1952 and went to a Brixton comprehensive on his arrival in London in 1963, Berry has long been settled in the UK.

Most Caribbean collections include 'Black British' poetry; but the term usually refers to African and Asian as well as Caribbean communities in contemporary Britain. Much of what I say about language and identity is applicable to the concerns of poets such as Jackie Kay (b. 1961), who first came to notice in *A Dangerous Knowing: Four Black Women Poets* (1984), edited by Prathiba Parma, and whose sense of herself as a black child adopted by white parents informs her work – for example in her stunning first collection, *The Adoption Papers* (1991). Like 'post-colonial', 'Black British' is a problematic term; but in line with my overall attempt to focus

closely upon writings selected in terms of shared historical as well as
cultural-geographic and linguistic experience, I will concentrate upon a
few contemporary Caribbean and Black British poets whose origins,
preoccupations and audiences broadly coincide. This is not to smooth over
or essentialize varied and distinct backgrounds: as Roberto Marquez
argues, 'the coincidence of thematic preoccupation (if not of ideological
response)' found in the work of Caribbean authors 'underscores the pan-
Caribbean scope of their defining experiences' without 'in the least
diminishing the force of clearly manifest regional identities'. Or I could
invoke Paul Gilroy's idea of a 'Black Atlantic', an 'intercultural and
transnational formation' which links black communities across the sea,
while acknowledging their differences.[6]

The tension between local, regional and diasporic identities is central to
the writings I deal with here, which bestride independence from Britain
for Caribbean nations in the 1960s and 1970s. Official independence was
in any case part of a continuum of change, including the arrival in Britain
of significant numbers of West Indians between the end of the Second
World War and the early 1960s, after which successive governments, both
Conservative and Labour, severely limited the opportunities of Commonwealth, particularly 'New' Commonwealth, citizens seeking the right to
live and work in Britain. The multiple ironies of the situation were neatly
encapsulated in one of Louise Bennett's famous ballads, 'Colonisation in
Reverse' (most immigrants came from Jamaica, the most densely populated
island):

> An week by week dem shippin off
> Dem countryman like fire
> Fi immigrate an populate
> De seat a de Empire.
> Ooonoo see how life is funny,
> Oonoo see de tunabout?
> Jamaica live fi box bread
> Out a English people mout.
>
> . . .
>
> What a devilment a Englan!
> Dem face war an brave de worse;
> But ah wonderin how dem gwine stan
> Colonizin in reverse.
>                           (Markham, pp. 62–3)

As David Dabydeen (b. 1956, from Guyana, also settled in the UK) remarked in *Slave Song* (1984), a mutual misrepresentation of Otherness has been going on – perhaps for a very long time:

> 'England' is our Utopia, an ironic reversal, for Raleigh was looking away from the 'squalor' of his homeland to the imagined purity of ours whereas we are now reacting against our 'sordid' environment and looking to 'England' as Heaven. All is a criss-cross of illusions, a trading in skins and ideals.[7]

But the result has been, at least since the 1950s, the fastest growing area of literary experimentation and achievement among all the former colonized peoples of the old Empire. According to Ramchand, in the fifteen years from 1952 to 1967 alone, West Indians published 137 novels, beside a considerable volume of short stories, plays and poems.[8] Since the 1970s, poetry has become the fastest growing branch of this activity. The most prolific, as well as the most honoured poet is Derek Walcott.

## Walcott: 'Either I'm Nobody, or I'm a Nation'

Identity is the product of history; on the personal level, of memory. For Caribbean writers, according to Walcott (in a lecture given at Columbia University in April 1971), 'history is fiction, subject to a fitful muse, memory'; and servitude to this muse

> has produced a literature of recrimination and despair, a literature of revenge written by the descendants of slaves or a literature of remorse written by the descendants of masters. Because this literature serves historical truth, it yellows into polemic or evaporates in pathos. The truly tough aesthetic of the New World neither explains nor forgives history . . . The shipwrecks of Crusoe and of the crew in *The Tempest* are the end of an Old World . . . But to most writers of the archipelago who contemplate only the shipwreck, the New World offers not elation but cynicism, a despair at the vices of the Old which they feel must be repeated . . . Their malaise is an oceanic nostalgia for the older culture and a melancholy at the new, and this can go as deep as a rejection of the untamed landscape, a yearning for ruins.[9]

The sense of lack, or loss, of living in a cultural vacuum, may have held back achievement – which in literary terms has meant until relatively recently a rather limited concern with the effects of colonialism, written in the derivative forms derided by Fanon as the first phase of awareness among the colonized. For Fanon, 'the Peloponnesian War is as much mine as the invention of the compass . . . what I have to recapture is the whole past of the world' ; for this West Indian, 'it is insufficient to dedicate myself to the revival of an unjustly unrecognised negro civilization'.[10] Walcott's resistance to the 'Black Power' politics of the immediately post-independence period, and the astounding range of his writing, redefining himself simultaneously as a Caribbean artist and a figure in world history, suggest how far these words may still ring true – at least for him.

Abjuring revenge and remorse, cynicism and despair, Walcott espouses the 'truly tough aesthetic' of the New World. He sees himself in the line of 'great poets of the New World, from Whitman to Neruda', who have 'paid [their] accounts to Greece and Rome' and walk 'in a world without monuments and ruins'.[11] He is not so much rejecting history, as rejecting those versions of it which are insufficiently alive to the potential of the present, versions locked into a colonised past too appalling or insecure to generate the renewal which he aims to celebrate. Probably the best known writer of Caribbean origin since he won the Nobel Prize for Literature in 1992, Walcott comes from a tiny island in the Windwards whose control swung fourteen times between the French and the British before St Lucia finally became a British colony in 1814; by which time the language of the place was a French-based 'patwa', and the islanders were preponderantly Roman Catholic. Walcott was born in the island's small capital, Castries, along with a twin brother, Roderick. Their father, who died the following year, was a clerk in the District Court; their mother, headteacher of a Methodist infant school, and a lover of literature who used to recite great swathes of Shakespeare. Having an Englishman as paternal grandfather, and a Dutchman as maternal grandfather, while the women in his ancestry were predominantly of African origin, makes Walcott's descent intriguingly mixed – 'hybrid' and 'mongrel' he calls himself, identities which, like his English Protestant background, set him at a distance from the French 'patwa'-speaking, Catholic, black majority.

Rather than trying to retrieve his own past, Walcott forges a new present and future out of many pasts. For this, he manipulates the language of the English literary tradition, increasingly accommodating Creole – including both the French-based speech of his island, and the English-based Jamaican and Trinidadian dialects. Like one of his finest poetic creations, his alter ego the 'bastard' seaman Shabine, in 'The Schooner *Flight*':

I'm just a red nigger who love the sea,
I had a sound colonial education,
I have Dutch, nigger, and English in me,
And either I'm nobody, or I'm a nation.[12]

Walcott proudly confesses both his mixed descent and, with a hint of scorn, the 'sound colonial education' which overlay, without muting, his native dialect – represented in the Creole verbal form 'love', in 'who love the sea'. He claims the nation of the imagination, as a poet riddled with the poetry of others. By the time he became a student in Jamaica, he was already a known and published poet – if at his mother's expense: she gave him $200 to publish *Twenty-Five Poems* in Trinidad when he was 18. With the next two (privately published) volumes, a precocious talent was revealed, as was the influence of Dante, Shakespeare, Donne, Marvell, Eliot, Auden, Hart Crane – a range both 'classical' and modern, both wide and profound. In 1962, *In A Green Night: Poems 1948–60* was published in London, and his international reputation began – in terms which immediately universalized him: as P.N. Furbank put it in *The Listener*, 'history has made him a citizen of the world';[13] three years later, when Philip Larkin compiled *The Oxford Book of Twentieth Century English Verse*, he broke his own rules to include poems from this collection.

The title of Walcott's first, landmark book alludes to a line from Marvell's 'Bermudas', a poem referring to some of his own early and abiding themes: colonialism, exploration, the sea, time past and present, the responsibility of the imagination. One of the most well-known of the forty-two poems in this book, 'Ruins of a Great House' has been widely anthologized, including by Markham (pp. 95-6). It remains a challenging starting-point. It is a meditation upon a plantation slave-owner's decaying mansion, invoking a long tradition of European verse upon the transience of greatness, as opposed to the permanence of poetry. It raises a question central to Walcott's writing: how far does the poem contradict itself by mimicking the inherited 'high art' rhetoric of the imperializing, slave-based power whose decay it celebrates?

There is no doubt about the almost overwhelming intertextuality of the verse: explicit in an epigraph from Sir Thomas Browne's treatise *Urn Burial* (1658), in the Horatian tag in the first line ('Stones only, the *disjecta membra* [scattered remains] of this Great House'), and references to Raleigh, Donne, Kipling and Faulkner – all involved in one way or another, in one part of the world or another, with the 'remains' of empire – living or writing its greatness, but also its brutality, corruption and waste. 'Ancestral murderers and poets, more perplexed / In memory now by every ulcerous crime.' Implicit allusions refer to Old English poetry, Donne (again), Shakespeare and Blake – and there may be more. Topographical poems about great houses appear in English writing from the Renaissance onwards – one of the most well-known, Ben Jonson's 'To Penshurst' (1616), describes walls which were 'reared with no man's ruin, no man's groan / There's none that dwell about them wish them down', interestingly raising the possibility of wishing them down even as it is denied – a possibility realized in Walcott's poem. In short, 'Ruins' is replete with the language and associations of the English literary tradition. But if so, perhaps the detached, intellectual elaboration of this language, confirms the view that it is all too difficult, high-flown and demanding, hence out of touch with the currents of everyday life? What, then, about lines like these – ?

> It seems that the original crops were limes
> Grown in the silt that clogs the river's skirt;
> The imperious rakes are gone, their bright girls gone,
> The river flows, obliterating hurt.

The condensed clarity, the richness of sound texture, reinforce rather than undermine a profound yet simple paradox: good and bad, beauty and cruelty co-exist – now, as they have always done. The poem aims to arouse, then overcome anger:

> Ablaze with rage, I thought
> Some slave is rotting in this manorial lake,
> And still the coal of my compassion fought:
> That Albion too, was once
> A colony like ours

Entirely characteristic of Walcott, and suggestive of his view of history, this recalls the rise and fall of empires through multiple perspectives, so as to engender detachment, then compassion. Equally characteristic is the poem's resistance to quotation or easy summary, its abrupt transitions: composed of fifty-one lines divided into nine unequal sections with varying iambic patterns and occasional rhymes and half-rhymes, almost clinched by a final full rhyme – upon 'ends' and 'friends', words appropriately framing a fragment from Donne's famous meditation, asking not 'for whom the bell tolls; it tolls for thee'. But Walcott quotes a less well-known part of the passage, allowing his poem to end without completion:

> All in compassion ends
> So differently from what the heart arranged
> 'as well as if a manor of thy friend's . . .'

Thus returning us to the idea of the great house and its estate, but with a new vision of what that signifies. The Donne passage runs:

> No man is an island, entire of itself; every man is a piece of the continent, a part of the main; if a clod be washed away by the sea, Europe is the less, as well as if a promontory were, as well as if a manor of thy friend's or of thy own were. Any man's death diminishes me, because I am involved in mankind; and therefore never send to know for whom the bell tolls; it tolls for thee.[14]

Does this finally resolve the poem's contradictions?

The jury is still out. The most convincing defence I have come across was made by Mervyn Morris, himself a distinguished poet, and teacher at the University of the West Indies. That word 'friends' in the last line, he says, is 'superbly ambivalent': it refers to the colonialists mentioned earlier, where the 'West Indian speaker' was angry, and yet leaves open whether or not their shared humanity makes them 'friends' after all. This unanswered question is 'important in the West Indies at this time', says Morris (writing in 1968).

> Walcott, some say, is not West Indian enough. He is too much concerned with world literature and international sophistication. Of course, the fact that Walcott has actually chosen to live in the West Indies is given little weight by West Indian pundits who assert their commitment from some address in London. The central content of Walcott's verse is not much examined. The accusers get stuck with allusions to world literature or with stylistic influences. Poems which happen to be about death, love, evil, art, the loss of faith, are not relevant enough for those who find compassion or complex ambiguity decadent luxuries in our emerging society, and call instead for poems which speak stridently of politics, class and race. Poems are fine if they are black enough. Walcott has written many poems about race, but usually they are exploratory enough to displease the propagandists . . . Like any worthwhile poet, Walcott speaks to people anywhere, but very often his primary significance is for his own West Indian people or for Negroes.[15]

Morris himself has written poetry of the kind he anathematizes here – 'I am the man' is a strong example: it begins

> I am the man that build his house on shit
> I am the man that watched you bulldoze it
> I am the man of no fixed address
> Follow me now
>                     (Markham, p. 171)

To some degree poetry like this, like Morris's criticism, reflects an engagement with the antagonisms of the time, the 1960s and 1970s, which saw 'assaults . . . on Caribbean artists then not deemed "black" enough' (qtd Markham, p. 159). It took a different kind of poet, such as Brathwaite, to counter as he tried to accommodate the criticism. Nevertheless, Morris highlights the continuing problem with poetry as sophisticated and demanding as Walcott's, poetry perhaps inevitably creating a gap within and between audiences at home and abroad.

Morris's most helpful point, though, is that Walcott's work is always and crucially *exploratory*. 'Ruins of a Great House' is not only exploratory in its own right as a poem – witness its open, fragmentary nature – but in representing only a stage, a moment in a much longer and larger exploration, which has issued in Walcott's ever-increasing range and clarification of purpose. On one level, 'I will always remain, as long as I write in the West Indies, I will always seem to be a visible imitator, and superficially *I will* always be an imitator', he told Dennis Scott in 1968; but at the same time, as the revisionary inflection suggested by 'visible' and 'superficially' reveals, his ambition goes beyond the mimicry so often identified with the colonial and ex-colonial artist; for instance, towards the new, unembellished style identified in 'Islands', a poem contemporary with 'Ruins'. 'I seek' he wrote there,

> I seek
> As climate seeks its style, to write
> Verse crisp as sand, clear as sunlight,
> Cold as the curled wave, ordinary
> As a tumbler of island water[16]

Genuine simplicity is apparent elsewhere, as in 'Sea Canes', or the touching and unadorned 'Letter from Brooklyn':

> An old lady writes me in a spidery style,

> Each character trembling, and I see a veined hand,
> Pellucid as paper, travelling on a skein
> Of such frail thoughts its thread is often broken
>                    (Markham, p. 97)

it begins. This is a long way from the convoluted and calculated metaphoric development of 'Ruins'; although the poem's very 'ordinariness' relies upon a deft use of the web metaphor (which continues after these lines), as well as a personal tone which later becomes central to the poet's maturing aesthetic.

This aesthetic is centrally a matter of language:

> I do not consider English to be the language of my masters. I consider language to be my birthright. I happen to have been born in an English and a Creole place, and love both languages. It is the passion, futility and industry of critics to perpetuate this ambiguity. It is their profession. It is mine to do what other poets before me did, Dante, Chaucer, Villon, Burns, which is to fuse the noble and the common language, the streets and the law courts, in a tone that is true to my own voice, in which both accents are heard naturally.[17]

Both accents may be heard even in a poem which seems to be in standard English, 'Mass Man', from *The Gulf* (1969, reptd Markham, pp. 98–9), a recreation of Carnival in Trinidad (forerunner of the Notting Hill Carnival in London), and written during Walcott's years on the island as a dramatist, critic and freelance journalist. The title 'Mass Man' has a triple reference: to people in the mass; to a man who attends the Catholic mass; and, in creole, to a carnival masquerader. The subject is transformation: of the ordinary to the extraordinary; a metaphor for the poetry itself, as well as an evocation of the popular annual event, originally a white planter-class diversion appropriated by former slaves and their descendants, who brought into it their steel bands and Calypsonian spectacle. The poet explores the paradoxes, the historical realities theatricalized, the tears within the joy: in the second stanza we see

> Hector Mannix, waterworks clerk, San Juan, has entered a lion,
> Boysie, two golden mangoes bobbing for breastplates, barges
> like Cleopatra down her river, making style.
> 'Join us,' they shout. 'Oh God, child, you can't dance?'
> But somewhere in that whirlwind's radiance
> a child, rigged like a bat, collapses, sobbing.

This asks to be read with the rhythms and intonation of Caribbean English, if not precisely Creole: 'making style' (posing), and 'you can't dance?' suggesting the rising sound of local speech, as in 'meckin style' and 'yuh cyaan dance?'. The Trojan warrior Hector is recalled, alongside the television hero Mannix (= no man?), in the name of the clerk who, like Bottom the weaver, would roar us a lion. The complex duality of Walcott's inheritance is further caught by the juxtaposition of cross-dressed Boysie and Shakespeare's Cleopatra, the Calypsonian on the one hand, the literary classic (in Shakespeare's time played by a boy) on the other – invoking a post-colonial interrogation of the European tradition, as the black man dressed up implicitly reflects upon the conventionally 'white' Shakespearian actress who displaces the original Cleopatra's race.

Like Yeats, Walcott increasingly takes on disguises and masks to find his way as an artist, most obviously to begin with in his second early collection *The Castaway* (1965): Crusoe, Friday, Adam all feature in that book's deepening exploration of the isolated figure identifying himself in relation to the natural world of the islands and the surrounding sea. In one poem, 'Laventille' (named after a Trinidad slum and dedicated to V.S. Naipaul) however, there is no intervening mask, as the poet engages with the traumas of colonialism, which leave him driven to 'hopelessness and rage' by the 'apish mimicry' of the Caribbean people, by their 'grinding poverty', a cultural and material lack ultimately brought about by the 'deep, amnesiac blow' of the Middle Passage.[18]

This closed, imprisoning sense of identity – widely shared by Walcott's contemporaries, responding with cynicism and despair to the continuing sterility and violence of West Indian politics – is eventually transformed when we come to Walcott's Shabine, who leaves his Laventille slum at the start of his story of 'The Schooner *Flight*'. Shabine's perspective enables him to transcend as he accepts the wounds of the past: from the original annihilation of the Carib Arawak people, slavery, the decline of empire, through present post-colonial neglect – all referred to in his long narrative (some five hundred lines). 'I met History once', Shabine declares,

> but he ain't recognize me.
> a parchment Creole, with warts
> like an old sea-bottle, crawling like a crab
> through the holes of shadow cast by the net
> of a grille balcony; cream linen, cream hat.
> I confront him and shout, 'Sir, is Shabine!
> They say I'se your grandson. You remember Grandma
> your black cook, at all?' The bitch hawk and spat.

A spit like that worth any number of words.
But that's all them bastards have left us: words.[19]

Shabine is not white enough to be accepted by those in power before independence, inheritors of the cream linen version of history; nor, it turns out later in the poem, is he black enough for those who took over after independence, and whose corruption disgusts him. But because 'I have Dutch, nigger, and English in me', an identity bespeaking mixed blood, race, language, the potential insult of 'nigger' overcome by its syncopated placing in the line – this sense of identity releases the huge claim of 'either I'm nobody, or I'm a nation'.

Shabine is the Everyman of the Caribbean, the poem he inhabits its masterpiece. Walcott's long autobiographical poem in standard English, *Another Life* (1973, extract in Markham, pp. 102–4) prepared the way for Shabine's burden of criticism, fact and self-analysis; while earlier attempts at Creole voices in poetry (e.g., 'Parang') and drama (*Dream on Monkey Mountain*, 1967), prepared for the complex and varied blend of speech registers, the wonderfully telling version of the local idiom, which permits Shabine his combination of low-life humour and bardic lyricism. Ultimately, as Shabine tells us, he speaks in the 'common language' of 'the wind', is 'satisfied / if my hand gave voice to one people's grief'.[20] Walcott's lines are so resonant because they assert no superiority between the European and African languages which have helped create the different dialects available within the repertoire of English today. He offers instead a mixed and flexible dialect of his own, welcoming anyone willing to listen, and to accept that language may be greater than the confines of class, race and self.

I do not say 'gender' because, as Elaine Savory has argued, Walcott's women tend to be represented in stereotype, as either seductive or threatening, reflecting a patriarchy resisting the autonomy of those it has long tried yet failed to marginalize. Thus, after reflecting upon his escape from his wife and his mistress, Shabine tries other women, only to find that 'once they stripped naked, their spiky cunts / bristled like sea-eggs and I couldn't dive'.[21] Shabine's first and last love is the sea, and if its infinite generative power becomes personified in women, it becomes hostile to someone like himself when unprepared for the humility and acceptance which heals. Shabine has to be both realistic character and visionary; and the tensions of Walcott's culture, the fractures of its past and present, are difficult to overcome; and so we feel the uncertainty underlying this attempt, through Shabine, to embrace his hybrid origins. If at times it seems a 'vain search for one island that heals', nevertheless, the search goes on. If the wound of the past remains, it remains in language, hence, as the poet proposes in his most ambitious recent long poem, the epic *Omeros*, ordinary fisherfolk speaking demotic Caribbean, can assert that 'Like Philoctete's wound, this language carries its cure, / its radiant affliction'.[22] The multiple, fragmentary identities can be carried in this vision, which incorporates without erasing difference.

### Brathwaite: Caliban at the Carnival?

One reason why Walcott, unlike, say, V.S. Naipaul, can celebrate as he registers his uncertain identity, is his willingness to adopt the creolized perspective of the Caribbean, first offered by Louise Bennett, the founding mother of 'dialect verses'. At the same time, he locates himself in the mainstream of European and American poetry, with his invocation of the classics, and his continued echoes of Auden and Eliot, Berryman and Hart Crane. His possession equally of the 'centre' and the 'margin' undermines facile distinctions of difference – as Homi Bhabha, for one, has acknowledged in *The Location of Culture*.[23] Kamau Brathwaite, with whom Walcott is often (not always fruitfully) compared, has developed a poetic language more resistant to the Western high cultural tradition, and more narrowly engaged with local, especially African, roots. It is an engagement in its way as monumentally ambitious as Walcott's, and as evocative of multiple pasts: as Gordon Rohlehr pointed out when Brathwaite's first three books of poetry – *Rights of Passage* (1967), *Masks* (1968), *Islands* (1969), collectively *The Arrivants: A New World Trilogy* (1973) – began to appear, this was 'a kind of *Aeneid* or *Iliad* for Black people' exhibiting an 'epic sense' of exile, journey, arrival and return. More specifically – and the most critical point of difference between the two poets – Brathwaite's epic revealed his abiding concern 'with coming to terms with his own history'.[24] It is the central theme of this poet-historian, author of *The Development of Creole Society in Jamaica 1770–1820* (Clarendon Press, 1971) and the influential *History of the Voice: The Development of Nation Language in Anglophone Caribbean Poetry*, originally a lecture to students at Harvard in 1979, and published in 1984 by the leading Black British bookseller, John La Rose's New Beacon Books (named after the pioneering literary magazine *The Beacon*, published in Trinidad, 1931–3).

Unlike Walcott, Brathwaite places colonial history within a context which aims to empower the black population of the Caribbean. Not for him the detached perspective in which history may be rewritten as a hybrid myth of the rise and fall of empires; rather, he privileges the presence of

Africa, consciously reversing the given hierarchy of his society so as to enable the downtrodden – identified as the descendants of slaves – to identify themselves as the inheritors of past civilizations such as those of Egypt, Ghana, Mali, Songhai. However sophisticated and scholarly the medium in which this position is articulated, it emerges quite clearly as the product of his own personal history – a formative experience of departure, exile and return in many ways more characteristic of his fellow Caribbean writers than Walcott's long rootedness in the islands. In the autobiographical essay 'Timehri' (1970), Brathwaite claims that, though by birth and education 'nominally "middle-class"', he was not in a position to make any serious 'investment in West Indian middle-class values', since his childhood was spent mixing with 'beach-boys' or 'country boys and girls'. One of the sought-after 'island scholarships' took him to Cambridge. However,

> since I was not then aware of any other West Indian alternative (though in fact I had been *living* that alternative), I found and felt myself 'rootless' on arrival in England and like so many other West Indians of the time, more than ready to accept and absorb the culture of the Mother Country. I was, in other words, a potential Afro-Saxon. (qtd Markham, p. 117)

This is the familiar experience of the colonized intellectual, so persuasively theorized by fellow-Caribbean Fanon: unaware of their own independent culture, they strive to possess the imposed culture. For Brathwaite, self-awareness came later, during his stay in Ghana between 1955 and 1962, and after he had published his first poems in a Cambridge magazine – poems chosen, he says, for their 'exotic' flavour. He was 'a West Indian, roofless man of the world. I could go, belong, everywhere on the worldwide globe. I ended up in a village in Ghana. It was my beginning'. (Markham, p. 118).

In Ghana he came to an awareness 'of community, of cultural wholeness', identifying with the Africans, his 'living diviners'. This new awareness became his 'problem' when he returned to the Caribbean: how to relate it to the 'existing, inherited non-African consciousness of educated West Indian society' (p. 119). In Fanon's terms, he was trying to become an awakener of the people. And for him, the way to do this was to employ the language of the people, or, something more ambitious, 'nation language'.

Brathwaite's poetry aims to promote 'nation language', rather than standard English or Creole, so as to empower the black population of the Caribbean through the expression of its history in terms of its cultural heritage. What does he mean by this memorable term? 'Wings of a Dove', reprinted in Markham (pp. 120–3) from the first book of *The Arrivants*, *Rights of Passage*, effectively registers what is meant by it. In the opening stanzas, the narrator, speaking standard English, introduces

> Brother Man, the rasta
> man, beard full of lichens
> brain full of lice

in his poor, shanty-town kitchen. Upon smoking 'ganja', Brother Man is transformed into a voice speaking thus of himself: 'I / Rastafar-I', a 'prophet and singer, scourge / of the gutter', who then takes the reader/ listener through the 'silent streets of affliction', where he hears 'my people' shout:

> Down, down
> white
> man, con
> man, down

and then:

> Rise rise
> locks-
> man, Solo-
> man wise
> man

The poor, all of those who are 'down', are exhorted to rise again by this new voice; unlike the 'white black man', those who lack self-awareness, and who lack awareness of their rich spiritual heritage, a heritage going

> back back
> to Af-
> rica

The spiritual poverty of 'them clean-face browns' in 'Babylon town' is what the Rasta man fears most, and it is also they who fear him most. Finally, what Brathwaite calls the 'sound-structure of Rastafarian drums and the "Dry bones" spiritual' are introduced, so as to assert a triumphant conclusion:

Watch *dem* ship *dem*
come to *town* dem
full o' *silk* dem
full o' *food* dem

an' *dem* plane *dem*
*come* to *groun'* dem

full o' *flash* dem
full o' *cash* dem

silk *dem* food *dem*
shoe *dem* wine *dem*

date *dem* drink *dem*
an consume *dem*

*praisin' de glory of the lord*

The italics are Brathwaite's, quoting himself in his 'nation language' essay, to demonstrate that 'a nation language poem could be "serious" and employ not only semantic but *sound* elements'. Reading it aloud is the nearest we can get to the 'charismatic' first performance in the Cochrane Theatre, London, on 3 March 1967, recalled by Louis James.[25]

For this is 'performance poetry', in which occasion and delivery are at least as important as what's written. Yet even the written version of the whole poem with its extraordinary shifts and changes, its unexpected line-breaks – even this is comprehensible and compelling, since there is a clear progression of signals to the reader. The first signal in 'Wings of a Dove' is the introduction of the 'Rasta' figure, whose use of the pronoun 'I' in particular exemplifies the 'dread talk' of the black cultural minority which re-emerged during the 1960s in the Caribbean and the UK, calling themselves the Rastafarians, whose appearance, behaviour and language denoted their 'back-to-Africa' religious cult. The movement began in Jamaica in the 1930s with the work of Marcus Garvey (1887-1940), who encouraged black people to think of Africa, especially Ethiopia, as their religious and cultural home, from which everywhere else is Babylon, on the analogy with the Jews in exile. The Rastafarians think of themselves as the true Black Israelites, whose messiah, called Jah (from the Hebrew Jahweh), was the Emperor Haile Selassie (1892-1975), one of whose titles was 'Lion of Judah', in honour of which they wear 'dreadlocks', symbol-

izing a lion's mane. The 'I' is used in 'dread talk' as both subject and object
('I and I'), in both singular and plural forms, as well as a translation of the
second-person pronoun 'you', thus departing not only from standard
English lexis (as the Rasta does with 'ganja', i.e. cannabis, and 'Babylon',
i.e. non-Rasta territory) but grammar as well, breaking down the distinction between self and others.

The Rastaman's dream of escape from his squalid surroundings, and
from the forces which keep him there (it is usually 'him', not 'her'),
represents the dream of all who can share that striving – including,
momentarily, the poet, adopting the Rasta language. But then there
follows the 'nation language' section, rhythmically reinforcing the merging
of different 'Black' cultural traditions – from West African chant, Black
American spirituals and jazz to Caribbean Creole. This recalls the Négritude
movement of the pre-independence period, the poetry and politics of the
Martinican Aimé Césaire, for example, who used a stereotyping of race,
culture and language in an attempt to resist European metropolitan norms.
But what Brathwaite is doing here is more subtle: reinforcing his sense of
a submerged voice breaking the chains of formal, written verse in standard
English, through the use of many voices and perspectives. In 'Wings of a
Dove', there is a self-awareness which was absent from the Caribbean
Negritude-mongers, whose time had passed; reflected in the paradoxical
fact that the poet himself resembles most closely one of those 'clean-faced
browns' the Rastaman distrusts. Nor does this paradox deflect the success
of the poem, with its varied layout, rhymes, rhythms and registers, guiding
(in the first place Black British) readers through the liberation of expression
which 'nation language' allows. Brathwaite's emphatic delivery of the
'riddimic aspect', is central to his project of creating a poetic language
which validates the 'natural' language, that is Creole, of Afro-Caribbeans,
thought of as 'bad' or 'broken' English even by those that speak/spoke it.[26]
Yet he goes beyond the dialect, to some extent inventing his own, like a
latter-day Hugh MacDiarmid attempting to forge a new national consciousness.

There is no question of the large and liberating impact of Brathwaite's
poetry and his polemic upon Caribbean and Black British writings –
releasing 'the people's language from the imprisoning dungeon of "dialect"', as James Berry put it (qtd Markham, p. 176). Brathwaite's basic
premiss, that 'What our educational system did was to recognise and
maintain the language of the conquistador', [27] is shared by many poets,
from Louise Bennett and Martin Carter, to Olive Senior and James Berry,
all of whom have testified in one way or another to the point that imported
literary forms and traditions 'had very little to do, really, with [our]

environment and reality' (see Markham, pp. 48, 66–7, 176–7, 214–15). In Fred D'Aguiar's 'Papa T' (Markham, pp. 322–3), the poet recollects his Guyanese grandfather reciting Tennyson's 'Charge of the Light Brigade', interrupting himself to shout at the children in his audience in Creole: '*If yu all don't pay me mind, / I goin ge yu a good lickin an sen yu to bed*'. In the final line, the child-as-adult remarks, in an ironic echo of Tennyson, 'to hear, to disobey'; turning disobedience into a more fundamental resistance, resistance to the colonial language – in which, however, the poem itself is couched. For Brathwaite, the mainstream of English poetry since Chaucer, with its (usually iambic) pentameter-based model, 'carries with it a certain kind of experience, which is not the experience of the hurricane'; recent Caribbean poets try to break out of this model and 'move into a system which more closely and intimately approaches our experience' through an English which 'is not the standard, imported, educated English, but that of the submerged, surrealist experience and sensibility', in short, 'nation language'.[28]

For Brathwaite's own work, this idea released a sustained rhythmic and tonal audacity which continues up to the present; and which has yet to be adequately recognized. Edward Said's 1994 'Afterword' to *Orientalism* refers to the 'daring new formal achievements' of Walcott's poetry, in re-appropriating and transforming 'the historical experience of colonialism';[29] but it is Brathwaite who is formally the more daring, while re-writing the colonial narrative: witness 'The Journeys' section of *Rights of Passage*, which begins with this startlingly fragmented line of names, cracked to emphasize and relish their strange yet homely sounds, encouraging listeners/readers to explore and recognize these ancestral places:

> E-
> gypt
> in Af-
> rica
> Mesopo-
> tamia
> Mero-
> ë[30]

As the places between which the African has journeyed through history approach the present, so the verse lines broaden out, delineating the series of migrations which criss-cross the whole book, moving about with the figures of African descendants, in their various roles, from 'the Negro' to 'Uncle Tom' and 'the Rasta / man', in Europe and the Americas. Brathwaite evokes these roles, 'these New World mariners / Columbus coursing kaffirs' ('The Emigrants') in order to replace them with a new sense of self, celebrated in the *Masks* book, while admitting that, as the title implies, this identity is not final, but taken on, a project in history –

> So for my hacked
> heart, veins' mem-
> ories, I wear this
>
> past I borrowed; his-
> tory bleeds
> behind my hollowed eyes

the final section of *Masks* begins, evoking the recurrent imagery of slavery.[31] In the last book, *Islands*, the multiple, overlapping flashbacks, the African cities, drums and rituals of *Masks*, resolve themselves into a Caribbean vision, 'Caliban at the Carnival', where the poet uses the Creolized sounds of the New World to register the multifarious survivals of its African heritage.

These 'New World' poems begin with an invocation of the Rasta Emperor, 'Jah', in terms of the triumphant, trumpeting music from Africa to all corners of the Americas, the Caribbean:

> Nairobi's male elephants uncurl
> their trumpets to heaven
> Toot-Toot takes it up
> in Havana
> in Harlem

but these are also and always the blues, lamenting at the end of this poem that

> The sun that was once a doom of gold to the Arawaks
> is now a flat boom in the sky.[32]

This historically inevitable 'doom', this sense of loss, undermines the hopeful, celebratory struggle, even to the last words of the entire trilogy, which concludes with the poem 'Jou'vert' (Creole: the morning before Carnival, from French, pre-British Trinidad):

*bambalula bambulai*
*bambalula bambulai*
. . .

with their

rhythms some-
thing torn

and new[33]

Brathwaite's passionate journey between language and history has taken him into a second trilogy, the even more fragmentary *Mother Poem* (1977), *Sun Poem* (1982), and *X/Self* (1987), which reveal a Blakean, neo-apocalyptic struggle to reorder history as it is rewritten into the present, based on Brathwaite's birth-place, Barbados. The black diaspora is no longer the focus; rather, it is the possibility of spiritual wholeness, latent even in a world torn apart by imperialism and its latter-day equivalent, international capitalism.

Is this trajectory so far from Walcott's after all? As Michael Dash has observed, the redemptive, quasi-mystical role the poet is apparently developing for himself places him closer to certain modernist English poets, such as T.S. Eliot, than the speech patterns and rituals of the Caribbean 'folk' he otherwise seeks to adopt.[34] *Mother Poem* opens with an evocation of the porous limestone landscape of Barbados:

The ancient watercourses of my island
echo of river, trickle, worn stone,
the sunken voice of glitter inching its pattern to the sea,
memory of foam, fossil, erased beaches high above the eaten
boulders of st philip[35]

The island's 'sunken voices' are also the voices of its women, who are – and this places him favourably against Walcott's (and Eliot's) masculinist writing – shown to be central to the experience discovered and defined in *Mother Poem*. Consider the much-anthologized 'Horse Weebles' (i.e. weevils, Markham, pp. 130-2), from the second section of the book, beginning

Sellin biscuit an sawlfish in de plantation shop at pie
corner, was another good way of keepin she body an soul-seam
together

This woman shop seller is part of a community projected in *Mother Poem*,
a community which relies on its women to attend to its everyday, material
needs. They also voice themselves, in Barbadian (Bajan) Creole, which the
poet modulates into historical perspective, as he registers their cruel
circumstances

> but then is cries an hungry faces: children
> who can hardly shit: tin bones of ancient skeletones
>
> the planter's robber's waggon wheels and whips
> and she trapped in within her rusting canepiece plot

Walcott's isolated male figures look limited beside this large vision, in
which oppression is seen as part of the historical process, which the women
dream of escaping. Not that Brathwhaite ignores the male view: the
next book, *Sun Poem*, deals with boyhood, and the rituals of men, as
the other side of the coin. The final work, *X/Self*, its very title signifying the problematics of recreating the broken or split self, explores
forms of language 'calibanised' (as he dubs it) into more emphatically
assertive yet fragmented lines like these, from 'Mont Blanc' (Markham,
pp. 125–7):

> chad sinks
>
> sa
> hara wakes out slowly
>
> the dry snake of the harm
> attan the harmattan reaches into our wells into our smiles in

Taking revenge on coherence, delighting in the erosion or slippage of
meaning, 'Mont Blanc' begins with the central fact of the sequence, 'Rome
burns / and our slavery begins', defining 'the pivot of the Euro-imperialist
/ Christine mercantilist aspect of this book', as Brathwaite calls it in a note
– where he goes on to explain that the 'harmattan' of the Sahara, the
'seasonal climate-changing wind and starting-point of much of my poetry
since *Rights of Passage*' has its origin in a place become the focus of Western
humanitarian concern, 'where thousands perish in full view of the
television cameras, a visible hell'.[36]

It is hard to find any redemptive qualities in *X/Self*'s vision of desolation
and absurdity, a vision in which post-colonial realities around the world are

linked through allusions to the defeated or unborn revolutions of the New World and Africa (including 'aparthate' South Africa). The collection ends with an invocation of 'Xango', the pan-African thunder-god Shango, healer as well as destroyer, associated with both male and female principles, whose breath, whose blast, whose blues will 'shatter outwards to your light and calm and history'.[37] The reverberations set up by the preceding poems help to generate a sense of reaching beyond the time of history; and to hear the poet's vibrant, incantatory performances (in public and on recording) is to experience some shared sense of restorative forces. More recently, however, personal griefs and public disasters, such as an attack upon him in his Jamaica home, and the stoning to death of Mikey Smith during the 1983 Jamaican election, have generated a gloomier image of the poet as an isolated, sacrificial figure – as in 'Stone' (*Jah Music*, 1987, reptd Markham, pp. 133–5), Brathwaite's elegy for the Jamaican dub poet. After giving Smith's own famous extended word 'lawd' ('Me Cyaan Believe It', Markham, p. 286) across an entire line seventy-seven letters long, 'Stone' concludes, 'i am the stone that kills me'. Brathwaite's even more recent verse, 'writing in light' on the screen of the word-processor, may enable yet more remarkable shifts of word-shape and pattern, gaining visual effects as violent and discordant as the most modern jazz, as in *Middle Passages* (1992). However, as Louis James has well said, the resultant effect

> is hard to describe, and impossible to illustrate, for any excerpt loses the meaning found only within the whole. It is illogical to complain that Brathwaite is attempting the impossible, using the printed page as if it were sound. All written poetry is a raid on the border between the inner and outer voices, what is heard and what remains in the mind. In these brave, profoundly disturbing poems, Brathwaite pushes to the limits the jazz concept in poetry to express the cycle of destitution and protest of the Caribbean peoples.[38]

In his attempts to integrate the acoustic and the graphic, Brathwaite continues to reveal himself as probably the most technically innovative and adventurous poet of the Caribbean diaspora, being led by his own work towards ever new horizons of communication. He wants to outwit language, even as he uses it to further his project of creating a sense of meaning and identity beyond the conspiracies of history.

### New Voices, New Memories: Johnson, Berry and Nichols

The most important aspect of 'nation language' is its emphasis upon, and validation of orality: the communication medium of the ordinary people of the Caribbean and its diaspora. Hence, poetry as it is derived from speech, not writing; poetry as it is derived from the communal and historic, not the individual experience. If, as Brathwaite promotes it, this privileges the influence of 'the African model, the African aspect of our New World/ Caribbean heritage',[39] then it is also a way of dislodging the pejorative overtones still attached to Creole – although, as I have been suggesting, his poetic voice takes nation language well beyond everyday speech. One problem with his position is that it appears to promote polarities: between 'native' and imported, 'folk' and learned, Creole and standard, above all and potentially most damaging, between African and non-African. This is obviously inaccurate in terms of the 'book' learning present throughout Brathwaite's work – he owes more to T.S. Eliot than Walcott does – but it is also a denial of non-African histories and experiences. In terms of language, the more useful concept, identified by Gordon Rohlehr in his Introduction to the *Voiceprint* anthology

> is that of a 'continuum' stretching between Creole and standard English, from which speakers naturally selected registers of the language which were appropriate to particular contexts and situations. The notion of a continuum made sense of what West Indian novelists had been doing for some time, that is, exploring the whole range of language and speech registers open to them. The poets also needed to recognise that alternative registers were accessible to them and to liberate, through an openness to all available voices, such word-shapes as these voices might suggest.[40]

The dangers of dividing 'oral or performance' and 'literary' practices need to be avoided, as do those of exaggerating the importance of the African ancestry of the submerged majority in the Caribbean when talking about language. On the other hand, emphasizing the diversity of the Caribbean and diaspora experiences in theory, should not blind us to the specific, historic demands met by poets such as Brathwaite, and those whose poetry he liberated.

Thus, Brathwaite was also linking himself in with, as he was promoting, the movement of Black British poetry of the 1970s and early 1980s, displayed by the new 'reggae' and 'dub' poets, whose radical, streetwise politics and use of popular music took their writings as far from the learned history professor's as they were geographically distant from him as well. Poets such as Linton Kwesi Johnson, whose popular anthology *Dread Beat an' Blood* (Bogle L'Ouverture, 1975) contained highly politicized, performed poems, first printed like this (from 'Five Nights of Bleeding', 1974):

> night number one was in BRIX/TON:
> SOFRANO B sounn sys/tem
>
> was a–beatin out a riddim / wid a *fyah*,
> commin doun his reggae-reggae *wyah*;
>
> it was a sounn shakin doun you spinal col / umn,
> a bad music tearin up you *flesh*;
> an th'rebels-dem start a-fightin,
> th'yout dem jus tunn *wild*.
>
> it's *war* amongst th' rebels:
> mad / ness . . . mad / ness . . . *war*
> so wid a flick
> a de wrist
> a jab an a stab
>
> th'song of blades was *soun* / ded
> th'bile of oppression was *vom* / ited
> an two policemen *woun* / ded
>
> *r*ighteous *r*ighteous *war*[41]

The powerful, mesmerizing rhythms, with their jabbing, stabbing physicality, are unmistakable, as is the aggressive message. This 'dub' text has been smoothed down by Markham (pp. 264–5), but even the later anthologized version remains a challenge to English literary norms, as it remains a challenge to establishment ideologies about the 'place' of black or ethnic minorities in Britain in the post-war era.

Johnson saw himself as speaking primarily on behalf of a young Black British audience: ' to show the black youth of England . . . that you don't have to be immersed in classical literature or to have been to a university to be able to write poetry that strikes a common chord of response among your peer group' (Markham, p. 261). Certainly the success of his music and poetry suggests that a common chord was there, although how far his aim to present 'a hurting black story' ('Reggae Sounds', Markham, p. 262) was achievable beyond his peer group is hard to know. Perhaps only poems such as the elegiac 'Reggae fi dada' (as performed on TV: Markham, pp. 266–9), can and have reached further. Nevertheless, a positive awareness of Black poetry in Britain has for some time now been promoted in school curricula, visiting writer schemes, public readings and performances, and Johnson still plays a part in this – witness his 1996 return to the stage, when younger writers like Caryl Phillips and Fred D'Aguiar recalled his importance as *the* 'dub' poet. A Jamaica-born Londoner who, like Brathwaite, added an African middle name, and founder-member of the Brixton-based Race Today Collective, Johnson's career originated in the mobilization of black youth when clashes with fascists and police were leading up to the country-wide disturbances of 1981. His dub form, derived from reggae music and Rastafarian religion, was one form of expression which Brathwaite's cultural initiative was in part about legitimating. 'I was', he remembered, 'influenced by Fanon – the internalising of oppression'.[42]

The anger and violence of the form was – is – that of a post-independence generation whose ties with the Caribbean, much less with Africa, were less important than their sense of being second-class citizens within their own country, ostracized by whites and bullied by the authorities. In 1976, the year after the appearance of *Dread Beat an' Blood*, the Chair of the Race Relations Commission warned that Britain's black population (40 per cent of whom were by then born in Britain) thought of themselves as British, and took 'the phrase "equality of opportunity" for what it means'. According to Arthur Marwick, race had become 'a more significant, and certainly a more dangerous divide in British society than class'.[43] This is arguable; unarguable is the fact that, after the 1979 Conservative victory, the government was increasingly concerned to stamp its authority over areas of the country perceived as unstable or resistant to control, with the result that confrontation became an increasingly common experience for those in the urban areas who felt rejected or devalued. Pitched battles between the police and rioters (often, but far from exclusively 'black') throughout the country in July 1981 brought a new urgency to the issue of race, often misidentified as the source of the problems associated with a declining imperial nation looking for a new role in the world.

For poets such as Johnson, who identified themselves with the activists, class and race were interrelated factors. 'Di Black Petty-Booshwa' (Markham, pp. 269–70) was dedicated to the 'Railton Youth Club members' of Brixton, and it attacks

> dem w'i gi' whey dem talent to di State
> an di' black workin' class andahrate
> dem wi' side wid oppressah
> w'en di goin' get ruff
> side wid aggressah
> w'en di goin' get tuff

The response to liberal, reformist attempts (exemplified by the Scarman Inquiry) to address the issues which brought about 'Di Great Insohreckshan' of 1981 was to claim that the 'plastic bullit' and the 'waatah cannon'

> will bring a blam-blam
> nevah mine Scarman
> will bring a blam-blam

The limitations of dub poems, 'heavy with testimony, warning and prophecy'[44] are the limitations of the time, when the frustrations of urban black communities were especially acute, and the sounds and speech of the streets important to use in solidarity against the oppressor.

   Brathwaite's own agenda was always broader and more inclusive than that of the dub poets, but his programme also involved important exclusions: Caribbean writers of Amerindian or Asian descent, for example. Nor did it recognize that in Guyana and Trinidad the population is almost 50 per cent of non-African ancestry – implicitly marginalizing the achievement of work like Dabydeen's *Slave Song* and *Coolie Odyssey* (1988), based on Guyanese–Indian patois. In their joint *Reader's Guide to West Indian and Black British Literature,* Dabydeen and Nana Wilson-Tagoe (both at the new Centre of Caribbean Studies in Warwick University), asserted that

> The business of the writer is to break through the confines of narrowness, whether it be the political narrowness of nationalism, or the cultural narrowness of localism, or the imaginative narrowness of social reality, or even the existential narrowness of reality itself.[45]

The book was the first of its kind, published by two specialist Black/Third World publishers: Hansib and Anna Rutherford (later Dangaroo). For Dabydeen and Wilson-Tagoe, harking back to C.L.R. James and Fanon, the actual, historical hybridity of people's backgrounds meant that European philosophy, aesthetics, and languages, were as 'native' to the

Caribbean as to Europe itself; and to pretend otherwise was narrow and sentimental.

The great strength of James Berry's work since the early 1970s has been its lack of narrowness, although it is occasionally sentimental in its affirmation of Black British experience and culture. Widely known in Britain for his promotion of fellow Black poets and their work, especially in performance and for schools, Berry preceded collections of his own poetry (*Fractured Circles*, New Beacon, 1979 and *Lucy's Letters and Loving*, New Beacon, 1982) with the anthology *Bluefoot Traveller* (New Beacon, 1976), and then went on to produce *News for Babylon: The Chatto Book of Westindian-British Poetry* (1984), which included 40 poets and 154 poems. *News for Babylon* further helped establish the presence of an important and growing body of poetic expression ignored or marginalized by the arbiters of 'English' poetry – who, if they allowed any Black writing into their anthologies, ensured it was cleansed of Creole. Even D.J. Enright's *Oxford Book of Contemporary Verse: 1945–1980* (Oxford University Press, 1980), which was supposed to shake up the notion that British poetry was (in his words) 'pitiably provincial or parochial' by including Commonwealth, Irish and American poets, included just seven of Walcott's most easily assimilable, standard English poems as the Caribbean contribution. Britain was represented by many good poets, none Black.

Berry's poetry addresses the historic experience of Black British people of his own generation, whose settlement in Britain began with the 492 Jamaican immigrants who arrived at Tilbury in June 1948 on the SS *Empire Windrush*, in response to the demand for labour in key areas of the postwar reconstruction programme, such as the transport and catering industries, and the new National Health Service. There have been Black people in Britain for centuries, but West Indians only began arriving in large numbers in the 1950s, when immigration to the United States became more difficult, the vast majority coming to find work, not to settle permanently (immigration from India and Pakistan began later, and peaked in the 1960s). Nevertheless, pressures for immigration control mounted, until immigration from the New (i.e. mainly Black) Commonwealth, already restricted by a series of measures from 1962 onwards, was virtually ended by the Immigration Act of 1971, except for (limited) family reunion. The 1971 Act's definition of 'patriality' (having a parent or grandparent born in the UK), allowed some millions of Old Commonwealth citizens to settle in Britain if they chose. Ever more complicated ways of becoming (or not becoming) British were later introduced, the most obviously racist in 1981, making British citizenship dependent not on birth in Britain, but conditional upon the citizenship of one's parents. Black Britons have had to survive the humiliations of the changing law, as well as the deprivations of the inner city.

Describing himself as a 'transplanted root, I need the right depth to survive', Berry says his poetry is for 'discovering' and 'celebrating the truth of myself relevant for survival' (Markham, p. 176). This truth is the truth of those whose first experience of Britain is of confusion and alienation, a sense that their identity has come into question. Novelists such as George Lamming (*The Emigrants*, 1954), Andrew Salkey (*Lonely Londoners*, 1956), Alvin Bennett (*Because They Know Not*, 1961) and, of course, V.S. Naipaul (e.g. *The Mimic Men*, 1967) recreated the common experience of 'double exile', the struggle to come to terms with the present, and to resist dehumanizing definitions of their otherness by the 'host' culture. Poets took up this theme, too, if tempted at times into prosaic reportage, as in Berry's well-known vignette, 'On an Afternoon Train from Purley to Victoria, 1955', which touches on both the innocence of some forms of racism, and its continuity –

> Where are you from? she said
> Jamaica I said
> What part of Africa is Jamaica? she said
> Where Ireland is near Lapland I said[46]

Berry's best work uses Creole or 'nation language', above all through his 'Lucy' persona. She is 'a Caribbean woman who came to England in the 50s [and who] writes letters back to her friend who has never left the village' (Markham, p. 177). 'Lucy's Letter' begins with an expression of nostalgia which at the same time validates the use of the 'home' dialect, or 'labrish' (literally, gossip: also alluding to Louise Bennett's landmark collection, *Jamaica Labrish*, Kingston, 1966): 'Things harness me here / I long for we labrish bad', it begins. The opening lines of the third verse capture the sense of being caught between cultures:

> London isn't like we
> village dirt road, you know
> Leela: it a parish
> of a pasture-lan' what
> grown crisscross streets,
> an' they lie down to my door.
> But I lock myself in.
> (Markham, pp. 183–4)

The poem contrasts the longed-for better life of London, represented by the National Health Service and money for holidays, with vivid recollections of a poor but freer life left behind. The poet's fragile sense of identity needs a Creole-speaking female persona to express his sublimated longings.

It is striking that Berry and others (such as Fred D'Aguiar) use a woman's voice for negotiating such complexes of feelings and identities through language. More effective at engendering language, are the women poets themselves – who, however, also find the adoption of a persona a way of reconstituting the self in a situation of multiple cultural and linguistic influences and practices. Louise Bennett's traditional, ballad-like narratives of popular aspiration and acceptance become only one, if a potent, model in this scenario. For Grace Nichols, a 'regular book hound' whose young ears were filled with the sounds of traditional English poetry from Shakespeare to Christina Rossetti, but who as an adult began collecting Guyanese folktales and Amerindian myths, the whole rich variety of Caribbean cultures and connections – to Africa, Europe, Asia and the Americas – led her to call herself 'a poet of the world' (Markham, p. 296). But it is precisely the Caribbean inflection of these various historic criss-crossings which impress her work, written in both standard English and Creole, sometimes within the same poem. Gender is on her agenda, too, and the series of monologues dramatized in her first collection, *i is a long-memoried woman* (published by Caribbean specialists, Karnak House, 1983) survey the long oppression of Caribbean women, while honouring their capacity for survival. Her characteristic wry humour is evident from the start

> From dih pout
> of mih mouth
> from dih treacherous
> calm of mih smile
> you can tell
>
> *I* is a long memoried woman
> (Markham, p. 299)

Her long memories serve to speak on behalf of

> we the women
> whose praises go unsung
> whose voices go unheard
> (p.300)

and like several other woman poets of Caribbean origin – such as Lorna Goodison, Jean 'Binta' Breeze, Amryl Johnson and Olive Senior – Nichols finds that singing the woman in her work leads to a position challenging not only the old imperial master-narrative, but the new critical, anti-imperial narratives of Fanon and Said as well. As Jane Miller has demonstrated, the seductive strength of the position articulated by those concerned to expose the continuing force of colonial attitudes in terms of class, race and language excludes or at least compromises women's histories, their status as producers and critics.

According to Miller, the central idea of the other in theories of colonization and its aftermath can be used to displace the patriarchal aspect of anti-imperialist post-colonial attitudes so that 'women's vulnerabilities and the injuries they attract to themselves . . . become metaphors for the injuries suffered by whole societies and for the consequent humiliation of their men'.[47] A more complex approach to the issue of gender in this context, as developed by theorists like Trinh T. Minh-ha and Sara Suleri, suggests the need for continuing vigilance towards articulations of 'Otherness'. Although the poetry of most women writing out of the experience of the Caribbean and Black Britain challenges the masculinist assumptions of the developing canon in fairly obvious ways, Nichols's 'natural fear of anything that tries to close in on me, whether it is an ideology or a group of people who think that we should all think alike because we are all women or because we are all black' drives her to resist facile identifications of her position as either 'feminist' or 'black' – or, indeed, as the 'long-suffering black woman', whether at the hands of 'white society or at the hands of black men'. Sharing the commitment of Caribbean and Black British poets to her past and to the 'valid, vibrant language that our foremothers and our forefathers struggled to create', does not mean that the only reason she uses Creole in her poetry is to preserve it, but also because 'I want something different; something that sounds and looks different to the eye on the page and to the ear. Difference, diversity, and unpredictability make me tick'.[48]

But, then, in what way does difference, diversity, and unpredictability correspond to the experiential geography of a specific poem? The 'long memoried woman' breaks the victim stereotype by being 'Quivering and alert' ('Night is her Robe', Markham, p. 300), unexpectedy shifting identities as she shifts between Creole and standard English, between male and female. In 'Sugar Cane' (pp. 301–3) the cane's growth cycle is imagined as a little erotic odyssey, ending with the wind caressing him 'shamelessly'. The whole collection needs to be read sequentially to be fully understood and appreciated; as does Nichols's next, *The Fat Black Woman's*

*Poems* (Virago, 1984); although the sheer enjoyment in herself, at the same time as she creates an image that questions the stereotypical thin white model of Western woman, can be well enough recognised in 'Tropical Death', 'The Fat Black Woman's Instructions to a Suitor' ('Do the boogie-woogie / Do the hop . . . hope you have a little energy left / to carry me across the threshold') and 'Small Questions Asked by the Fat Black Woman', which concludes with the tongue-in-cheek

> Will I like Eve
> be tempted once again
> if I survive
> (Markham, pp. 304–5)

Nichols is a satirist (traditionally in English the male poet's role), whose manner is sly, brash, exuberant, laid-back and wonderfully economic, refusing cliche while drawing on the myths of old and new worlds to articulate a complex, fluid vision. No single voice or perspective is inhabited for long, as she constructs and deconstructs versions of her self, returning always to the exciting potential of language, Creole or standard, or both at once: 'Don't be a kyatta-pilla' she instructs, in a voice you cannot read without picking up or hearing the Caribbean inflection, 'Be a butterfly': which is immediately undermined by the fact that this little maxim is 'screamed' by an old preacher to illustrate his sermon; but then finally: 'That was de life preacher / and you was right' (Markham, p. 309). Was the complexity of the relationship of gender to the representation of the Other more poignantly, yet briefly summed up? The displacements of the uprooted writer are overcome by the ability to adapt, to mould identity as she moulds language. The strong representation of women among the writers of the Caribbean and Black British diaspora is an increasingly important fact about that writing, reflecting 'the beginnings of a female crossing of the barriers of race, class, language and history, which have existed among us for the chief benefit of the colonizer', as Ramabai Espinet asserted in the Introduction to *Creation Fire: a CAFRA Anthology of Caribbean Women's Poetry* (1990), published by the activist Sister Vision, Black Women and Women of Colour Press.

## Summary

For Caribbean and Black British poetry the central issue is how to use the double inheritance of the colonizer's tongue and the hybrid Creoles or 'nation languages' which have developed locally and in the diaspora. If the first important upsurge of creativity from the West Indies has been in the novel, poetry has become a central fact of the 'Black Atlantic' – especially, but far from exclusively, poetry which registers the power and continuing historic relevance of everyday speech forms, and associated popular cultural activities and festivals, from jazz to Carnival. Walcott and Brathwaite may seem the dominant figures, and their development of a new aesthetics of the Caribbean the most striking aspect of recent poetry from there; but, as the work of such varied but historically and culturally related Black British poets as James Berry, Linton Kwesi Johnson and Grace Nichols shows, there are many concurrent and emerging voices which testify to the growth and potential of this area. The most important aspect of the post-colonial touched on here is how varieties of language articulate problematic identities.

## Notes

1 C.L.R. James, 'From Toussaint L'Ouverture to Fidel Castro' (1962), in *The C.L.R. James Reader*, ed. Anna Grimshaw (Blackwell, 1992), p. 306.
2 V.S. Naipaul, *The Middle Passage,* first publ. 1962 (Penguin, 1975), pp. 45, 73.
3 Stuart Hall, 'Cultural identity and diaspora', *Identity: Community, Culture, Difference*, ed. Jonathan Rutherford (Lawrence & Wishart, 1990), reptd in *Colonial Discourse and Post-Colonial Theory*, eds Patrick Williams and Laura Chrisman (Harvester Wheatsheaf, 1993), pp. 392–403 (p. 402).
4 Henry Louis Gates, Jr, *Figures in Black* (Oxford University Press, 1989), pp. 176–8, 187.
5 E.A. Markham, *Hinterland: Caribbean Poetry from the West Indies and Britain*, ed. E.A. Markham (Bloodaxe, 1989), p. 18. All further references to this anthology are given within parentheses in the text.
6 Roberto Marquez, 'Nationalism, nation and ideology: trends in the emergence of Caribbean literature', in *The Modern Caribbean*, eds F.W. Knight and C.A. Palmer (University of North Carolina Press, 1989), pp. 293–340 (p. 295); Paul Gilroy, *The Black Atlantic: Modernity and Double Consciousness* (Verso, 1993), p. ix.
7 David Dabydeen, Introduction, *Slave Song* (Dangaroo, 1984), p. 9.
8 See Kenneth Ramchard, *The West Indian Novel and Its Background* (Faber, 1970), pp. 274–89.
9 Derek Walcott, 'The muse of history', in *Critics on Caribbean Literature*, ed. Edward Baugh, (George Allen & Unwin, 1978), pp. 38–43 (pp. 38, 39, 42).
10 Frantz Fanon, *Black Skin, White Masks*, 1952, tr. C.L. Markmann 1967, foreword by Homi Bhabha (Pluto Press, 1986), pp. 225–6.
11 Walcott, 'The muse of history', p. 39.

12 Derek Walcott, *Collected Poems 1948–1984* (The Noonday Press, Farrar, Straus & Giroux, 1986), p. 346.

13 Derek Walcott, 'New Poetry' (5 July 1962), qtd Robert D. Hamner, *Derek Walcott Updated Edition*, Twayne's World Authors Series (Twayne, 1993), p. 28.

14 John Donne, Meditation XVII, 1624, reptd in *The Literature of Renaissance England*, eds John Hollander and Frank Kermode (Oxford University Press, 1973), p. 557.

15 Mervyn Morris, 'Walcott and the audience for poetry', reptd in *Critical Perspectives on Derek Walcott*, ed. Robert D. Hamner (Three Continents Press, 1993), pp. 174–92 (pp.178–9)

16 Walcott, *Collected Poems*, p. 52.

17 Leif Sjoberg, 'An interview with Derek Walcott' (1983), in *Conversations with Derek Walcott*, ed. William Baer (University Press of Mississippi, 1996), p. 82.

18 Walcott, *Collected Poems*, pp. 87–8.

19 Ibid., p. 350.

20 For 'Parang' see Walcott, *Collected Poems*, pp. 33–4, 347, 360.

21 See Elaine Savory Fido (as she then was), 'Macho attitudes and Derek Walcott' (1986), in *Literature in the Modern World*, ed. Dennis Walder (Oxford University Press, 1990), pp. 288–94; *Collected Poems*, p. 350.

22 Walcott, *Collected Poems*, p. 361; Derek Walcott, *Omeros* (Faber & Faber, 1990), p. 323.

23 Homi Bhabha, *The Location of Culture* (Routledge, 1994), pp. 234–5.

24 Gordon Rohleher, 'Blues and rebellion: Edward Brathwaite's *Rights of Passage*' (1971), in *Critics on Caribbean Literature*, ed. Edward Baugh (George Allen & Unwin, 1978), pp. 63–74 (p. 63).

25 Edward Kamau Brathwaite, *History of the Voice* (New Beacon, 1984), pp. 33–4; Louis James, 'Brathwaite and Jazz', in *The Art of Kamau Brathwaite*, ed. Stewart Brown (seren/Poetry Wales Press, 1995), p. 67.

26 Brathwaite, *History of the Voice*, p. 34.

27 Ibid., pp. 8–9.

28 Ibid., pp. 9–13.

29 Edward Said, *Orientalism* (1995), p. 353.

30 Edward Kamau Brathwaite, *The Arrivants: A New World Trilogy* (Oxford University Press, 1973), p. 35.

31 Ibid., pp. 52, 148.

32 Ibid., p. 164. See also Markham, *Hinterland*, pp. 14–15, although Markham does not give the complete poem.

33 Ibid., p. 270.

34 See Michael Dash, 'Edward Kamau Brathwaite', *West Indian Literature*, ed. Bruce King, 2nd edn (Macmillan, 1995), pp. 201–4.

35 Edward Kamau Brathwaite, *Mother Poem* (Oxford University Press, 1977), p. 3.

36 Edward Kamau Brathwaite, *X/Self* (Oxford University Press, 1987), pp. 118–19.

37  Ibid., p. 111.

38  James, 'Brathwaite and Jazz', in *The Art of Kamau Brathwaite*, ed. Brown, p. 73.

39  *History of the Voice*, p. 13.

40  Gordon Rohlehr, Introduction, *Voiceprint: An Anthology of Oral and Related Poetry from the Caribbean*, eds Stewart Brown, Mervyn Morris, Gordon Rohlehr (Longman, 1989), pp. 1–2.

41  This is the version as heard and transcribed by Brathwaite in *History of the Voice*, p. 35, from the LP *Dread beat an blood* (Virgin Records, 1978), the text of which was given in Linton Kwesi Johnson, *Dread Beat an' Blood*, intro. Andrew Salkey (Bogle-L'Ouverture, 1975), pp. 15–17.

42  See Peter Fryer, *Staying Power: The History of Black People in Britain* (Pluto Press, 1984), pp. 391–9; and Maya Jaggi, 'Mi Revalueshanary Fren', *Guardian* (24 September 1996), p. 13.

43  See Arthur Marwick, *British Society Since 1945*, 3rd edn (Penguin, 1996), pp. 219–20.

44  Rohlehr, Introduction, *Voiceprint* (1989), p. 20.

45  David Dabydeen and Nana Wilson-Tagoe, *Reader's Guide to West Indian and Black British Literature*, eds Dabydeen and Wilson-Tagoe (Hansib/Rutherford, 1989), p. 170.

46  James Berry, *News for Babylon*, ed. James Berry (Chatto, 1984), pp. 190–1.

47  Jane Miller, *Seductions* (1990), p. 120.

48  Grace Nichols, 'The battle with language', in *Caribbean Women Writers: Essays from the First International Conference*, ed. Selwyn R. Cudjoe (Calaloux Publications, 1990), pp. 283–9 (pp. 284–5).

# 7

## South African Literature in the Interregnum

My teacher says we've got nothing. No literature, no drama, no culture, no home . . .

*The Fantastical History of a Useless Man*,
Junction Avenue Theatre Company, 1976

We all know where South Africa is, but we do not yet know what it is

Albie Sachs, 'Preparing ourselves for freedom', 1989

We are in unexplored territory, developing a new and uniquely national aesthetic in literature

Barbara Masekela, 'We are not returning empty-handed', 1990

### Colonial or Post-Colonial?

On 14 October 1982 the South African writer Nadine Gordimer began a lecture in New York by referring to a 'heady' vision of her country 'swaying with the force of revolutionary change' at 'the end of the colonial era in Africa'.[1] It is a vision which has come to dominate Gordimer's own writings, as it has those of her compatriots, all of whom, in more or less direct ways, have been preoccupied with 'Living in the interregnum', the lecture's title, and an echo of Gramsci's well-known remark (used as an epigraph for her novel *July's People* the year before): 'The old is dying, and the new cannot be born; in this interregnum there arises a great diversity of morbid symptoms.' Literature under these circumstances seems symptomatic: of the end of colonialism, and the beginning of a new era; which is what gives such literature its interest, and power, although it also suggests its potential narrowness. The most important reason for choosing South African literature in English for my final case study, is that its major writers say this is where colonialism, in one of its most persistent if not its worst forms, is finally dying. But is it?

To Gordimer,

It's inevitable that nineteenth-century colonialism should finally come to its end there, because there it reached its ultimate expression, open in the legalised land- and mineral-grabbing, open in the labour exploitation of indigenous peoples, open in the constitutionalised, institutionalised racism that was concealed by the British under the pious notion of uplift, the French and the Portuguese under the sly notion of selective assimilation. An extraordinarily obdurate cross-breed of Dutch, German, English, French in the South African white settler population produced a bluntness that unveiled everyone's refined white racism: the flags of European civilisation dropped, and there it was unashamedly, the ugliest creation of man, and they baptised the thing in the Dutch Reformed Church, called it *apartheid*, coining the ultimate term for every manifestation, over the ages, in many countries, of race prejudice. Every country could see its resemblances there; and most peoples.[2]

South Africa offers a kind of mirror in which people can see themselves; a uniquely bare and ugly vision of the mix of social, economic, political, religious and racial forces which have affected all of us in the post-colonial dispensation. If, as Fanon said,[3] apartheid is a form of colonialism, its disappearance, too, can be understood as a form of decolonization.

But has it disappeared? Less than a decade after Gordimer's speech, the head of the banned liberation movement, Nelson Mandela, had been released after 27 years in prison; the State President F.W. De Klerk had publicly committed himself and his government to end apartheid; and a new, post-colonial country seemed indeed about to be born. Yet, as the playwright Athol Fugard remarked at the time, if South Africans like himself who had attacked apartheid for many years felt 'a lot more hopeful', they were also aware of 'how precarious the moves towards a new dispensation are'. And, according to a survey, despite the overwhelming endorsement of the reform process by an all-white referendum, the feelings of people of all races remained at best mixed about 'the new South Africa'.[4] The elections of April 1994 which followed, were conducted remarkably peacefully, but the transition from white minority rule to a non-racial, democratic state in South Africa remains a time of trauma, confusion and violence, although the dominant mood is optimistic. Colonialism does not cease overnight, any more than it begins at a stroke.

This touches on my second reason for taking South Africa as my last case study. In terms of history, language and theory, its situation challenges any simple notions of post-colonial literatures in English. One should be wary of any group or country wishing to claim for itself uniqueness, even a uniqueness of evil; and there are many ways in which South Africa resembles other 'white settler' colonies, for example in relations between the colonizers and the colonized, those 'intimate enemies' as Ashis Nandy calls them.[5] Said reminds us that despite the shared effects of colonial exploitation, 'to be one of the colonized is potentially to be a great many different, but inferior, things, in many different places, at different times'.[6] It may surprise some to know the degree to which, for example, the predominantly white, Afrikaans-speaking descendants of the original settlers see themselves as the colonized, the victims first of British imperialism, and then of worldwide threats to their identity.

Anne McClintock, a South African protégé of Said's at Columbia, has protested against linear historical definitions of the post-colonial, which, she argues, reinforce rather than undermine the ideology of empire, with its implicit assumption of progress towards metropolitan, European civilization.[7] But even a straightforward historical approach reveals telling contradictions: would anyone, for example, want to argue that South African literature from 1910 was an instance of post-colonial writing, that being the moment when the semi-independent Boer Republics (the Transvaal and the Orange Free State) and the Cape and Natal Colonies were merged as a result of the Anglo-Boer War into the Union of South Africa; which thereby took its place beside such self-governing former colonies of the British Empire as Canada and Australia? Unlike the other 'white dominions', however, South Africa has since then been governed by the minority settler community (at most 20 per cent of the total population), exerting a colonial or at least 'quasi-colonial power' with 'subject peoples living within [the country's] own boundaries', characteristics confirmed by the creation of formally distinct but dependent ministates or 'Bantustans' as part of the apartheid master-plan during the 1960s and 1970s.[8]

Certainly South African history displays features common to many other territories subject to Western expansion since the late fifteenth century, when Columbus 'discovered' America, and the Portuguese 'discovered' the Cape. Like the Americas, South Africa had long been settled by numerous distinct peoples.[9] But unlike the Americas, South Africa was not then settled by Europeans until a further two centuries had elapsed, and the Dutch East India Company reluctantly began a colony to feed their sailors en route to India. One of the first acts of the new colony's leader, van Riebeeck, in 1660, was to plant a hedge to keep the colonists in and the indigenous Khoikhoi out. Bits of that hedge still stand today, a reminder

– as more than one observer has remarked – of the country's first failure in apartheid.[10]

Another reminder has been the development of the Afrikaans language itself. While Dutch was the official language of the colony, indigenous people continued speaking in their own languages, and various pidgins and creoles began to develop – including, for example, a Portuguese Creole among the Asian slaves in the Cape. Ironically, the first book published in the developing Dutch Creole, Afrikaans, was written by descendants of those slaves about their Islamic faith, and it appeared in 1856, in Arabic script; while today it is the many Black or 'Cape Coloured' Afrikaans-speakers who will guarantee the survival of what became during the apartheid years the hated language of white supremacy. The 1976 Soweto rising was sparked by resistance to the imposition of Afrikaans upon black township schools; nearly two decades later, Afrikaans has been granted the status of just one, with English, of eleven official languages, including seven indigenous African languages. Meanwhile English, for nearly a century after its arrival in the 1820s, had been the only authorized language for government offices, law courts and public (state) schools. South African English has subsequently developed to the extent that the first fully historical dictionary (1996) runs to some 800 pages. Its liberal and international associations suggest English will survive as the lingua franca, if not the dominant form of communication between the different ethnic groups, who already use it as their own in a variety of local forms, some of which have entered literary expression, especially in spoken poetry and performed drama.

The obvious and immediate complexity of the South African context highlights the problematics of the post-colonial, whether viewed from within or outside the country's borders – and there is a large discourse about the country from outside in which, as Rosemary Jolly maintains, a word like apartheid risks reification into a 'reactionary measure at a historical moment in which the break from apartheid and its constructions requires a profoundly different strategy' for succesful critical articulation. Like Spivak before her, Jolly argues for a self-aware approach: 'As critics, teachers, and students, we need to forge a language beyond apartheid that refuses to hypostasize South Africa as the model in which the colonized black and the settler white eternally confront each other in the "ultimate racism"'.[11]

This should not mean that we expect people to forget Sharpeville 1960, or Soweto in 1976, or the more recent atrocities of the Third Force, set up to sow terror among the predominantly black electorate in the run-up to the 1994 elections. The legacy of one of the most extreme and complex systems of racial exploitation yet devised continues to be felt – in the texture of everyday life, from social habit to individual behaviour – as it is in the structures of the state, still divided and deformed on largely racial grounds. Theorists need to remember these matters, too. Contemplating the South African situation and its history helps us realize the limitations of thinking of 'colonial' and 'post-colonial' as distinct, rather than intermingled conditions which vary according to the historical and cultural specifics of the place. Just as it is possible to identify 'colonial' perceptions and behaviour surviving in a supposedly 'post-colonial' society, so too one can identify 'post-colonial' or emerging resistant features in 'colonial' society.

These boundaries are not easily fixed, the processes of change and resistance to change don't proceed in any smooth, unilinear way. The theories offered by critics and observers from Fanon (long banned in South Africa), or those who follow him, such as JanMohamed, whose *Manichean Aesthetics: The Politics of Literature in Colonial Africa* (1988), tries to fit South Africa precisely into Fanon's paradigm, or Benita Parry, who still argues that 'nativism' is relevant, to the post-structurally aware McClintock or Jolly, are just that – theories; which depend for their persuasiveness upon how they make us think about the matter at hand, and about our own positions in relation to it.

### What is South African Literature?

One problem critics and theorists still stumble over as a result of the continuing history of division and cultural fragmentation is identifying what constitutes South African literature. There have been three book-length studies (all by South Africans) of the subject. The first, Manfred Nathan's *South African Literature* (1925), was a bold chronological survey of literature 'which is *in or of South Africa*' (his italics), taking in travel, biography and history as well as the more usual literary genres, but assuming that all this literature is English or Dutch, and mainly the former. Black writing in English or indigenous tongues was ignored, even as a possibility. The second book, Stephen Gray's *Southern African Literature* (1979), included a wider geography (taking in, for example, Rhodesia/ Zimbabwe), and a whole chapter on 'The emergence of black English', while developing Nathan's multi-genre approach. But Gray rather disabled his book by admitting on page one that by the late 1960s, when the post-Sharpeville wave of repression had ebbed somewhat, 'as many as half of South Africa's English-language writers of all colours had been expelled over the borders into an international diaspora', splitting South African literature in English 'so irremediably and bitterly into two' that it only made sense to talk of 'two distinct literatures at present'. And this while focusing only on South African writing in English.[12]

Of the eleven official languages in South Africa, at least five (including the two of European origin) have produced substantial bodies of creative writing over the last hundred and fifty years. If, as Albert Gérard indicated in the first survey of its kind, *Four African Literatures* (1971), the Xhosa, Sotho and Zulu writings of Southern Africa have suffered from missionary and government control, English and Dutch-Afrikaans have, too; although the overseas links of English cultural traditions have always helped as much as hindered the development of independent expression – hence many black writers have (especially since the 1960s) chosen English as their preferred medium. All of which ignores the indigenous oral creative forms, which go back many centuries before they were first recorded in the nineteenth century, for instance by W.H. Bleek, whose versions of early San songs may be found in most poetry anthologies, such as Gray's *The Penguin Book of Southern African Verse* (1989).

It is premature to talk of any single identifiable entity as South African literature. Gray resorted to metaphor and identified an 'archipelago' of literatures, a grouping of literary islands of different size and significance, associated simply by being where they are. But Michael Chapman's *Southern African Literatures* (Longman 1996) has now brought together a range of material interpreted in terms of the whole field of southern African history and literature, including the writings of all South Africa's recently independent neighbours, Angola, Malawi, Mozambique, Namibia, Zambia and Zimbabwe; adopting a progressive, historicist approach which, however, knocks anything which doesn't contribute towards the forward march of the shared national culture. While this new engagement with the subcontinent is praiseworthy, it subsumes the specifics of local traditions, languages and cultural forms, implying regional renewal through a redefinition of power and control by – South Africa.

It may be that, as Jean-Philipe Wade concludes his contribution to *Rethinking South African Literary History*, only by recognizing a plurality of voices, celebrating 'difference' *against* oppressive totalities, but simultaneously (to avoid old apartheid fall-back positions) accepting the post-structuralist point that the meaning of difference is unstable, always deferred, that a history of South African literature can be articulated.[13]

At least we can say here that one voice, South African literature in English, starts by the 1820s, when settlement by the British began in earnest, and English became the official language of the region. Further, that a broad definition of literature is required for a literature predominantly subgeneric for the first hundred years or so – diaries, travel, tales, journalism, sketches and hybrid oral forms (such as the *Kaatje Kekkelbek* song mentioned in chapter 3) – although important individual poems, novels and (to a lesser extent) plays also appeared. Further, that this body of writings, whoever produced it, has arisen in part as the product of an imported culture, self-consciously 'liberal' in persuasion, but bearing the mark of its early, even pre-Victorian origins. Beyond that, everything is still subject to fierce debate.

Such as that provoked by Barbara Masekela's 'We are not returning empty-handed' (1990), a speech delivered at the National Arts Festival – founded at Grahamstown in 1966 to celebrate the cultural contribution of the British settlers, and funded by Anglophone commercial enterprises. Her speech was the first to be delivered by an activist and former exile to the festival (by then enlarged if not broader in approach); it was reprinted in *Die Suid-Afrikaan*, a bilingual (English/Afrikaans) publication founded in 1984 by liberal Afrikaners based at the University of Stellenbosch, once the intellectual cradle of apartheid.

Masekela was building on a paper delivered by Albie Sachs to an ANC in-house seminar the previous year – 'Preparing ourselves for freedom', which can be found alongside a range of comments and responses in *Spring is Rebellious*, edited by Ingrid de Kok and Karen Press, 1990, and in which Sachs announced that 'our members should be banned from saying that culture is a weapon of struggle', because of the impoverishing effect that had had on art and literature, 'obsessed by our oppressors and the trauma they have imposed, [so that] nothing is about us and the new consciousness we are developing'. Masekela elaborated on this (exaggerated) view by arguing that the arts needed redefining as a carrier of the community's values, as opposed to the oppressive and patriarchal view of culture implicit in the position of the ruling white groups. 'English and Afrikaans-based cultures', she said, were 'a valid part of the whole rich tapestry of South African culture – but a part – not the sun around which the whole cultural universe revolves'. Instead of continually looking to 'ersatz European high culture' for guidance, what was needed was 'an aesthetic which is uniquely South African'.[14]

This is the familiar theme in post-colonial theory of the contestation of values between distant metropolis and local centre; familiar, too, is the demand for a more broadly based and therefore authentic, national culture. According to Masekela, the culture of the English-speaking community has been 'the most exclusive and resistant' to other voices; and as poets Jeremy Cronin and Mongane Wally Serote had pointed out, language was a key factor. But so too was education, including such basic problems as

illiteracy, and the erosion of 'our own folk tradition . . . by the fragmentation of the family system under migrant labour', a situation explored, for
example, by storyteller Gcina Mhlophe. The voice of the well-financed
'cultural elite' who have 'disproportionate access to national and international media . . . is often assumed to be our voice, simply because it is the
only one anyone has heard'.[15]

Masekela did not spell out the criteria for what counts as 'the people's
voice'. Nor did she seem aware of some contradiction between attacking
the Eurocentrism of the English-speakers' cultural attitudes from a position
based on a European, neo-Marxist form of cultural analysis, mediated in her
case by the writings of Ngugi wa Thiong'o. But the point remains: that
there are many different voices – some of them new – being heard during
the interregnum, as part of the evolving, multifarious culture of English
expression in South Africa.

### Decolonizing the Colonial Imagination: The Conservationist

Nadine Gordimer's work can be said to represent what Masekela calls the
historically dominant, elitist English tradition, validated by external,
metropolitan cultural media. Gordimer herself has acknowledged many of
Masekela's points in her critical writings since the early 1980s, and we are
bound to ask: are things really quite so straightforward? How, for example,
should a novel like *The Conservationist* be read today – as the work of a
'white liberal' South African novelist, disqualified by her race and class if
not gender from attention? Does it still have something to say, or does it
inevitably, in the post-colonial context, obscure the voices of others, more
important? I have to a degree pre-empted the answers by starting with
Gordimer, but my analysis should reveal why.

Nadine Gordimer's writings have changed radically over her career:
from traditional, social realism, towards a modernist narrative poetics – first
evident in *The Conservationist*. When the Swedish Academy awarded her
the Nobel Prize for Literature in 1991, they announced that it was for her
'great, epic writings centring on the effects of race relations in her
country'.[16] However her kind of writing is defined, her achievement by
now, as the author of eleven novels and more than two hundred short
stories, not to mention dozens of critical essays and reviews, stands alone.
There are few if any living writers in English worldwide who can approach
it. Within South Africa, where her works have been almost as often banned
as praised, recognition has been much slower in arriving, and even now
appears grudging. On the one hand, she has come to be seen as a betrayer

of those white liberal values which were promoted even as they were dissected in her early fiction; not only has a more radical position become evident in her essays and her fiction since the mid-1970s, but during the 1980s she openly espoused the liberation movement and associated cultural bodies, such as the Congress of South African Writers. On the other hand, whatever the direction of her recent pronouncements or her work, she can also be seen as the most obvious example of that Eurocentric, English-language, culturally exclusive tradition which obscures the voices of the black underclass, and makes it more difficult for local writers who derive from other traditions to gain publication, much less wider acceptance and status.

One of three novels described by the academy as 'masterpieces' was *The Conservationist*, which also won the Booker Prize when it was first published in 1974. But how, and in what ways, does it represent the workings of the colonial imagination during decolonization? My answer would be that it makes us think about and question the continuing pressure and presence of the colonial past in the present, offering a representation of the individual psyche in these circumstances, specifically a version of the white patriarchal viewpoint, which embodies a critical perception of consciousness during decolonization.

According to Abdul JanMohamed, *The Conservationist* 'eschews history', or at least attempts to 'escape' it, which results in an unbalanced, 'highly subjective and ambiguous novel'; a view opposed by the South African critic Stephen Clingman, who argues that there is 'no contradiction between the "subjectivity" of or in the novel and its broader, "objective" historical significance'.[17] I haven't space to develop a complete or even very full critical account of *The Conservationist* here, much less of Gordimer's work as a whole. But a large and increasing volume of commentary and criticism is available: Michael Wade's *Nadine Gordimer* (1978), for instance, gives an account of her career up to *The Conservationist* in terms of her 'extensive creative probing' of the 'governing notions of European liberalism' in South Africa;[18] but apart from the chapter in JanMohamed's *Manichean Aesthetics* and Clingman's richly contextual analysis of her work up to the mid-1980s when *The Novels of Nadine Gordimer* was published, the only other book-length study I'd recommend would be Judie Newman's brief introduction in the Contemporary Writers Series (*Nadine Gordimer*, 1988). Newman treats Gordimer as a writer engaged with the current of Western thinking about politics and culture, except in her account of *The Conservationist*.

All these critics draw to some extent on what JanMohamed calls the 'generative ambience' essential for any understanding of the nature of 'colonial literature and the rise of the African novel'.[19] This trend in Gordimer criticism helps to counteract the stock response of critics and reviewers in South Africa and abroad, which has been to treat her work as if it simply exhibited 'universal' criteria − meaning Western, liberal humanist criteria. The result has been the kind of contradiction revealed most dramatically by the Nobel Award for her treatment of 'race relations' which also, according to the Nobel secretary, had 'nothing to do with political relations in South Africa'.[20] Of course all Gordimer's work, on her own admission, takes its force, its point, from the fact that it testifies to the quality of life in South Africa in recent years, life dominated by the politics of a specific form of colonialism. Even when, as in her fifth novel *A Guest of Honour* (1971), the setting is elsewhere − an anonymous, recently independent African state − South Africa, as a moment in the history of decolonization, is the source of her concerns.

During the 'interregnum' 1980s Gordimer acknowledged this herself (for example, in the title essay of *The Essential Gesture*). But to begin with she seemed oblivious of her context, or at least to feel that, as she observed in 1961: 'The novelist in South Africa does not live in a community and has begun to write from scratch at the wrong time.'[21] And yet, there had appeared as long ago as 1883 *The Story of an African Farm*, a founding text of the colonial experience, and the first successful novel by a white writer born in the country, who also happened to be a woman − Olive Schreiner (1862–1920); and in 1930, Plaatje's *Mhudi*, the first novel in English by a Black South African; and by the time of Gordimer's remark, there had also appeared powerful and acclaimed works such as Sarah Gertrude Millin's *God's Step-children* (1924), William Plomer's *Turbott Wolfe* (1925), Peter Abrahams's *Mine Boy* (1946), Alan Paton's *Cry, the Beloved Country* (1948), Dan Jacobson's *A Dance in the Sun* (1956) − not to mention Gordimer's own first two novels, *The Lying Days* (1953) and *A World of Strangers* (1958). If, like Gray and Chapman, we include Rhodesia/Zimbabwe, there had also appeared Doris Lessing's *The Grass is Singing* (1950), and beyond that, a novel that made African writing in English a force which could no longer be ignored by the outside world: the Nigerian Chinua Achebe's *Things Fall Apart* (1958). So it seems odd, even bizarre, that in 1961 Gordimer should have said that the novelist in South Africa starts from scratch.

The point is, even though Gordimer went on to mention some of these works (not Achebe's), that is how it felt for her kind of colonial writer, a kind familiar in Canada and Australia as well: lacking a sense of tradition, alienated from their own, colonial culture, uncertain of their identity, they look towards an ideal which − as Masekela says − has its origins in the metropolitan centres abroad, and so they cannot see what is around them.

No wonder Gordimer's public utterances are even now replete with the names of European artists and writers. Of all the novels I've just mentioned, only two display any real sense of history, and they are both by black Africans: Achebe's *Things Fall Apart*, set, as we've seen, in the early twentieth century, and showing the impact on traditional society of the arrival of the European; and Plaatje's *Mhudi*, set in the 1830s, and with the same basic theme. Plaatje also wrote *Native Life in South Africa* (1916), attacking the Natives Land Act of 1913, which reserved a mere 10 per cent of South Africa for the majority of its inhabitants and which has only now been repealed. The question of the land and who owns it is central to the colonial imagination in general, and to *The Conservationist* in particular.

Gordimer was born in 1923, the second daughter of English-speaking, Jewish immigrants in Springs, one of several gold-mining, semi-industrial towns that run east and west of Johannesburg. Her first published work for an adult audience was a short story in one of many English liberal journals, *The Forum* (18 November 1939). (There were no specifically literary magazines for which to write.) The story, about a crisis in the life of an elderly man from the poorer white class, was rooted in her early environment, whose values she accepted without question. Not until her first published novel, *The Lying Days* (1953), does any sign emerge of a deeper, more challenging awareness of the fragmented colonial culture in which she grew up.

To begin with, that awareness seems no more than an awareness of lack. As the central character and narrator of the semi-autobiographical *The Lying Days* puts it:

> In nothing that I read could I find anything that approximated to my own life; to our life on a gold mine in South Africa. Our life was not regulated by the seasons and the elements of weather and emotion, like the life of peasants; nor was it expressed in movements in art, through music heard, through the exchange of ideas, like the life of Europeans shaped by great and ancient cities, so that they were Parisians or Londoners as identifiably as they were Pierre or James. Nor was it anything like the life of Africa, the continent, as described in books about Africa; perhaps further from this than any. What did the great rivers, the savage tribes, the jungles and the hunt for huge palm-eared elephants have to do with the sixty miles of Witwatersrand veld that was our Africa? . . . We had no lions and we had no art galleries, we heard no Bach and the oracle voice of the ancient Africa did not come to us – drowned, perhaps, by the records singing of Tennessee in the Greek cafés and the thump of the Mine

stamp batteries which sounded in our ears as unnoticed as our blood.[22]

That 'unnoticed' thumping of the mine batteries which drowns out the voices of Western high culture suggests there *is* a recognition, on some obscure, unconscious level, of the source of this community's energies, its life, in the work of the mine, work that precedes, as it shapes, the actual culture of the place – and which, it is precisely not-said, is primarily the work of black people, uprooted and turned into abstract units of labour. But on the conscious level, without this recognition, the passage simply clarifies why the writer's earliest acknowledged mentors should have come from abroad; why they were short story writers such as Maupassant, Chekhov and D.H. Lawrence, and novelists such as Turgenev and Proust.

It was these later nineteenth- and early twentieth-century European writers who helped Gordimer define for herself what the role of the writer should be. When she cites Turgenev, for example, it is to offer as her own creed his reply to left-wing attacks on his unflattering portrait of a revolutionary: 'in the given case, life happened to be like that'.[23] Paradoxically, it was these great, liberal humanist European voices that helped Gordimer find her own voice and, eventually, through her commitment to writing in South Africa, a commitment beyond anything they would have dared. *The Lying Days*, like all her work before *The Conservationist* and indeed like most South African fiction before *The Conservationist*, operates within the familiar, 'classic realist' mode of mainstream nineteenth-century fiction. It is a *Bildungsroman* about the first faltering steps towards independence of a young, white, South African woman, Helen Shaw, brought up like her author in the lower middle class of a Rand town. Her search through friends and lovers for a relationship both sensually and intellectually fulfilling leads her first to question the values of her own, illiberal, small-town white society, and then those of the Johannesburg white liberals who seem to question their society – but not far enough. Finally, she decides to leave the country but, as she tells herself on the last page: 'Whatever it was I was running away from – the risk of love? the guilt of being white? the danger of putting ideals into practice? I'm not running away from now because I know I'm coming back'. She has, she says, 'accepted disillusion as a beginning rather than an end'. The self-justification closes off the narrative in a way that doesn't do justice to its more subtle and resonant moments, partly because of the demand for closure of the classic realist genre, but also because of the author's failure to acknowledge the more subversive implications of her fiction at this early stage.

To me this relates to a failure in the whole tradition of colonial, English liberal writing – what I call *a failure of admission*. In the preface to *The Story of an African Farm*, Olive Schreiner rejected colonial writing about 'ravening lions and hair-breadth escapes', in favour of painting what lay before her. Yet the documentation of local fact was something she could not herself manage: instead, the surface realism of everyday life on a farm in the Karroo is disrupted – not indeed by adventures with wild animals – but by 'dreams and phantoms'; mysteriously powerful, uncanny experiences from which it is a relief to turn 'to some simple, feelable, weighable substance; to something which has a smell and a colour, which may be handled and turned over this way and that'. This yearning to escape from what Schreiner calls 'writhing before the inscrutable mystery' of the environment is echoed just sixteen years later by Conrad's *Heart of Darkness*, in which the mystery is revealed as fear – a fear of 'your remote kinship' with the 'incomprehensible' indigenous inhabitants.[24]

What the colonial writer in the liberal tradition cannot begin to admit is the possibility of intimate, not merely 'remote' kinship with Africans. Why not? Because this would mean admitting the racial basis of the whole power structure of colonization. It would mean admitting that the colonizers' fear is ultimately a fear that the colonized will do in turn to the colonizers what has been done to them. The 'heart of darkness' for Gordimer's heroine-narrator in *The Lying Days* is a black township on the outskirts of Johannesburg, where she waits for a black fellow-student to whom she has given a lift in well-meaning, liberal patronage; suddenly 'the grasp of my imagination let go'; she becomes frightened in the 'gathering darkness', sensing the 'awfulness' of township life. Later she recalls her experience as 'an almost physical sensation of being a stranger in what I had always taken unthinkingly as the familiarity of home. I felt myself among strangers; I had grown up, all my life, among strangers: the Africans, whose language in my ears had been like the barking of dogs or the cries of birds'.[25]

This sense of estrangement from the known and familiar, of the uncanny, recurs in Gordimer's succeeding novels, as the presence of black people becomes more powerful and challenging – until, in *The Conservationist,* it reaches its fullest if not final expression. By the time of the novel's publication, Gordimer had come to recognize that in an increasingly polarized situation, with Afrikaner nationalists on the one hand, and the rising Black Consciousness Movement on the other, the liberal politics of individual reform had become irrelevant. For the liberal writer this meant that the traditional European realist novel was no longer adequate either. Significantly, 1974 also saw the publication of the first novel by a major new writer of anti-realist persuasion: J.M. Coetzee's *Dusklands*. *The Conserva-*

*tionist* marks a crisis in the way the colonial imagination deals with the reality it perceives; a crisis that leads to the collapse of the traditional narrative relationship with society, now imagined as a mere surface, through which writer and reader fall towards a radically new form, more responsive to impersonal, psychological and historical forces which, as Gordimer comes to acknowledge, are struggling to be born.

The conservationist of the novel's title is a very wealthy, self-made Johannesburg industrialist named Mehring, who has bought a 400-acre farm as a tax dodge. He visits it at weekends, when he is not jetting around the world on business. These visits are rendered in the present tense, disrupted by past flashbacks which reveal that his adolescent son Terry is in Namibia (where, as his German name suggests, Mehring himself originates); his divorced wife is in America, and his 'left-wing' mistress has escaped to London. So, he is alone; with the black farm workers, his white Afrikaans neighbours, the Indian shopkeepers and, on the periphery of his property, the blacks of the 'location' or township. Life on the farm proceeds as a separate narrative thread in the past tense, largely from the perspective of the black foreman Jacobus. We gather there has been a long drought; and the novel registers the changing seasons, from the sharp dry highveld autumn, through winter, summer (including Christmas), to a cataclysmic last storm 'from the Mozambique Channel', presaging spring.

This story of an African farm, like Schreiner's earlier narrative (which it recalls) has obvious symbolic overtones, but it is written in a complex, multilayered and elliptical modernist manner, dispensing with the usual external indices of time, place and character. What we have instead is the more or less direct presentation of consciousness: predominantly the white man's consciousness, although that is interwoven with the thoughts, voices and views of others – ultimately and most subversively, the uncanny presence of 'the other', the black man – who is, however, already dead. Nevertheless, the dominant narrative is increasingly pervaded by this anonymous man, killed in some fracas near the farm. The authorities do nothing, so, instead of a proper burial, he is unceremoniously dug into the ground of the third pasture, near the river, where Mehring likes to walk about enjoying the feel of ownership, while inwardly conversing with himself and his wife, mistress and son. The end comes when a flood brought by the storm cuts the farm off and disinters the body, Mehring gets trapped in some ambivalent sexual misadventure, and the black man is finally reburied with due ceremony.

The agenda for the whole novel is established early on, from a curiously abrupt, elliptical beginning:

Pale freckled eggs

Swaying over the ruts of the gate of the third pasture, Sunday morning, the owner of the farm suddenly sees: a clutch of pale freckled eggs set out before a half-circle of children. Some are squatting; the one directly behind the eggs is cross-legged, like a vendor in a market. There is pride of ownership in that grin lifted shyly to the farmer's gaze. The eggs are arranged like marbles, the other children crowd round but you can tell they are not allowed to touch unless the cross-legged one gives permission.[26]

The fundamental theme of ownership, or possession, has been immediately established: who owns the eggs, and who really owns the land, whose product they are? The question recurs throughout, until the last line of the novel, when it is answered by the reburial of the dead black man, who thereby takes 'possession' of the earth. This is also an issue of language, which here means race and power, as we can tell from the farmer's 'many gestures' to protect 'his' game birds, who have produced the eggs, but which the children who hold them don't understand any better than they understand his language. When the foreman appears, speaking his own creolized African English:

– No – everything it's all right. One calf he's borned Friday. But I try to phone you, yesterday night –
– Good, that's from the red cow, eh? –
Each is talking fast, in the manner of a man who has something he wants to get on to say. There is a moment's pause to avoid collision; but of course the right of way is the farmer's. (p. 11)

This invites us to feel the continuous assertion of the white man's point of view, as his concerns impose themselves upon his employee's. But Jacobus comes to tell the farmer of the discovery of the dead man, and so the matter of the eggs must give way, suggesting the vulnerability of the white man's discourse, despite its apparent power. Mehring's thoughts are offered in all their increasingly manic certitude: 'A whole clutch of guinea fowl eggs. Eleven. Soon there will be nothing left. In the country. The continent. The oceans, the sky' (p. 11). The large irony is that the white man's urge to 'conserve' the land is a delusion; what he really wants to conserve is a way of life, his way of life, with an intensity of desire that blots out everything else.

Desire, especially sexual desire, is the other major theme of the novel: the farm is primarily 'a place to bring a woman' (p. 47). Mehring's interest in women and land as interchangeable objects of desire is repeatedly caught, for instance by his stereotyped image for the desert: 'Golden reclining nudes' (pp. 103, 126). The second time it enters his mind he is flying back from Europe, looking down at 'the home that is the earth itself', from which he is so detached – a detachment chillingly reinforced by the sequence that follows, in which he 'fingers' a young Portuguese immigrant girl beside him in the plane, their secret contact described in the metaphors of exploration and possession, but also as an unarticulated relationship in which the girl's body 'takes up the narrative', his hand proposes. All this in 'an hour between the hour of Europe and the hour of Africa', something 'happening nowhere' (pp. 126–9). But when he leaves the aircraft, he is aware of her 'fluid on his hand as one says a man has blood on his hands' (p. 131); his sense of guilt anticipating the last moment of his narrative, when another 'poor white' young woman seems to invite sexual encounter in the nowhere between motorways and minedumps, with more traumatic results, as his guilt overwhelms even his sense of the securities of self.

Mehring's view of the farm-children at the start is scored by the emblem on his car's bonnet, suggestive of the gun-sight of the European observer's viewpoint imposed on the rural scene. But by the conclusion of the novel, this destructive vision is challenged, the 'flashing emblem whose prism is always there' (p. 256), as the desire leads to nightmare. The young woman he's picked up – or has she picked him up? – is noticed to have 'rough curly hairs' on her face, like 'sideburns', 'Coloured or poor-white, whichever she is', suggests further, racial uncertainty; and suddenly there is a man watching, a 'thug' or a 'mine detective' (pp. 260–4). Ambivalence has replaced certainty. Nor can he escape: he thinks he will

> make a dash for it, a leap, sell the place to the first offer . . . They can have it, the whole four hundred acres . . . no no. No no, what nonsense, what is there to fear – shudder after shudder, as if he were going to vomit the picnic lunch, it's all coming up, coming out. That's a white tart and there was no intent anyway, report these gangsters or police thugs terrorizing people on mine property, he's on a Board with the chairman of the group this ground still belongs to . . . No, no, no. RUN.
> – Come, Come and look, they're all saying. What is it? Who is it? It's Mehring. It's Mehring, down there. (pp. 264–5)

The traditional, historical role of the white, male hero of colonial fiction has been subverted, indeed reversed: defining the world around him, so as to possess and ultimately destroy it, he is now coming to be defined himself, and so be destroyed. I don't think this means that Mehring dies by the end, although some critics have taken it as so (JanMohamed says it is impossible to determine whether he has really been murdered or whether he has gone mad). Rather, his consciousness has lost its dominance, its ability to intervene in the narrative, and to possess (note his last futile attempt to claim the power of ownership, through his role on the mine Board). So this is not the end of the story; *that* comes with the perspective of the black farmworkers, burying their dead. This is the end of *his* story.

Like most modernist fiction, *The Conservationist* asks to be re-read, and it is hard to imagine a second reading that isn't influenced by the next, finally concluding sequence on the farm, which reminds us we should have been attending to the 'black' point of view, too – to such matters as the drought, the assault on farmworker Solomon, the fire, the spirit-possession of one worker's wife and its attendant feast, and the flood – all framed by the appearance of the body to the farmworkers, and their reburial of it. There is a continuing preoccupation within this 'black narrative' with practical, everyday concerns, normally on the periphery of white experience – and, I might add, on the periphery of the readings of the novel so far provided by its critics. These concerns have to do with the struggle to obtain work, with the pass laws, with ways of operating in the gaps between different forms of authority under apartheid, from the English industrialist to the Afrikaans farmer, from the police to township gangs. Even Clingman, whose historicist reading allows him to note how *The Conservationist* registers the rise of the Black Consciousness Movement, the increase of guerilla activity on the borders, and the nearness of liberation for the adjoining Portuguese colonies (the army officers' coup in Portugal took place on 25 April 1974) – even Clingman fails to notice this direct admission into the narrative of the texture of everyday life for black people, mediated by a writer whose commitment to her writing has itself brought this into range for her readers – predominantly white and overseas as they were/are.

One may be misled by contemporary post-structuralist accounts of post-colonial discourse, as Homi Bhabha indicates in 'Representation and the colonial text':[27] not only into avoiding the strength of the counter-discourse potentially on offer, but into permitting the inescapability of neo-colonial readings. As I remarked in relation to Spivak, maybe there is no escape from the discourse we are using. But we should be aware of the reactionary, or at least politically dubious overtones effectively encoded in recent Eurocentric critical language. Clingman concludes that with revo-lution at stake, the very basis of reality is at stake in the novel, so justifying its post-modernist intertextuality; but this implies a view of the relation between history, society and literature which is both too simple and too complicated: deleting the level and force of social or critical realism in the book, on the one hand, while overvaluing its modernist tendencies, on the other.

### Other Voices: Poetry and its Formation

The work of South African writers and their critics, like that of Indian, Caribbean and Black British writers has to find a place in a huge international market, dominated by Western publishers not particularly interested in 'local' concerns, especially as expressed in the more accessible, less literary genres of poetry and drama. The most comprehensive survey of South African poetry until recently was Jacques Alvarez-Péreyre's *The Poetry of Commitment in South Africa*, a doctoral thesis published in France in 1979, unavailable elsewhere until translated for Heinemann's Studies in African Literature in 1984. Similarly, the most comprehensive survey of South African theatre until recently was South African Robert Kavanagh's Leeds University doctorate of the same vintage, later published as *Theatre and Cultural Struggle in South Africa* (1985). Within South Africa, the first serious full-length study of black writing was made by a white academic: Ursula Barnett's *A Vision of Order: A Study of Black South African Literature in English: 1914–80* (1983); and the first account of South African poetry to allow adequate space to black poetry was Michael Chapman's *South African English Poetry* (1984); while the first to give adequate space to the contribution of black South African dramatists was Martin Orkin's *Drama and the South African State* (1991).

As I've already suggested, the long-term, colonialist compartmentalization of South African life and culture has led to the formation of partial, fragmentary or patently biased accounts of what constitutes the literature(s) of the subcontinent – Gray's *Southern African Literature* ended with 'The emergence of black English' – up to the 1930s! Such distortions appear within the study of every genre, in each of which they take on a configuration to some extent typical of that genre. The notion of genre is itself a Western formulation subject to question or subversion. The more important distinction may be between written and oral forms; certainly the greatest upsurge in 'new' or hitherto unheard voices has appeared in those areas of literary production least subject to the constraints of the publishing industry, and most closely linked with the relative freedom of the domain of the spoken or performed.

Of equal importance has been the primacy of the 'consciousness-raising' function of literature in a situation of political instability. Protest poetry, recited at the funerals of victims of police or vigilante killings, workers' participation drama with little if any script – these are the forms of literary production which became familiar in the last decades of apartheid as 'weapons of struggle', until more positive, inclusive and complex approaches began to emerge – from Masekela, for example, or critic Njabulo Ndebele (*Rediscovery of the Ordinary*, 1991). It used to be argued, for instance by South African exile Lewis Nkosi, that, when it came to poetry, Black South Africans seemed to benefit from writing inside the country, their 'rage and bitterness' fuelling their verse.[28] And certainly some surprisingly 'unpoetic' material has appeared, such as 'In defence of poetry', by Mafika Gwala (b. 1946). Direct, colloquial and obviously oral in tone and structure, it involves a cumulative rhetoric of questions, followed by blunt assertion:

> What's poetic
> about Defence Bonds and Armscor?
> What's poetic
> about long-term sentences and
> deaths in detention
> for those who 'threaten state security'?
> Tell me,
> what's poetic
> about shooting defenceless kids
> in a Soweto street?
> Can there be poetry
> in fostering Plural Relations?
> Can there be poetry
> in the Immorality Act?
> What's poetic
> about deciding other people's lives?
> Tell me brother,
> what's poetic
> about defending herrenvolkish rights?
>
> As long as
> this land, my country
> is unpoetic in its doings
> it'll be poetic to disagree.[29]

The title alludes to a long metropolitan tradition of defending poetry, from Sidney to Shelley, while the poem itself conspicuously lacks the traditional features of rhythm, metre and image – clung to by most white, English-speaking writers from the 1820s onwards, when the Scottish settler Thomas Pringle (1789–1834) wrote 'Afar in the Desert I love to ride / With the silent Bush-boy alone by my side' – who speaks at last in Gwala's poem, his 'voice' finally admitted.

If the English liberal humanist tradition long opposed the discourse of state power attacked by Gwala and other protest poets, by the 1960s the bankruptcy of its position seemed sharply evident, the immorality of those whose wealth and relative freedom was guaranteed by the system they attacked. This ambivalence can be detected from early on. Pringle's poetry was most known for expressing indignant concern on behalf of the plight of those it unconsciously helped to silence. It still commonly opens anthologies of South African poetry in English (for example, Chapman's *Paperbook of South African English Poetry*, 1990). Pringle was the first poet writing in English to be acclaimed overseas; acclaim that stemmed also from the liberal politics which made him unpopular with the colonial (British) authorities, and which clearly distinguished his position from that of the earlier, Dutch-speaking settlers. Pringle, who founded the Cape library, one of the first English schools and, with another British immigrant (John Fairbairn), the liberal English Cape Press (where 'Afar in the Desert' was first published), returned home, to become Secretary to the Anti-Slavery Society. His poetry began as oppositional; but it became the dominant voice.

That voice was defined for 'white liberal' English-speakers by Guy Butler (b. 1918), poet and professor of English at Rhodes University in Grahamstown. This he did in his anthology *A Book of South African Verse* (1959) dedicated to the most famous South African poet of the preceding fifty years, Roy Campbell (1901–57), who with William Plomer (1903–73) had most space in the collection. The title didn't add 'in English', although as Butler confessed in the introduction, his volume was devoted to only one of three 'strands' he identified in the community – his own 'linguistic, political and cultural minority'. He included nothing in Afrikaans, nor in 'any one of a dozen African tongues, or the hot, new argot of the townships' whose existence he acknowledged, without admitting, even in translation. South African poetry was 'an educated man's affair', trying to transform landscape and the 'primitive' into something assimilable to 'European origins'. The work Butler selected testified to a feeling of rootlessness, but not the experience of mere 'tribesmen', who had lost their 'vital culture' in the cities.

Ten years later, Jack Cope and Uys Krige's *Penguin Book of South African Verse* (1968) registered a crucial shift in perception. Cope, founder of the liberal Cape literary magazine *Contrast* in 1960, and his co-editor the Afrikaans poet/translator Krige, were well-known literary mediators (Krige helped Gordimer first get published abroad). By joining forces they set a precedent for collaborative anthologies, although their embattled liberalism led to a contradictory editorial policy. They allowed in many of those excluded from Butler's anthology, acknowledging the contribution of Afrikaans and African verse; but they slotted them into their separate linguistic groupings, with the white English-speakers (led by Roy Campbell) in front, and taking up more than half the space. The now-familiar despairing or dissociated voices dominated the 'English' section, with one inspired newcomer the exception: Douglas Livingstone, probably the leading poet in the urbane Campbell line.

A whole tradition of Afrikaans poetry came next, from Eugène Marais to the 'Coloured' Adam Small (whose Afrikaans-based argot was however lost in translation); and it included eight poems by the disturbed and brilliant Ingrid Jonker, who committed suicide in 1965, aged thirty-two. Then, at last, came the so-called 'African Section', including five sub-sections, from 'Bushman' and 'Hottentot', through Sotho, Xhosa and Zulu, each represented by so-called 'traditional' verse in translation, thereby insulated from the currents of recent South African history as well as from each other. This was an advance, despite the compartmentalizing, and the exclusion of all those silenced after Sharpeville – such as Dennis Brutus (b. 1924), whose first collection, *Sirens, Knuckles and Boots* (1963), was published abroad long before the Cope/Krige anthology, and was awarded the prestigious Mbari prize. At the time, however, Brutus had already been arrested for his political activities and sentenced to eighteen months' hard labour on Robben Island; after which, banned from writing, publishing or teaching, he left for permanent exile in America. His work has only become available in South Africa since 1990, forty years after he began.

If anyone fits Butler's notion of the poet as an 'educated man', it is Brutus, the clever son of schoolteacher parents who loved Wordsworth and Tennyson, and who was educated at Fort Hare and Witwatersrand University. But his background and politics ensured almost permanent exclusion. A further irony is that his poetry is quite consciously within the broadly European literary tradition, while attempting to give shape to urgent contemporary realities. His poem 'A troubador, I tráverse all my land' wittily explores the metaphoric potential of bringing together the erotic and the political, turning a love-lyric in the manner of a seventeenth-century English poet comparing his mistress to a new land (as in 'O my America, my new found land' in Donne's poem 'To his Mistress Going to

Bed') into a 'protest' poem against 'Saracened arrest' (a Saracen is an infidel; and an armoured car used by the police to quell township disturbance). The 'unarmed thumb' alludes at once to an erection and the gesture of the 'comrades'of the liberation movement.

> A troubadour, I tráverse all my land
> exploring all her wide-flung parts with zest
> probing in motion sweeter far than rest
> her secret thickets with an amorous hand:
>
> and I have laughed, disdaining those who banned
> inquiry and movement, delighting in the test
> of will when doomed by Saracened arrest,
> choosing, like unarmed thumb, simply to stand.
>
> Thus, quixoting till a cast-off of my land
> I sing and fare, person to loved-one pressed
> braced for this pressure and the captor's hand
> that snaps off service like a weathered strand:
> − no mistress-favour has adorned my breast
> only the shadow of an arrow-brand.[30]

Brutus at his best is austere, ironic and controlled; although signs of bitterness and fatigue have crept over his later poems. Arthur Nortje (1942–73), a former student of Brutus from the Eastern Cape, was also left out of the Cope/Krige anthology, despite having begun to publish in the early 1960s. His work was identified by another writer abroad, Cosmo Pieterse, as 'poetry of the committed exile, the work of the "ex"-South African who writes, not, as many earlier South African poets did, with a sense of spiritual exile from a European home, but out of a conviction that something is rotten under the Southern Cross'. This was in Pieterse's preface to the first of a number of anthologies introducing the work of writers from South Africa living abroad, *Seven South African Poets* (1971). Nortje himself lived in self-imposed rather than enforced exile; he died from a drug overdose while a research student in Oxford. His intense, verbally sophisticated and ironic verse clarified how he saw himself and others sharing his relation to 'the malaise of my dear land': 'for some of us must storm the castles / some define the happening' ('Native's Letter'). In this and other poems which appeared posthumously in *Dead Roots* (1973), Nortje defined the happening while he remained unknown to his generation back home.

If Cope and Krige had no choice but to exclude Brutus and Nortje, their inclusion of eight poems by the Afrikaans poet Ingrid Jonker was bold. Women poets loom large in the Afrikaans tradition; so do suicides. But Jonker betrayed her heritage, in two of her best-known poems, 'Pregnant woman' and 'The child who was shot dead by soldiers in Nyanga', both first given wide currency in the Cope/Krige anthology. They challenged the sexually repressive, racially violent, Calvinist culture of Afrikanerdom, as much in the directness and urgency of her vision of herself as a woman, as in her testimony to the growing power of the black children who would survive those being murdered in the townships.

The appearance of Jonker's poem on the Nyanga child was timely, and prophetic: the year of the Cope/Krige anthology (1968) was also the year of the beginning of the Black Consciousness Movement, whose origins and support lay with the younger black generation – doubly disaffected by the brutality of their treatment at the hands of the police and an education system which now forced them into separate, all-black, so-called 'tribal' schools and colleges. 'Black man [*sic*] you're on your own' was their slogan. The movement was, in a way, the creation of apartheid; but its aims transcended separatism. Their ideology was explicitly Fanonist. They rejected what they perceived as the 'elitist' take-over of the 'struggle' by 'bourgeois' black collaborators and white liberal journalists, churchmen, educators and artists alike; and the effect on artists and writers of the late 1960s and early 1970s was immediate and profound.

According to Mafika Gwala, 'today's blacks have taken the literary initiative into their own hands', because they are experiencing

> directly or indirectly, the decolonization of Africa, the emergence of bourgeois values in the African community and the seeking after certain alternatives . . . Although we must of necessity adapt ourselves to South Africa's brand of Western Civilization, we have by all means possible to assert our cultural past and our cultural present – despite the non-existence of a national culture within the apartheid society.[31]

How had it come about that poets such as Gwala were being published locally? The main source of black poetry (and also of short stories, criticism, and pieces on drama and music) was the quarterly *Staffrider*. *Staffrider*'s first issue in March 1978 contained Gwala's 'In defence of poetry', among three other poems by him. The magazine took its name from the Black South African English label for the non-paying, daring riders of township trains, youths who cling perilously to the doors and even carriage roofs. It was put out by Ravan Press, founded in 1973, the most prominent of the small group of radical local publishers who emerged during the period of the cultural boycott (including also Ad Donker, David Philip, and Renoster).

Since 1991 *Staffrider* has become the national journal of the Congress of South African Writers (COSAW). Its initial aim was to provide a forum for writers, to 'encourage and give strength to a new literature based on communities', in the dangerous times after June 1976. At its peak, the magazine touched sales of 10,000, and was read by many more. Individual issues (including the first) were banned, but never the magazine itself. The majority of its contributors have been black, although early association with the BCM was succeeded in the 1980s by a more open, non-racial policy.[32] A whole new generation of black poets of the 1970s was named after it, 'the Staffrider poets'. They might equally well have been called 'the Soweto poets', although not all of them came from or lived in the massive, sprawling township outside Johannesburg. Before 1976, their poetry was directed as much at liberal whites as at black audiences, which helps explain how so much of it obtained publication for all its apparent rejection of the mainstream English literary tradition.

Thus the seminal figure was not Gwala or one of the other Black Consciousness poets, but a scooter-messenger from Soweto named Oswald (later Mbuyiseni) Mtshali (born 1946), whose first collection of poems, *Sounds of a Cowhide Drum* (1971), opened a new era in South African poetry in English. His work had been quietly appearing in a scattering of small poetry magazines, but it was not until the publisher Renoster took the chance of putting together a book with a commendatory foreword by Nadine Gordimer that Mtshali became widely known – indeed astonishingly so, for often prosaic and sometimes poorly crafted work. The first edition sold out at once, and within a year 16,000 copies had been printed, a record for a book of poetry in South Africa. His publishers made a profit (also unheard of), Oxford University Press took the book up, and employment as a newspaper columnist, and an American scholarship, soon followed. Despite white liberal patronage and the attacks of black radicals, Mtshali's early poetry created a space to be heard, while drawing on his Zulu background rather than the South African English tradition. Here is 'Boy on a swing':

> Slowly he moves
> to and fro, to and fro,
> then faster and faster
> he swishes up and down.
>
> His blue shirt
> billows in the breeze

like a tattered kite.
The world whirls by:
east becomes west,
north turns to south;
the four cardinal points
meet in his head


          Mother!
Where did I come from?
When will I wear long trousers?
Why was my father jailed? [33]

An everyday situation is quietly evoked and worked towards a climax with the rhythm of the swing itself until we hear the simple questions which can undermine a state. Rhyme and metre are ignored for the uncluttered rhetoric of statement, question and answer, and occasional images from nature. Mtshali's range is wider than it seems: from the retrieval of his people's history in 'The birth of Shaka', to the horror of township life, as dogs tear at a baby's corpse in 'An abandoned bundle' – which Gordimer called one of the most shocking poems ever written, and yet a triumph 'of steely compassion' (Foreword, *Cowhide Drum*). The point about Mtshali is not to whom he spoke, but *for* whom. As Mongane Wally Serote (b. 1944) said:

          White people are white people,
          They must learn to listen.
          Black people are black people,
          They must learn to talk.

This was in the long poem 'Ofay-watcher, throbs-phase', which appeared in *Yakhal'inkomo*, published by Renoster Books a year after *Sounds of a Cowhide Drum*. 'Ofay' is a black Americanism for 'white'; and the book's title means the cry of cattle entering the slaughterhouse (later paralleled by Gwala's *Jol'iinkomo*, which means the call to bring the cattle home safely). Serote's book opened with an implicit, ironic appeal to white liberals

          Do not fear Baas,
          My heart is vast as the sea
          And your mind as the earth.
          It's awright Baas,
          Do not fear.

and concluded with the assertive tone, and loose, repetitive structure of his 'Ofay-watcher', a long poem suggesting just how near to militant black American verse the township poets had moved. The work of poets like Serote, who knew at first-hand the violence and brutality of the regime, exhibits a violent response – as in the scatological vocabulary, the tone of disgust, in 'What's in this black "shit"'. The disrespect is not only aimed at whites; the poet is doing 'A thing my father wouldn't do'. By the time of the book-length, sixty-page poem *No Baby Must Weep* (1975) a lyrical and reverential strain had become apparent. As Njabulo Ndebele confirmed in a study of Mtshali in 1973, 'Our poetry . . . should go beyond the confirmation of oppression to reveal the black man's attempt to recreate himself'.[34]

For Douglas Livingstone, 'merely blurted out angers' against 'Whitey', are a weakness in the poetry of Mtshali, Serote, Sepamla and the others; while their energy, humour and intelligence challenged the 'internationally established yardsticks' of poetry. Most astounding is the fact that, writing at the time of the risings against apartheid education in the townships, Livingstone did not pause to consider *why* the work of these poets might exhibit limitations, what deprivations the pervasive structures of his country enforced while granting him his privileges. The struggle between 'settler' and 'indigenous' discourses, itself part of the larger struggle for supremacy of different cultures and power-groupings in post-colonial society, is at the heart of this kind of response.[35]

It's not a simple matter of written versus spoken forms: the 'Soweto poets' did not come from an entirely 'oral' society; nor did their poetry appeal to a homogenous, performance-oriented audience. It sought and achieved publication, and was read, or at least eavesdropped upon, by the literate and 'educated'. There is no absolute division between oral and written poetry anyway, 'for a poem may be orally composed then later transmitted in writing, or perhaps written initially but then performed and circulated by oral means'.[36] And most oral poetry this century is likely to be produced by people who have some contact with the wider world. In South Africa, the borderline or marginal case is more central to the culturally mixed and diverse situation of the majority of South Africans.

This is where the 'new black poetry' of the interregnum emerged, a 'hybrid' form most obvious in poems like Gwala's 'Getting off the ride'. It is less the imported jazz idiom that suggests their vitality, than the sheer physicality of Gwala's 'khunga-khunga man', the dancer whom we hear and feel moving from side to side ('Untshu, Untshu!') until the climax in the last line:

And the sounds of the Voice come:

>        Khunga, Khunga!
>    Untshu, Untshu!
>            Funtu, Funtu!
>    Shundu, Shundu!
>        Sinki, Sinki!
>            Mojo, Mojo!
>    O-m! O–o—m! O——hhhhhhhhhmmmm!!! [37]

Less directly but more wittily expressed is the voice of the flashy township seducer of Sipho Sepamla's 'Come duze baby' – also the name of a 1950s township jazz number drawing on a subculture going back decades. Sepamla's celebration of cultural and linguistic hybridity, using the slang 'tsotsitaal' (gangster-speak, a mix of American, English, Afrikaans, Xhosa and Zulu), invites his 'baby' to 'come duze' (come closer, from 'duze' in the Nguni – Zulu, Xhosa, Swazi – languages). Although 'Come duze' was written down and printed, its oral, township roots were obvious. The township codes were mediated by these poets; reshaping the colloquial as a poetic, literary, cultural and political act, comparable to the work of Caribbean and Black British poets such as Brathwaite and Kwesi Johnson.

Stephen Gray's *The Penguin Book of Southern African Verse* (1989), was the first of a series of anthologies unapologetic about including the oral tradition and translated material. Nowadays, more and more writers from the educated, liberal elite are eager to show similar willingness – some, like the poet and ANC activist Jeremy Cronin (b. 1949) want 'To learn how to speak / With the voices of the land',

>    To parse the speech in its rivers,
>    To catch in the inarticulate grunt,
>    Stammer, call, cry, babble, tongue's knot
>    A sense of the stoneness of these stones
>    From which all words are cut.

The self-consciousness about this way of writing (learned during Cronin's seven years *Inside,* as his collection's title proclaims) seems to patronize the non-standard, marginalized forms he goes on to include, representing the desire to speak the land, to hear

>    Syllables born in tin shacks, or catch
>    the 5.15 ikwata bust fife
>    Chwannisberg train, to reach

The low chant of the mine gang's
Mineral glow of our people's unbreakable resolve.[38]

Does the inclusion of that 'ikwata bust fife' train really engage with his black 'other' to the extent that the 'our' which succeeds it is convincingly inclusive? It sounds a false note, although bearing witness to its time, the desperate 1980s.


### Other Voices: Drama and Its Formation

In the final part of this case study I take up an area of literary practice – drama – which has, more than any other, testified to the condition of interregnum South Africa. This testimony is evident not merely in the written, or printed and published medium; but also, and often more effectively, in the performed or theatrical medium in which plays are first communicated. This makes it difficult to refer to anything that is easily available. I will refer to the available version of a performance by the South African actress, playwright and storyteller Gcina Mhlophe (b. 1958), of her work *Have You Seen Zandile?*, commissioned for a festival of women's plays at the multiracial Market Theatre in Johannesburg in February 1986, during the State of Emergency. The festival failed to come off; but the play was a surprise success, offering the story of a young Black South African woman's growing self-awareness to enthusiastic and largely black local audiences, followed by overseas (albeit non-mainstream) success.

What kind of testimony does such a work offer? This is partly a question of how it is located within tradition. Although a tradition of playwriting in the European sense and in European languages (mainly English but also Afrikaans) has arisen over the last century or so in South Africa, there is a strong tradition of theatre in the African sense too, more directly and immediately related to its public, functional roots, and which persists even in the culturally mixed urban environment. The result is a hybrid form, relatively freed of the preconceptions of most Western drama today, which appeals not only to fringe or experimental theatre groups in search of inspiration, but also to a broader public at home and abroad – although it makes its quality more difficult to judge.

Thus 'interregnum' plays by South Africans have been astoundingly successful in such local venues as the Market in Johannesburg; and abroad at such venues as the Lincoln Center in New York, or the Hackney Empire in London – where, for example, the township musical *Sarafina!* had its UK premiere in May 1991. This production, while focusing on the story of the young heroine of the title, had a cast of thirty-six, and was designed to commemorate the children of the Soweto rising by means of a mix of song, dance, mime, and role-play, adapted from popular township forms like *mbaqanga*, a 1950s jazz style. The appearance of *Sarafina!* in the UK coincided with a television documentary about its hugely successful American production, and interviews with the scriptwriter, co-composer and choreographer, Mbongeni Ngema (b. 1955) – who first made an impact abroad with his part in the Market Theatre production *Woza Albert!* in 1982, and was until a recent (1996) financial scandal the most prominent South African theatremaker after Athol Fugard (b. 1932).

Many Western theatre critics are unimpressed by such mixed productions: Michael Coveney called *Sarafina!* a 'rather peculiar commercial operation', combining 'classroom subversiveness' and 'gloriously unsanitised' township music and dancing; Michael Billington found it a 'fantastically disciplined and energetic hymn to liberation that the audience greeted with a roar', but disliked its 'sloganizing approach' to politics and education.[39] The subversive potential of the play's climax, when the schoolgirl Sarafina plays the role of a freed Nelson Mandela addressing Soweto, is missed by such criticism. There are important questions to be asked about its commercial and political implications, not to mention its aesthetics; but such questions should be grounded in a proper sense of the mixed or hybrid, mainly non-Western origins of the work, and the changing context of its production, reception and status.

The roots of the different forms of South African drama go back a very long way, if we think in terms of the oral traditions from which they derive. Even if we limit ourselves to the varieties of English which have developed locally, there are discernible traditions which have only recently been unearthed by researchers imbued with a new sense of their relevance – mainly white academics (such as the aforementioned Barnett, Kavanagh, Coplan and Orkin) whose work has shown, for example, that long before the township theatre of today, whether 'popular musical' or 'committed', a form of theatre existed in the cities which was an extension of traditional narrative, ritual and entertainment. But it is possible to over-emphasize these anonymous, communal traditions. One of the most important figures in the new history of South African drama, is H.I.E. Dhlomo (1903–56), a journalist and poet whose literary work was consciously set apart from this township culture.

'Drama is the reconstruction, recreation and reproduction of the great experience of a people', Dhlomo wrote in 1936, 'and it helps them to live more abundantly'. He explained how the roots of Western drama and African drama were the same: the basic urge to recreate through imitation, action, rhythm and gesture the sacred and secular stories of the community, illustrative or symbolic of their lives and the forces which ruled them. He recognized that African and Western drama had developed differently; but argued that the former 'must borrow from, be inspired by' the latter, indeed be 'tainted by exotic influences'. The African playwright must dramatize African 'Oppression, Emancipation and Evolution'; yet to do this, 'he must be an artist before being a propagandist, a philosopher before a reformer; a psychologist before a patriot'.[40]

Dhlomo himself wrote some twenty-four plays, none of them very successful or lasting, apart perhaps from *The Girl Who Killed To Save*, about a nineteenth-century Xhosa prophetess, who declared that the spirits had instructed her to tell her people the European invaders would be driven into the sea if they killed their cattle and burned their crops (a prophecy with disastrous results for the Xhosa). The play included such 'traditional' features as praise songs. But *The Girl Who Killed To Save* (1936) was probably inspired by an earlier play he saw while performing at the launch of the Bantu Dramatic Society in – *She Stoops to Conquer!* This helps remind us that, until recently, theatre in English in South Africa has been influenced primarily by British and other Western models, and has been on the whole a very conservative enterprise, focusing on 'light entertainment' (farces, musicals and thrillers), with the occasional 'heavy' piece from Shakespeare, Ibsen, O'Neill, Shaw or Beckett, often performed by touring companies from abroad – at least until the international playwrights' boycott of 1963 put a stop to that. Ironically, the boycott helped encourage the development of local theatre. Apart from *Kaatje Kekkelbek* (1838), and the early twentieth-century Cape satires of Stephen Black (a protégé of Kipling), none of which was published at the time, there is little of interest until the late 1950s and early 1960s, when the young Athol Fugard's work first began to appear.

But by then, there had also emerged a much more popular and genuinely mixed form of dramatic entertainment in the townships, mainly on the Rand and starting in the 1920s with Esau Mtetwa's Lucky Stars, a semi-professional group who emphasized traditional cultural values by performing a series of standard scenes enlivened with improvised dialogue, song and dance. As the musical side of this became more sophisticated and successful, white involvement became more pronounced. This process culminated with the creation of a multiracial group to protect the rights of black performers, Union Artists, which also engineered the boycott by British Equity of segregated shows in South Africa. Union Artists organized an African Music and Drama Association (AMDA), funded by the success of its promotion of *King Kong*. But by then it was 1960, *Kong* had gone abroad with its cast (many remained in exile), the Sharpeville massacre had taken place, and a tight grip descended on the country, with mass arrests, detentions and bannings. Segregation in the theatres became a fact. Black artists and entertainers were forced to lie low or go abroad, when they were not in prison or banned. One notable exception was Gibson Kente, probably the most important single influence on black South African drama.

Kente (b. 1932), based in Soweto but originally from East London in the Eastern Cape, began with Union Artists, writing and producing musical melodramas reflecting township life. As the apartheid barriers went up, Kente left to take the lead in writing and producing successful township theatre with and for blacks only. He toured the country with a few crudely painted flats, simple costumes and young, newly trained actors in an old bus. By combining shrewd business talent, training for all his own performers and collaborators, and the use of traditional storytelling, mime, song and dance to create productions rooted in township experience, he became very successful. Until, that is, he saw the arrival of a new group from Port Elizabeth called Serpent Players. Their production of a play about the pass laws, *Sizwe Bansi is Dead* (1972) received local and international acclaim, and led Kente to produce a series of political dramas of his own: but by then it was 1976, and the protest element got him arrested. He was later released, to carry on with his career as a one-man black drama school and, finally, independent tv producer. Meanwhile, other black groups arose during the 1970s and 1980s, despite continuous police harassment; all uncompromising, highly politicized, and all severely curtailed. Some of their work (including Kente's) can be found in Robert Kavanagh's *South African People's Plays* (1981).

The voice of Athol Fugard was one of the few to be heard after the 1960 clamp-down. He had produced two township plays with amateur, largely black casts in rough conditions, and went on to make a name with a small new play, acted by himself and a jazz musician called Zakes Mokae, *The Blood Knot* (1961). Fugard is South Africa's most well-known – probably its *only* well-known – playwright, with more than fifteen full-length published plays to his name, several films, and a novel. All his work focuses on the fears and torments, as well as the small celebrations, of the people of his country. He has been criticized for addressing a predominantly white and overseas audience. And although it is true that the Western tradition of drama has been of great importance for his work and its reception, equally important has been its involvement in local drama traditions. He has often turned to black performers to mediate their experiences by risky playmaking across the racial divide.

The best-known of these jointly created plays were overtly political: the aforementioned *Sizwe Bansi is Dead,* and *The Island* (1973), which explored the pain, humiliation and ability to survive of the political detainee – not heroes of the resistance such as Mandela and Sisulu, but their anonymous fellows. Workshop improvisation was the key to the activities of the Serpent Players, a group from the New Brighton township near Port Elizabeth, Fugard's home town. The local success of *The Blood Knot* had led them to approach Fugard, with whom they produced drama out of the barest essentials. Accustomed to the restrictions of life under apartheid, they used whatever space or resources came to hand, often illegally. Brecht and the Polish director Grotowski's theories, as well as their own familiar storytelling techniques, were fused. Two performers in particular, John Kani and Winston Ntshona, proved remarkably talented; two decades later, Kani is Executive Director of the Market Theatre in Johannesburg; a living testimony to the changes that people like himself and Fugard helped bring about. The first black director of the Market, however, was a woman – Gcina Mhlophe – in 1989–90.

The Market Theatre Company was formed in 1974 by Barney Simon (1933–96), a Johannesburg friend of Fugard's and a theatre practitioner committed to the idea of workshop theatre established in the 1950s in Britain by Joan Littlewood, with whom Simon worked briefly before joining Union Artists. With Mannie Manim, whose background was in the white, mainstream, subsidized theatre, Simon converted a fruit market in downtown Johannesburg for use as a multiracial theatre complex. From its opening in 1976 it has hosted productions of some of the most important theatreworks in South Africa. This included Fugard's later and more personal plays (such as '*Master Harold*' *and the Boys, 1983*), the satire of Pieter-Dirk Uys (for example, *Paradise is Closing Down*, 1977), and above all the work of playwrights, directors and performers such as Mbongeni Ngema, Maishe Maponya, and Zakes Mda from Lesotho. Other alternative theatres had already developed, such as The Space Theatre in Cape Town, where *Sizwe Bansi* and *The Island* were premiered with their co-creators, Kani and Ntshona, and the first play by a black South African woman, Fatima Dike's *The Sacrifice of Kreli* (1976). The Market remains the most significant theatre stimulus and showcase in the country.

Unsubsidized until 1995, the Market's aim was to raise the awareness of racially mixed, but predominantly white audiences, into admitting the textures and perceptions of the world about them, for instance in workshop productions like *Born in the RSA* (1985), a typical Simon production (in which Mhlophe appeared), involving the collective realization of interwoven monologues derived from recent events, researched and explored by the cast. It made a strong impression at home and abroad (where it was televised), especially in terms of its suggestion that the different 'voices', experiences and languages in the country could be orchestrated to express a perspective on what was happening. The basic argument against the Market phenomenon is that, whatever its overt intentions, its white backers and management, in combination with its local middle-class and overseas Western audiences, compromised any role it might have had in the political struggles of the time.[41]

A perspective on the argument is provided by *Have You Seen Zandile?*, which was first performed at the Laager in the Market from 6 February to 8 March 1986. Gcina Mhlophe played Zandile; a Market actress Thembi Mtshali took on the roles of her grandmother, mother and friend, under the direction of an experienced theatre practitioner, Maralin Vanrenen. The writer was the driving force, as well as the provider of the subject, drawing on different traditions of her own. *Have You Seen Zandile?* is short, fast, continuous, multilingual, and multicultural. Based on role play and song, a series of successive brief scenes reveal the situation of a young Black South African schoolgirl living with her grandmother in Hammarsdale, near Durban. Almost the only action is her abduction by her mother's family to live with them in the rural Transkei, where she comes to question traditional views of women's destiny.

The creator of the play is also the main performer, who seems at first to address an audience familiar with her specific, hybrid culture and traditions; a mixture of Western popular music and literature ('Sugar, Sugar' and Barbara Cartland) South African education ('the great trek, the great trek, every year it is the same'), Christianity (prayer and hymn-singing) and local oral forms, ranging from lullabies, popular urban jazz songs, to a full praise poem. The play appeals beyond its immediate audience, being presented predominantly in English, while we understand that the characters speak their own languages (Zulu in the first half, Xhosa in the second) throughout – acknowledged with exclamations of glee by African members of the first Market audiences. But its use of English enables it to appeal across local linguistic as well as racial barriers, and over the heads of the censors to an international audience.

The plight of the young girl in *Zandile* evokes pathos and laughter. Her story is simple, but the telling of it complicated, in the way that traditional oral narrative often is; the stage is peopled with different characters by its protagonist, who can imitate her schoolmistress teaching the children to sing (scene 4a) as easily as she can enact the reply of an agony Aunt to 'Confused' of Port Elizabeth in the popular magazine *Bona* (scene 11), with equally comic results. The play's attitude towards its subject seems balanced between this humorous, even satirical tone, and the pain of the illegitimate girl's yearnings for friendship and family, for her mother and grandmother. Men do not feature except offstage: Mr Hlatshwayo, the revered school principal and object of Zandile's praise-poem (scene 12) is the major figure; otherwise brothers, fathers, musicians and prospective husbands appear as the source of generally patriarchal, constraining attitudes towards women, although not unloved.

There is more to be said of the play's shape and texture, but what of its politics? During the Emergency's first two years, according to the government's own figures, over 13,000 people, many of them children, were detained; some died in custody, many were hospitalized.[42] So it is understandable that a play exploring the inner world of a young woman, without overt sign of outrage or protest, should not have been well received by activists. But what about, for example, the scene in which Zandile addresses her grandmother's flowerbeds as if she were her teacher instructing the class on how to behave when the inspector visits? She tells them:

> You know the inspector does not understand our language (*she starts giggling*) and we don't want to embarrass him. (*Puts her hand over her mouth and laughs.*) He cannot say our real names so we must all use our white names in class today. Hands up those of you who don't have white names. We'll just have to give them to you. Wena you can be Violet . . . Do you know what name the inspector gave me in class today? Elsie. And I don't even look like an Elsie! Don't laugh! At least you are flowers. And do you know what he called Bongi? Moses! He couldn't even tell that she is a girl. (Scene 4(a))[43]

What this reveals is how, then as well as now, when the emergency has ended, and apartheid dismantled, inherited structures of power remain, including those which persist in placing women, especially black women, as a nameless, dependent underclass.

*Zandile* has been seen by South African feminist critics, such as Dorothy Driver, as a challenge to the very 'illusions of identity' upon which such power-structures rest. Mhlophe's work, she said

> is about finding a position from which to write, which is to say, about constructing an identity from which to speak, a place from which she may view herself . . . and from which she may dream of a world which offers, through acting, the assumption of many more roles than a wife.[44]

Driver compares apartheid to the 'phallocentric model' which underpins patriarchy, in that it posits 'black and white as distinct categories, with black as the negative of white, a position that becomes reversed in Black Consciousness. In both models the categories of feminine and black exist as the "other" of the masculine/white self, functioning primarily to define for that self his/her sense of authority and identity'. The subjectivity explored in Mhlophe's work is what makes it radical, expressing the 'voice of difference' that enables us 'to slip out of the repressiveness of orthodox alignments' and takes us beyond the 'rigid categories' of different forms of patriarchy.[45]

For Mhlophe, refashioning a culture of silence means more than allowing new voices to be heard, it means creating a medium for those voices – a process she now furthers by reactivating oral, folk traditions eroded by the (colonial and apartheid) migrant labour system, if not also to a degree by the cultural predominance of the English-speaking elite – to which, of course, someone like Driver also belongs. In *Zandile*, Mhlophe performs herself as a child learning the art of storytelling from her grandmother, thereby resisting both the dominant discourse of the ruling whites, and the alternative, masculinist discourses of black protest. More: as an itinerant storyteller, performing and assisting new (especially young) audiences to perform traditional stories, with her group Zanendaba ('Bring me a story'), in a mix of languages determined by the audiences, she moves towards a form of cultural intervention which offers a space for both retrieval and growth.

## Summary

Trying to identify some of the most important trends in literature in English in South Africa today, from the most obviously dominant, 'white liberal' tradition, to some of the recently emerging, contesting or alternative voices raises unsettling questions. How far does reading Gordimer's *Conservationist* now involve the subversion of the patriarchal colonizer's consciousness by 'other' voices? Turning to hear those voices in the poetry and drama of the 1970s and since, reveals that the claim for space in culture as in society, is stronger than ever, and that 'protest' was always limited. Gcina Mhlophe, like Jeremy Cronin and Mongane Serote, is among the 'other voices' quoted in Masekela's key 1990 speech, but does her voice reach beyond apartheid, beyond the colonizing structures reflected by protest? It certainly touches on the 'double oppression' of black women. Who, then, is being decolonized in the decolonizing process in South Africa?

## Notes

1 Nadine Gordimer, 'Living in the interregnum', reptd in *The Essential Gesture: Writing, Politics and Places*, ed. Stephen Clingman (Cape, 1988), p. 262.

2 Ibid., p. 262.

3 Frantz Fanon, *The Wretched of the Earth* (Penguin, 1967), p. 40.

4 Athol Fugard, *Cape Argus* (20 June 1991); (12 May 1992).

5 Ashis Nandy, *The Intimate Enemy: Loss and Recovery of Self under Colonialism* (Oxford University Press, 1983).

6 Edward Said, 'Representing the colonized: anthropology's interlocutors', *Critical Inquiry*, 15, 2 (Winter 1989), pp. 205–25 (p. 207).

7 Anne McClintock, 'The angel of progress: pitfalls of the term "post-colonialism"', *Social Text* (Spring 1992), pp. 1–15, reptd in Williams and Chrisman, eds, *Colonial Discourse and Post-Colonial Theory*, (Harvester Wheatsheaf, 1993), pp. 291–304.

8 G.H.L. Le May, *Black and White in South Africa: The Politics of Survival* (BPC, 1971), p. 68.

9 See Leonard Thompson, *A History of South Africa*, rev. edn (Yale University Press, 1995), pp. 1–30, for the best recent account.

10 Freda Troup, *South Africa* (Penguin, 1975), p. 40; Allister Sparks, *The Mind of South Africa* (Heinemann, 1990), p. xvi.

11 Rosemary Jolly, 'Rehearsals of liberation: contemporary postcolonial discourse and the new South Africa', *PMLA*, 110, 1 (Jan. 1995), pp. 17–29.

12 Stephen Gray, *Southern African Literature: An Introduction* (David Philip/Rex Collings, 1979), p. 1.

13 See Jean-Philipe Wade, 'Introduction: disclosing the nation', *Rethinking South African Literary History*, eds J.A. Smit, Johan van Wyk and Jean-Philippe Wade (Y Press, 1996), p. 9.

14 Albie Sachs, 'Preparing ourselves for freedom', in *Spring is Rebellious*, eds Ingrid de Kok and Karen Press (buchu books, 1990), pp. 19–21; Barbara Masekela, 'We are not returning empty-handed', *Die Suid-Afrikaan*, 28 (August 1990), pp. 38–40 (p. 39) – Masekela was at the time head of the 'cultural department' of the ANC.

15 Masekela, 'We are not returning empty-handed', pp. 38–40.

16 *The Guardian* (4 October 1991).

17 Abdul JanMohamed, *Manichean Aesthetics: The Politics of Literature in Colonial Africa*, first publ. 1983 (University of Massachusetts Press, 1988), p. 126; Stephen Clingman, *The Novels of Nadine Gordimer; History from the Inside* (Allen & Unwin, 1986), p. 161.

18 Michael Wade, *Nadine Gordimer* (Evans Brothers Ltd, 1978), p. 228.

19 JanMohamed, *Manichean Aesthetics*, p. 2.

20 *The Guardian* (4 October 1991).

21 Nadine Gordimer, 'The novel and the nation in South Africa' (1961), in *African*

*Writers on African Writing*, ed. G.D. Killam (Heinemann, 1973), pp. 36–7.

22 Nadine Gordimer, *The Lying Days* (Virago, 1983), pp. 96–7.

23 Nadine Gordimer, 'The essential gesture' (title essay), in Clingman, *The Essential Gesture*, p. 108.

24 Olive Schreiner, *The Story of An African Farm* (Penguin 1971), pp. 28, 105. Joseph Conrad, *Heart of Darkness*, ed. Joseph Kimborough (Norton, 1988), pp. 37–8.

25 Gordimer, *The Lying Days*, pp. 175, 186.

26 Nadine Gordimer, *The Conservationist* (Penguin, 1978), p. 9. All further references to this edition given in parentheses in the text.

27 Homi Bhabha, 'Representation and the colonial text', in *The Theory of Reading*, ed. Frank Gloversmith (Harvester, 1984), pp. 93ff.

28 Lewis Nkosi, *Tasks and Masks: Themes and Styles of African Literature* (Longman, 1981), p. 167.

29 Mafika Gwala, 'In defence of poetry', in *The Penguin Book of Southern African Verse*, ed. Stephen Gray (Penguin 1989), p. 333.

30 Dennis Brutus, 'A troubadour, I tráverse all my land', in *A Simple Lust: Collected Poems of South African Jail and Exile* (Heinemann, 1973), p. 2.

31 Mafika Gwala, 'Black writing today' (1979), in *Soweto Poetry*, ed. Michael Chapman (McGraw-Hill, 1982), pp. 169–70.

32 See Michael Vaughan, '*Staffrider* and directions within contemporary South African Literature', in *Literature and Society in South Africa*, ed. Landeg White and Tim Couzens (Longman, 1984), pp. 196–212.

33 Oswald Mtshali, 'Boy on a swing', in *Sounds of a Cowhide Drum* (Renoster Books, 1971), p. 3.

34 Njabulo Ndebele, qtd Chapman, *Soweto Poetry*, p. 193.

35 See Douglas Livingstone, 'The poetry of Mtshali, Serote, Sepamla and others in English: notes towards a critical evaluation' (1976), in Chapman, *Soweto Poetry*, pp. 157–61.

36 Ruth Finnegan, Introduction, *Penguin Book of Oral Poetry* (Penguin, 1982), p. 2.

37 Mafika Gwala, 'Getting off the ride', in *Jol'iinkomo* (Donker, 1977), p. 67.

38 Jeremy Cronin, 'To learn how to speak' (1987), in Gray, *The Penguin Book of South African Verse*, p. 365.

39 Michael Coveney, 'Flagging behind the barricades', *The Observer* (12 May 1991); Michael Billington, 'Class war', *The Guardian* (13 May 1991).

40 H.I.E. Dhlomo, qtd Ursula Barnett, *A Vision of Order: A Study of Black South African Literature in English* (Sinclair Browne, 1983), p. 228.

41 See Martin Orkin, *Drama and the South African State* (Manchester University Press, 1991), pp. 185–6, 212–13.

42 Thompson, *A History of South Africa*, pp. 235–6.

43 Gcina Mhlophe, Marilin Vanrenen, Thembi Mtshali, *Have You Seen Zandile?* 1988 (Heinemann/Methuen, 1990), p. 20.

44 Dorothy Driver, in Martin Trump, ed., *Rendering Things Visible* (Ravan, 1990), pp. 251–2.

45 Ibid., pp. 251–3.

# 8

## *After Post-Colonialism?*

I think the real problem is of course using any theory for any practice
Gayatri Spivak, *The Post-Colonial Critic*, 1990

How do we keep the past alive without becoming its prisoner?
How do we forget it without risking its repetition in the future?
Ariel Dorfman, Afterword, *Death and the Maiden*, 1991

Sometimes we can be strangers to ourselves
V.S. Naipaul, *A Way in the World*, 1994

### *Where are 'We' Now?*

Is there an 'after' the post-colonial? Should there be? I began this book by saying that writers resist the imposition of terms like post-colonial which, they feel, belong to the discursive regime of critics, academics and theorists. The common objection is that here we have yet another universalizing, Eurocentric, authoritarian approach to the world. Another common objection is that the term seems to imply that colonialism is over and done with. However, even among novelists as sceptical as Sahgal, an awareness of the historic impact of their own specific kind of colonial – and hence post-colonial – inheritance, infuses their work, its language, context and address. Caribbean and Black British poets like Kamau Brathwaite, Walcott or Grace Nichols are less shy of asserting both the centrality of the colonial experience, and their own emancipatory agenda. The position for South African writers of all genres is less clear, suggesting that although their particular version of the colonial experience is unquestionably lasting, a dramatic, even revolutionary process of transformation is taking place which throws open once again the question of what we mean by 'post-colonial', and how the term might be usefully employed in a present when its indeterminacy is more obvious than ever, although more and more claims are being made in its name.

If I cannot avoid the discourses of the critic, academic or theorist, I nevertheless do want to avoid the familiar trajectory according to which the reader is positioned so as to progress along a line from dimness and uncertainty to clarity and conviction. Of course I am not seeking to baffle, and I have tried to be clear about what I am about. But if there now seem to be more rather than less possibilities about how, when and where to use the term post-colonial, or whether or not it should be used at all, then I feel I have achieved something. If your use of the term is not empowering, then what use is it? The main thrust of my argument has been to propose that 'post-colonial' carries an unignorable historic weight which, if thought about coherently in relation to a particular cultural-geographic time and space, can help develop an appropriate – but not appropriating – sense of the themes, issues and values with which the literary texts of those areas are concerned. These areas have been released from the sway of the British Empire, while inheriting various forms of its language, cultural practices, and power structures, as well as their own languages, practices and structures. As far as new or at least more recent, post-Second World War global power-structures are concerned – well, negotiations continue.

On one level, my concern has been for what Raymond Williams once called 'the real human dimension in which works of art are made and valued'.[1] That dimension can only be reached through a sense of history, which is a form of collective memory, continually revised. If, as I believe, history articulates the struggle between different groups and interests, including the colonizers and colonized of yesterday and today, then it is by trying to understand the terms of such articulation that we may begin to understand ourselves and where we are; while conceding that this is inevitably a simplification of the actual, fissured and multifarious world in which 'we' (you and me), and 'others' live. In other words (returning to what I said in my first chapter) an awareness of the voices of others, important and inescapable as that is, must be brought back to a recognition of the forces – historical if nothing else – which have shaped their exclusion, as well as our own position(s).

Where then do literary works come in? The American critic J. Hillis Miller (who however also ignores the post-colonial) has put the position well:

> Works of literature do not simply reflect or are not simply caused by their contexts. They have a productive effect in history. This can and should also be studied. To put this another way, the only thing that sometimes worries me about the turn to history now as an explanatory method is the implication that I can fully explain every text by

its pre-existing historical context. But the publication of these works was itself a political or historical event that in some way changed history. I think that if you don't allow for this, literature is not much worth bothering with.[2]

Or as Walcott said of Auden's famous line in 'In Memory of W.B. Yeats' ('poetry makes nothing happen'), poetry *'does* make something happen because in the flow of the river which he talks about, the river touches many things as it passes by'.[3] Texts such as those I have been dealing with embody an important interventionary impulse, an impulse to shape as well as be shaped by the historical and the contingent, which distinguishes them from the typically post-modern work, with its lack of historicity, and implicit privileging of present Western cultural norms – evident in the commodification of colonial and post-colonial stories and cultures by, for example, Hollywood's version of Black South African township theatre (*Sarafina!* with Whoopi Goldberg), or, more recently, the Anglo-American transformation of Michael Ondaatje's 1992 post-colonial novel *The English Patient* into a timeless love-story – although there is more to it than that, as I shall show in what follows.

The point of taking up this filmic reworking of a text as my final example follows from my view that what you call post-colonial depends upon a specific cultural frame in time and space, which from most perspectives today (despite the significant silence on these matters among the most well-known theorists) should also include film, music, and other manifestations of contemporary culture. From the perspective of post-colonial writings, the decentring of orthodoxy and the characteristically elitist promotion of the post-modern, reflects a disturbingly unequal network of power relations: not simply the inevitable consumerist appropriation of old and new ways of life from around the world by the endless appetite of West European and American economies and their South East Asian overtakers; but also the unquestioning, institutional acceptance of that network.

### Producing the Post-Colonial Text

One way of locating what might be conceived of as post-colonial literary texts in this gloomy scenario is to locate their production – logically if not in other ways a more secure source of its subversive power – in the present, in terms of its past, without relinquishing the necessarily ambivalent or dialogic nature of that relationship. Consider, for example, the concluding moment of Ariel Dorfman's play, *Death and the Maiden* (1991), which faces the characters and the audience with a mirror, in which they and we see ourselves, as Schubert's piercingly sad music shifts the moral, political and emotional problems we have witnessed onto another, indefinable and enigmatic level. Is this moment a post-modern cop-out for *bien pensant* liberals? Or does it testify to the imaginative leap required from us (whatever our class, race and gender positions) to understand the world of the other, in which torture, including the torture of women and children, is an everyday event?

The answer depends on the nature of the moment as a definable, constructed event in politics and history, and how one relates to that. The play, originally in Spanish and by a Chilean citizen forced into exile in the United States after Pinochet's 1973 coup, uses the Hollywood thriller form to raise a series of questions facing the oppressors and the oppressed, and those who stood by, in a country at the turning-point from a (US-supported) dictatorship to democracy. One of the dictatorship's victims, a woman raped and tortured for opposing the regime, suddenly and unexpectedly confronts the man she believes carried out the crime; she overpowers him and tries to force a confession under threat of death. 'Whereupon the audience is caught in a neat moral trap and is made to confront choices that most would presumably rather leave to the inhabitants of remote and less favoured countries', as a reviewer of the first production at the Royal Court in London observed.[4] That is, it seems to me, the awkward, even occasionally question-begging position, in which the writings I have been interested in may well leave those of us who contemplate them from the comfort of distance, in time and/or place.

I say question-begging, because the position this reviewer outlines of course belongs to the liberal, patriarchal West, and if, as is sometimes the case, and for whatever reason (publishing demands, for instance) literatures in English are produced for this market, then that may undermine the validity of their claim upon conscience. On the other hand, it may be seen as a crucial part of Dorfman's project to 'decolonize' the West (Fanon and Sartre's project decades ago, without the gender dimension), which nobody can seriously claim has happened – witness the Falklands/Malvinas and Gulf wars, or, on a less distinct but more pervasive level, the continuing assumption that Britain is a racially and culturally homogenous nation state, or that the USA 'allows' Black or Chicano or other ethnic groups 'their place'. There is no doubt that *Death and the Maiden* generated considerable acclaim in the UK and US for its acknowledgement that there were no easy answers to the problems it posed, although it has subsequently became a Hollywood commodity of the kind I have been anathematizing as all too easy to consume, without significant or lasting effect.

This has to do with the wider problem of the cultural reception and status of what is designated as post-colonial, in which of course this book too plays its part: as does my writing of it, and your reading. In fact, Dorfman also put his play on in Chile, a year after the democratic government took over, and two days after their Commission on Human Rights published its report, when, as he put it, people were 'still censoring themselves'. The response was instructive.

> In the forums we held afterwards, those in the audience who were themselves victims said they had found the play liberating. But many who had been against the dictatorship, and were now part of the ruling group trying to take the country forward, felt that I had been irresponsible. Some of them said this was not the time, that it was too soon, that I was dwelling on the past. Others refused to see it. These were people in government who could have helped it tour schools and trade unions, so that it could be seen widely. Some of these people were my friends.[5]

None of the play's characters can offer a way out of the present, because they are living it, as the members of Dorfman's Chilean audience are too, and as those who refused to go testified by their absence. The play had the potential to intervene on a public as well as personal level, which is why it created such a stir; but perhaps also why it ended up as a Hollywood commodity, reducing that potential.

I chose this Chilean–American, cross-cultural product to reinforce the point that what can be called post-colonial literature in English depends upon the conditions of production and reception of any specific text – which may not itself begin or end up as, a written text in English, in the usual sense. The problems created by the dominance of popular cultural, media-based forms especially but far from exclusively in the West are demonstrated by another play-performance which, however, has no written text that I know of: Josie Ningali Lawford's Aborigine Australian one-woman show *Ningali*, which I observed in London's Queen Elizabeth Hall on 30 September 1995, after its success earlier in the year at the Edinburgh Festival and in 1994 in Australian venues. Comparable with Mhlophe's *Zandile* as a performance devised by three women which attempts to deliver a personal history through multiple role-playing, languages, song and dance (both popular-Western and indigenous), *Ningali* delivered a similarly powerful sense of the dislocating forces inherited from the colonial experience, against which there is a struggle to affirm a sense of identity for indigenous peoples.

The minority status of the Aborigine (or *Koori*) peoples, and within that context the powerlessness of women, however, may explain why Lawford's unscripted storytelling as a means of retrieving an alternate cultural frame came across to this viewer at any rate as altogether less confident or persuasive than Mhlophe's, the performer attempting to engage her metropolitan audience with near-racist jokes ('We'll have you sounding like a lotta blackfellows soon'), and finally offering herself in a bare-breasted body-painting ritual which was perhaps too comfortingly 'other', even voyeuristically 'exotic' altogether – as if legitimating the exploitative gaze which its production on the South Bank implied. Mhlophe's London performances were in a fringe venue advertised in the black press, which is part of what made the difference. But of course their backgrounds are different, too. For all the dislocation of Mhlophe's upbringing, her mixed Zulu–Xhosa, women's cultural inheritance is far more powerful and present in the South Africa of the interregnum than Ningali's fraction of the small minority indigenous cultures of Australia today. These sorts of differences in 'white-settler invader' cultures are too easily merged, I might add, as the so-called 'Second World' of some recent post-colonial theorizing;[6] that is, insofar as they are attended to at all, in any detail.

According to Lawford, who spoke no English until the age of twelve, when her father – one of the despised Aborigine labourers attached to a cattle-station in the outback (Fitzroy Crossing) – pushed her into attending the local school 'to survive', it was her subsequent departure from her country to take up a study scholarship in a place she had never heard of, Alaska, which alerted her to the need to recover the world she was losing, or already had lost. There she learnt to sing country-and-western, and met Black American and Inuit people, who, she says, helped her realize that her grandfather was right when he said 'if you lose your language, you're nothing: your songs, your stories, your dreaming, are all in your language'.

In a specifically local context, this could signify, indeed has apparently signified, a more interventionary product than appeared to me in London, and less of an entertaining pastiche for metropolitan consumption. It may become, then, more of a post-colonial play in the sense pursued by Helen Gilbert and Joanne Tompkins, Australians who have produced the first full-length comparative study of *Post-Colonial Drama* (1996). They agree with critics such as Anne McClintock (mentioned in my last chapter) that any useful theory of post-colonialism must respond to 'more than the merely chronological construction of post-independence' or 'the discursive experience of imperialism' as part of its public and political agenda, an agenda which is part of its defining characteristic. Post-colonialism 'has more affinity with feminist and class-based discourses than with postmodernism', despite the latter's brief to dismantle 'the often unwritten but frequently invoked rules of genre, authority, and value'.[7]

For Gilbert and Tompkins, this also means that theatre may have more of a capacity to intervene, while running a greater risk of interference from censors and the like, especially 'post-colonial theatre', as 'countless South African dramatists can attest'. In their view, the importance of *Ningali* lies in the storytelling base it shares with such earlier drama as Jack Davis's *The Dreamers* (1982), which established the storytelling figure as a repository of indigenous culture in the theatre.[8] But, as they also admit, the problem with live theatre is that the text is more variable and less easily tied down than with other genres, hence interpretation and value depend even more upon the moment and nature of production – which also varies in time and place. In short, this too must be historicized to be understood – although to aim to tie down a phenomenon labelled 'post-colonial drama' seems somewhat self-contradictory.

What a figure such as Ningali has in common with the performers, storytellers, artists who have some purchase upon post-colonial histories, languages, theories is *migrancy*: in person, in history, in language. What to make of her work in the world today becomes what to make of the multiple, overlapping and unstable identities in terms of race and gender, which characterize so many who have access to the media of another culture as well as, or instead of, their own.

One writer whose career has plunged through his own post-colonial writings into a kind of settled unsettledness offers an instructive comparison: V.S. Naipaul, hailed as a prize-winning British Writer, as well as (since 1990) a Knight of the Realm, while endlessly rewriting his identity as *not* British – nor, for that matter, Caribbean, nor Trinidadian, nor Indian, nor black, nor white. His is, on his own terms (which exclude gender), an identity always in process. Like Salman Rushdie, he is more interested in pursuing the question of his own voice through a range of narrative forms accommodated to neither Western nor local aesthetic paradigms exclusively; like Rushdie, he is almost careless about definitions of his procedures. His own definition of 'post-colonial' emerges in a 1994 book, *A Way in the World*, to describe writers 'like James Pope-Hennessy and Patrick Leigh-Fermor', as opposed to colonial writers like Trollope, Kingsley and Froude – who also offered their impressions of the West Indies.[9] The book itself ranges across the centuries, to the first moment of colonization and back, leaving its grave and artful narrator in a typically detached but troubled position. It is a position worth looking at, to clarify the position of this book as a whole, by another former colonial 'rooted' in the heartland of empire. As Aijaz Ahmad has forcefully demonstrated, you cannot exclude yourself from the area of enquiry; on the other hand, who, whether a well-paid academic in Delhi or London, can claim the moral high ground in this field? Naipaul's fictionalized struggle to locate himself in terms of the 'other' seems to me exemplary in suggesting both one possible mapping of a position, and the inevitable undecidability of its outcome.

### Others Again: Citizens of the World or Arrivants?

If any writings may be said to traverse the terrain of the post-colonial imagination, then Naipaul's do. And yet, his work penetrates and goes beyond the historical realities he engages, the realities of colonization, decolonization, and the 'free states' in which he – or rather, his semi-fictional persona – travels. Lacking the confidence in their own identities of a later generation of Caribbean and Black British writers, he alarmingly resembles the uncertain, guilty, racially self-aware and self-conscious figure of the South African liberal. Yet, obsessed by change and decay, by the otherness of himself as well as those he meets, he adopts the persona of a civilized stranger, to record – and, I would argue, question – his various encounters. This is where I find myself drawn in. Even as the author-narrator of *The Enigma of Arrival* (1987) remarks the convenience of his fictional status as a courteous and informed outsider, he also has to admit the disturbing colonial and post-colonial histories which shadow that position, and pursue new interpretations of it.

When, for example, he begins to relate the story told him by one of the English people he meets in the novel – the man tells a tale of childhood servitude and humiliation – he interrupts himself to remark that the man 'could talk to me' because: 'I was a stranger . . . I had discovered in myself – always a stranger, a foreigner, a man who had left his island and community before maturity . . . a deep interest in others, a wish to visualize the detail and routine of their lives, to see the world through their eyes.' But before the Naipaulian narrator gives us more of the world through the eyes of the other, he thinks of his own colonial childhood, a time when 'I found so many abuses I took for granted. I lived easily with the idea of poverty, the nakedness of the children in the streets of the town and the roads of the country. I lived easily with the idea of the brutalizing of the children by flogging; the ridiculing of the deformed; the different ideas of authority presented by our Hindu family and then, above that, the racial-colonial system of our agricultural colony.'[10]

A lacerating sense of being tied to his background, and of his early blindness towards its specific, colonial structures, continually undermines Naipaul's self-image as the gentleman-traveller, relaying the customs and peculiarities of the country in which he has arrived. As the title alone of *The Enigma of Arrival* implies, there is something enigmatic, unsettling and unfinished about Naipaul's arrival. The narrator wants to write a story on De Chirico's painting, *The Enigma of Arrival*, which he once saw in a schoolbook, and which shows the port of a 'dangerous classical city', a sail, a tower, and two figures, one of whom he imagines is a traveller whose feeling for adventure would give way to panic, as, 'led on by kindly people', he would find himself 'the intended victim' of 'some religious ritual'. Instead, the narrator writes the book in which, although he may find himself for the first time 'in tune with' the settled English landscape of Camelot and Constable, of church and manor, barrow and meadow, he is unable to forget that other landscape, of poverty and flogging, of huts and plantations, the ramshackle, incomplete colonial landscape from which he has come and to which, at the end of the book, he returns, for a family cremation.[11]

This is perhaps why, at the end of *In A Free State* (1971), the earlier narrative sequence deeply embedded within *Enigma* (which tells how it came to be written), he intervenes to prevent the flogging of a group of ragged Arab children. *In A Free State* remains Naipaul's most wide-ranging account of the 'casualties' of freedom, that is, of all those caught up in the shifting networks of power in the post-colonial world. He starts and ends that book in the voice of a gentleman-traveller journeying from one former, classical and imperial centre (Venice) to arrive in another, even more ancient (Alexandra). This traveller records overhearing among his fellow passengers an English tramp boasting of his journeys around the world, all to former British colonies: 'But what's nationality these days?' the tramp addresses the assembled, multinational audience. 'I myself, I think of myself as a citizen of the world.'[12]

This empty echo of Augustan, imperial and classical pasts appears to situate his observer, the Asian–Caribbean cosmopolite author, as a new citizen of the world, for whom nationality is an irrelevance. The irony of the situation is reinforced when three passengers of diverse nationalities bully the Englishman for some unspecified minor misdemeanour. 'It was', reports the author-narrator, 'like a tiger-hunt, where bait is laid out and the hunter and spectators watch from the security of a platform'. The comparison intensifies the historical irony: a member of the former imperial race has become the object of the detached, superior gaze of others, a victim of his victims. But our new citizen of the world is aware less of his power as spectator, than of fear, and powerlessness; feelings which return at the end of the book when he witnesses for the second time the easy brutality of the strong against the weak, and takes away the whip being used on a group of Egyptian children, only to be left feeling 'exposed, futile'.[13]

If Naipaul as author asks to be located in terms of the long literary and classical European traditions of cosmopolitan or internationalist imagining, he also suggests a permanent undertow of anxiety, of powerlessnes and futility, which effectively undermines this position, and creates the possibility of understanding, even intervening on behalf of, the other. The potentially subversive sense that he is, on some historically determined level, identifiable with the colonized, prevents him from becoming a fully paid-up citizen on the Enlightenment model. It is also what connects Naipaul with the much more recent, Caribbean tradition of locality and nation as the imagined source of an identity – a tradition typified by Kamau Brathwaite's *The Arrivants,* for example, in which, as we have seen, 'New World mariners / Columbus coursing kaffirs' search the wounds of their long history in the imperial centres of Europe, America and Africa, before returning to their Caribbean homelands. For Brathwaite and Walcott, the repossession of a national identity in the New World, through a redefining of history and language, does not entirely erase the trauma of the colonial past. For Naipaul, the possibility of that repossession haunts him, so that his assumption of the classical European canon is insecure, and in need of continual reinforcement. For myself, as a former South African, I can only say: how could that trauma be erased?

Despite himself, Naipaul carries around a yearning for the wholeness of home, which affects him like the dream of an exploding head which afflicts the narrator-author of *The Enigma of Arrival.* The crisis of self-questioning at the heart of *Enigma,* which is the crisis of the post-colonial, represents a new phase in Naipaul's exemplary struggle against the loss of a secure sense of self, against extinction; a struggle inherited – as he inherited his vocation – from his father Seepersad's defining experience of looking in the mirror one day and seeing nobody.[14]

Unfortunately, this existential, Lacanian, doomed attempt to create a secure self through language is also expressed in the compulsion to reject some of those whose histories Naipaul shares, but seeks to deny – like the 'Trinidad Negro' he met in Puerto Rico on the way to Harlem, or the other black man who refused to share his ship's cabin, 'men in whom (unwillingly, since I was Indian and Hindu, full of the tragedy and glory of India) I saw aspects of myself, echoes of my own journey and the yearning at the back of that journey'. These men have a vulnerability which echoes his own first migration, and after recoiling into an idea of ancestral

Indianness, he remembers how, on his return to Trinidad twenty years later, the rise of black nationalism alienated him. And yet, he admits his proprietary, exclusivist feeling to have originated in the flawed vision of his earlier writings.[15]

It was those writings, and especially the documentary he was commissioned by Eric Williams to write on his return, *The Middle Passage* (1962), which has made Naipaul one of the most problematic, if not actively disliked writers of the diaspora. If Sir Vidiadhar Surajprasad seems to accept the West's praise for his elegantly modernist, international fiction, there remains a chorus of dissent from those who perceive themselves to lie outside the dominant, international centres of power – those who, like Sivanandan, see him as at best a 'double-agent' for the colonizer, turning his acute understanding of the condition of the colonized into the means of betraying them, 'seeing history (his own included) through English eyes'. This is generally the response of fellow ex-colonials, many of whom (such as Rob Nixon, a South African based at Columbia) read all of Naipaul as if it were a repetition of his early position – whereas his more recent writings suggest not so much a double agent as an *agent provocateur* among those negotiating a space between the varying claims of national and international identity.[16]

What Naipaul reveals, in his peculiarly mordant and increasingly melancholy way, is that the history of the present is a history of disruption and discontinuity on a global scale. All of us, in some sense, belong to the diaspora; every nation is hybrid, becoming more so as migration increases and in despite of the rise of the archaic violence of 'ethnic cleansing' we have seen in Europe as in central Africa. The question is whether we – in the West as in Africa, Asia or the Pacific Rim – will *admit* this condition, which also means recognizing and respecting difference. Naipaul may find it easier to recognize than respect difference; but he does alert us to the complex ironies of our changing historic condition, even as he displays signs of its reactionary politics, its racial stereotyping.

And so, when in *Enigma of Arrival* he rewrites his arrival in the metropolitan, imperial centre, an arrival echoing that of so many others who established the Anglophone Caribbean identity as something neither strictly national nor international – when he now rewrites this arrival, he does so in terms which propose its representative historic force beyond even the large constituency of the Caribbean. Arriving in London in 1950 he was, he says, a raw colonial, unconsciously carrying his history, but without an 'idea of history', and so unaware of being at 'the beginning of that great movement of peoples that was to take place in the second half of the twentieth century', a movement between 'all the continents', which turned cities like London from being 'more or less national cities' into 'cities of the world, modern-day Romes, establishing the pattern of what great cities should be, in the eyes of islanders like myself and people even more remote in language and culture' – 'a great subject', he adds, 'if only I had had the eyes to see'.[17]

Naipaul now realizes that he was too absorbed in an idea delivered to him by his Eurocentric education, of the writer as a citizen of the world, to see his real subject, aspiring arrivants like himself. Behind the insight there lies also a vision of a hierarchy of dispossession, locating yet others, 'all the barbarian peoples of the globe' he calls them, 'people of forest and desert, Arabs, Africans, Malays' who are yet further from his imagined centres of civilization. Naipaul certainly transcends any simple English, European or even Western perspective; but, as Nixon points out, he here draws an alarming new distinction, between those who have *some* claim upon 'civilization', like himself, and those who do not.[18]

To rescue Naipaul from some of the more disturbing implications of his position means recognizing that his view of history changes. It's partly a function of the careful historical placing of his narratives – registering, for example, by means of the framing journal entries of *In A Free State*, that that book explores the specifically post-Suez phase of decolonization; but more important, that it involves a progressive exploration of a fundamental, paradigmatic historical narrative of empire, according to which civilizations sucessively rise and fall, and rise and fall again – the next to come, he says at the end of *In a Free State*, is China (particularly persuasive now, after Hong Kong's return). But even the African forest dwellers of that narrative, distanced and exoticized by the stereotyping white colonial imagination of Naipaul's two expatriate travellers – a stereotyping the narrator seems at times to share – even *they* were once 'a clothed people, builders of roads' comparable to Roman roads.[19] Now, they have been enslaved or abandoned by the nation-builders of the more powerful tribe. All that is left to individuals caught within this bleak vision of history – an amalgam of Hindu fatalism and modernist pessimism – is lucidity and withdrawal.

But this is not Naipaul's last word on history, as the attempt to recover by rewriting his fragmented past in *The Enigma of Arrival* shows. Contemplating his English landlord's inactivity, and the intimations of decline signalled by the interwoven histories of the dependents of the manor – the gardener, the housekeeper, the car-hire man – the intruding colonial discovers that there is new life here, too; that some of these rural English people are moving on with energy, if not conviction; and so, he says, the idea of 'human life as a series of cycles that ran together', itself replacing an earlier idea of inevitable decay, is now replaced by *another* idea, an idea of renewal and commitment. For Naipaul, this means 'committing one not only to travel but also to different explorations of the past'. Coming to terms with the past means coming to terms with a personal past, a past bound up with his own fractured sense of identity, his sense of being 'unlikely', an East Indian from the West Indies.[20] For the grandson of indentured labourers brought in to replace the freed slaves on the sugar plantations, that identity was, in the first place, created by Europeans from Columbus onwards; but it was also created by the African slaves brought in to replace the indigenous inhabitants, and who saw in their Asian successors a degraded people they could brutalize in their turn. If, as critics such as Adewale Maja-Pearce have pointed out, there is an undeniably racist tinge to Naipaul's African narratives (such as *A Bend in the River* and the title novella of *In A Free State*), then it is also true that, as David Dabydeen says, you can hear in Naipaul's anti-African asides 'the cry of the whiplashed coolie'.[21]

According to Naipaul, the Indian Trinidadian belonged to a group permeated with a sense of 'difference', which offered insulation from the racial politics of his society, but also imprisonment within a static, dying community.[22] It was to escape this community that Naipaul aspired towards becoming a writer and citizen of the world; but it also led him inwards, towards an arrival in his ancestral home of India – *An Area of Darkness* (1964) as he called it after his initial, year-long arrival there, *A Wounded Civilization* (1977) after the second and, after what he called his last visit, the place of *A Million Mutinies Now* (1990) all serving a 'central will, a central intellect, a national idea'. This sense of a common identity, gathered by Naipaul from long listening to people 'who have ideas now about who they are and what they owe themselves', has defused the old neurosis about India, the neurosis of a childhood when

> Growing up in far-off Trinidad, I had no idea of clan or region, none of the supports and cushions of people in India. Like Gandhi among the immigrant Indians of South Africa, and for much the same reasons, I had developed instead the idea of the kinship of Indians, the idea of the family of India. And in my attempt to come to terms with history, my criticism, my bewilderment and sorrow, was turned inward, focussing on the civilization and the social organization that had given us so little protection.[23]

By retrieving the individual history through memory, Naipaul rewrites the more general history, turning his earlier, often ferocious satire of colonial 'mimicry' or fantasy in India and other post-colonial countries, into the calmer, renewing awareness of the end of *Enigma* when, on the return to Trinidad, he realizes 'There was no ship of antique shape to take us back. We had come out of the nightmare; and there was nowhere else to go'. This last arrival brings a wish for 'things that were felt specifically to represent us and our past', a wish met by witnessing the renewal of the family's Hindu burial rites, and the recreation of a subjective 'composite history' of their communal past by an elderly relative. 'Men need history', the narrator adds, 'it helps them to have an idea of who they are'; and, like 'sanctity' it can 'reside in the heart'.[24]

Yet, according to the notorious remark in *The Middle Passage*, 'History was built around achievement and creation; and nothing was created in the West Indies'. If, like the language Naipaul uses, it originates somewhere else and its traditions are not his – if, as Walcott's Shabine snarls, 'that's all them bastards have left us: words', then his journey as man and writer will seem futile, his exile, unlike Rama's, permanent. But travel also gave Naipaul 'the changing world and took me out of my colonial shell', becoming the substitute for all that his background denied him. In the healing little allegory (as he calls it) at the centre of *The Enigma of Arrival*, he uses the De Chirico picture to rewrite the framing narrative of *In A Free State*. Once again a solitary traveller arrives in an ancient Mediterranean port, 'classical' from without, 'alien within'. But now the arrival is unending, or ends only in death.[25] Thus Naipaul recasts himself within the sophisticated and distancing format of the European classical tradition, while preserving a residue of alienation, of disaffection and resistance to incorporation, which ties him to his past, and through that, the multiple pasts of the diaspora. By admitting his overlapping, often anguished histories, Naipaul comes nearer to that ideal according to which, in the classic words of Francis Bacon, reminiscent again of Donne and Walcott: 'If a man be gracious and courteous to strangers, it shows he is a citizen of the world, and that his heart is no island cut off from other lands, but a continent that joins to them.'[26]

## The Cultural Mediation of the Post-Colonial Text

I have been arguing that we all need texts such as these to know where – and who – we are, in the long, decolonizing moment. That is if it is possible to find such a grounding: although, as it has been the whole thrust of this book to suggest, English literary texts broadly defined offer a lot more than their absence from recent theory implies. For Homi Bhabha, increasingly and conveniently dismissed as the producer of a form of critical and theoretical discourse both elitist and obfuscatory, it was in fact the struggle to come to terms with Naipaul's early novel, *A House for Mr Biswas* (1961) that first led to the move to theory, as a way of getting to grips with the anguish of displacement and loss he found in Mr Biswas's attempt to build a home in Trinidad.[27] The instability of home led to a sense of the instability of 'the colonial subject', and the desire for an identity. Naipaul's reiterated redefinition of himself implicitly acknowledges the constructedness of identity, through a recognition of difference and diversity. This key aspect of post-colonial theorizing, while demonstrating the need for continuing thought about how we define ourselves within our variously defined and positioned global condition, contains a trap, too: of defining the world solipsistically, as only real in terms of your own individual experience – hence allowing back the hegemonic (unexamined male liberal) position.

I want finally to demonstrate this danger by looking briefly at a popular cultural product, the prizewinning, star-studded, hugely popular film version (1996) of Sri-Lankan Canadian Michael Ondaatje's *The English Patient* (1992 ), and the relatively unknown (although Booker Prizewinning) novel-text from which it was taken. The film seems at first simply to gesture derivatively in the direction of such classic, exotic-romance films as *Casablanca*, *Ice Cold In Alex* and *Lawrence of Arabia*, while removing the complex, open-ended and decentring effect of the novel in order to promote itself in terms of nostalgic, popular fiction. The Italian–British director Anthony Minghella himself remarked: 'The first purpose of a film like this is to take people on a journey, whereas the book eschews destination.'[28] Exactly so: the audience is being invited to consume the familiar linear version of reality offered by the film, rather than being obliged to handle the interrupting, digressive mode of the novel-text, which throws uncertainty upon the present, as well as the past. In that sense, the post-colonial text becomes the submissively colonial again – even if in the post-colonial era.

In Ondaatje's book, as Jeanne Delbaere has put it, 'a new integrative paradigm is now emerging', to overtake 'early post-colonialism with its sharp polarizations' by creating 'hybridized sites of imaginative transformation'.[29] Her language may obscure the point: that the familiar political and historical concerns of post-colonial writing can be revitalized through such reconciling, visionary narrative modes. The English patient of the title, whose nameless and badly burnt body lies at the centre of the narrative, carries with him a copy of Herodotus's *Histories*, literally supplemented by personal diary entries, notes, newspaper clippings, extracts from other books, maps, even the leaf of a fern, which then become the metaphoric bridge across time and space that replaces simple historicist conceptions of time, through

> a poetic conflation of past and present, of facts and imagination, liberating stories, legends, images, myths or works of art from their rigid frames in a particular historical period so that, like seeds, they germinate and grow elsewhere in a ceaseless organic recreation of the mind counteracting the inorganic 'progress' of technology.[30]

This romantic conception of Ondaatje's project is plausible, as plausible as the novel's own resonant, profoundly intertextual quest for epiphanic connections across national, class, race and gender barriers. This very plausibility is what allows in the filmmaker's reworking, and displacement of the novel's restraining historical parameters in terms of sensual, visual images – as in the framing initial and concluding aerial shots of the Sahara, which represent north Africa as seductively feminine, offering itself to the viewer in much the same terms as those offered to the gaze of the overflying, proprietorial, desiring capitalist Mehring, in Gordimer's *The Conservationist*.

But in Gordimer's text the dominant gaze is challenged: by the reader's awareness that Mehring is a character, what's more a character whose inability to conserve what is truly valuable around him becomes a dimension of the radically upsetting unconscious, brought out by that narrative's ambivalent ending. Race, class and gender provide markers of identity in the Minghella film, perhaps primarily class, so as to feed a class nostalgia enjoyed worldwide. Thus the *Sydney Morning Herald* responded to the 'passion and allure' of the two supremely upper-class English performers, Ralph Fiennes and Kristin Scott Thomas, noting the latter's 'honey-coloured skin' and blonde hair, the emotions 'so often camouflaged by English paleness and self-deprecation', before remarking (this can serve as a summary of the plot) that

> Thanks to the surrounding hype, the story is now known to everybody who reads newspapers. It begins towards the end of World War II in a Tuscan villa where the 'English patient' lies dying from disfiguring burns received in an air crash in the Sahara. A charming, lucid character, he has a mind packed with information of all sorts, yet claims not to remember his name or his nationality. Out of fondness for him, a young French–Canadian army nurse, Hana (Juliette Binoche), has chosen to stay with him. She's also beginning to fall in love – with a Sikh sapper (Naveen Andrews) in the British Army, helping to rid the area of landmines.

Less kindly disposed to the burnt man is the fourth member of the group, David Caravaggio (Willem Dafoe). He's worked in Intelligence and knows that 'the English patient' is actually a Hungarian, Count Almasy – a former desert explorer suspected of an act of collaboration with the Nazis – but his affection for Hana makes him bide his time in trying to get to the truth.

Time is an elastic element in the novel, which ranges back and forth through the years to Almasy's affair with the Scott Thomas character, wife of another explorer, as well as taking in Hana's experiences as a nurse; Caravaggio's adventures as a thief and spy; and the young Sikh's feelings about England, his adopted country. Minghella chooses only what he really needs from these separate strands, concentrating his flashbacks on the Sahara of Almasy's prewar experience, which lives on as a golden world beyond the boundaries of nationality and the constrictions of ownership itself.[31]

This reviewer – like most – may have read the novel, yet conflates its different kind of characterization and narrative mode with that of the film; ignoring Hana's Toronto background, accepting at face value the patient's desire to avoid the claims of nationality and ownership, as well as the film's downgrading of 'the young Sikh's feelings'. In the novel a sapper named Kirpal Singh, nicknamed Kip by the English – whose country he doesn't adopt, rather, which has adopted him, is a member of the imperial army, trained in English ways as it has trained him in bomb-disposal; and it is to him, moreover, that the last words of the novel are given, from the perspective of a present in which, like a 'stone of history skipping over the water, bouncing up so she and he have aged before it touches the surface again and sinks', he has become a married doctor back in India, meditating upon his affair with Hana, fellow-colonial in a temporary space out of war, 'both international bastards – born in one place and choosing to live elsewhere. Fighting to get back to or get away from our homelands all our lives'.[32]

This ending defines a complex post-colonial position distinct from that enunciated by the patient's: 'Erase the family name! Erase nations! I was taught such things by the desert . . . By the time war arrived, after ten years in the desert, it was easy for me to slip across borders, not to belong to anyone, to any nation.'[33] His denial of origins, place and identity is also what enables him to betray the Allies to the Nazis; rather a different matter from saving them, as a sapper or a nurse. Wars, unfortunately for the patient's view of things, do involve taking sides, wherever you come from or are going to. Even the *New York Times* reviewer was seduced by the film's narrative of 'romance, danger, and adventure', into treating history as mere backdrop. It was not until Elizabeth Pathy Salett, President of the National MultiCultural Institute of America, and whose father knew the original Count Laszlo de Almasy, a 'committed Nazi collaborator' – it was not until she publicly charged the film with portraying Almasy as no more than an 'accidental spy responding to personal tragedy', that the question of history in both film and book was taken up publicly.[34]

Ondaatje, who collaborated with Minghella in the writing of the film script, defended both book and film by arguing that 'the facts are still murky and still uncertain . . . *The English Patient* is not a history lesson but an interpretation of human emotions – love, desire, betrayals in war and betrayals in peace – in a historical time'. The film includes a shocking scene of Nazi torture, when Caravaggio's thumbs are cut off, and the other central characters 'reflect and qualify' Almasy's character – which in any case, as an historical figure, was ambivalent.[35] Is this defence convincing?

Yes and no. Neither film nor book is simply a document, and it may be that the original figure was ambivalent. But Ondaatje's view denies the reality of the reception and interpretation of a film demonstrably different in structure, genre and tone from the novel, while reinscribing the novel as something both simpler and more universal than it is. Of course the author's reported words on this occasion are no more than one element of either work's cultural transmission, to be interpreted accordingly. But, contrary to what he does, by taking the book as different from the film, it is possible to acknowledge historical resonance and open-ness. One aspect of this (again, denied, this time by omission, in the film) is signalled by the remarkable moment in the novel when 'Kip' addresses the 'Englishman' as the colonizer, whose 'ships', 'histories and printing presses' ensured world power. 'And Indian soldiers wasted their lives so they could be *pukkah*. You had wars like cricket. How did you fool us into this? Here . . . listen to what you people have done'. They listen to the report of the 'tremor of Western wisdom' as 'the streets of Asia' fill with the fire of the atomic bombs which end the war.[36] The patient's non-English origins suddenly become less relevant than his shared European background, which makes him complicit with the technology which has wreaked such terrible vengeance upon the Asian people who made war against them.

This shift in perspective is startlingly anachronistic, and feels external to the book's narrative and its histories; yet it is prepared for by creating an awareness of the 'otherness' of the Sikh in relation to both the imperial and the settler nationals – primarily Almasy, Hana and Caravaggio, but also Hardy, his English army friend. And if, as I have been suggesting from the start, one fundamental element of reading as post-colonial the texts which confront us in the post-war period involves shifting perspective from the West, then you can see how *The English Patient* asks to be read in that way: a way which the film largely excludes. I say largely, because there *is* one moment when the post-colonial potential of the originating text is taken up, and that is when Kirpal Singh reads the patient's copy of Kipling's *Kim* to the burnt figure, who 'corrects' his non-standard, Indian English, only to be corrected back by his Indian reader.[37]

But on the whole, the cultural transmission of the novel by the film neutralizes the post-colonial potential of the book, both in terms of its exploration of racial 'otherness' and in terms of its even more interesting exploration of gender. This aspect of the original narrative is focused upon the figure of Hana, the French–Canadian nurse, whose independence – historically apt, since the war released many women from traditional roles – is confirmed by the novel, and is even written into it as a defeat for the male author at the end, when he remarks: 'She is a woman I don't know well enough to hold in my wing, if writers have wings, to harbour for the rest of my life.'[38] The patient's adulterous affair registers a familiar stereotype, although the narrative's complex structuring allows some questioning of that stereotype; but Hana is an outsider, a temporary sojourner on the European map, who approaches Kirpal Singh as a fellow hybrid. The film echoes her autonomy to some extent by visualizing her frequently on her own, either absorbed in her own actions and thoughts, or watching the men – especially Kip, whose long hair she glimpses on one occasion as he washes, creating a moment in which his otherness for her is sensually attractive. But the confirmation of Hana's independence as a desiring subject is foreclosed by the film, which ends – not with her and Singh's separate musings in an undefined present, but with a repeat of the opening shot of the desert as seen by Almasy from the plane.

The film finally insists on the primacy of the personal. Nations may take up arms against each other, who you are may determine which side you are on, but for lovers, who live in an eternal present, all that finally matters is whether or not they can find each other, even in death. If the film also captures something of the sense of Ondaatje's post-colonial perspectives, it reveals the problematics of this kind of mediation – which allows in, all too readily, a conservative, stereotyping, anti-historical urge.

### Summary and Conclusion

If there is an 'after' post-colonial space, maybe it is constructed like Ondaatje's patient's copy of the writings of Herodotus, 'the father of history': as a self-consciously self-referential mosaic of moments in the present and past – a structure repeatedly reinforced in the narrative by the images of Italian frescoes and other forms of fragmentary or ruined art – yet a structure interfered with by personal memories and historical event, in short by the changing world. Ondaatje's cast of four seem arbitrarily connected by the contingent, yet their multiplicity of identities suggests the direction post-colonial literary studies may go: recasting histories to create a set of achronic narratives which reach back and (allegorically at least) forward in order to rechart the world, testifying to what Ondaatje through the patient calls 'our communal histories. communal books. We are not owned or monogamous in our tastes or experiences'. Indeed not; and post-colonial theory still needs to account for this by registering the class and gender, as well as race dimensions of its subject. 'All I desired was to walk upon such an earth that had no maps', continues the patient.[39] This flawed desire carries with it the ambiguity of the writings I have been dealing with: resisting the mapping of themselves by the knowledges of the past, implicated as they are by the empires of the past; while reaching towards an uncertain future in which – is it conceivable? maybe we need new concepts for this – in which the silenced and oppressed reinscribe themselves in a changing history, language, and theory.

## Notes

1 Raymond Williams, *Problems in Materialism and Culture: Selected Essays* (Verso, 1980), p. 18.
2 J. Hillis Miller, *Hawthorne and History: Defacing It* (Blackwell, 1991), pp. 152–3.
3 William Baer, 'An interview with Derek Walcott' (1993), in *Conversations with Derek Walcott*, ed. William Baer (University Press of Mississippi, 1996), pp. 202–3.
4 John Butt, 'Guilty conscience?' *Times Literary Supplement* (28 February 1992).
5 Ariel Dorfman, 'Silence is the enemy of a free press', *Observer* (3 May 1992).
6 See, e.g., Stephen Slemon, 'Unsettling the empire: resistance theory for the second world', *World Literature Written in English*, 30, 2 (1990), pp. 30–41.
7 Helen Gilbert and Joanne Tompkins, *Post-Colonial Drama: Theory, Practice, Politics* (Routledge, 1996), pp. 2–3.
8 Ibid., pp. 3, 130–1.
9 V.S. Naipaul, *A Way in the World* (Minerva, 1995), p. 102.
10 V.S. Naipaul, *Enigma of Arrival* (Penguin, 1987), pp. 220–1.
11 Ibid., pp. 91–2, 25, 312–18.
12 V.S. Naipaul, *In A Free State* (Penguin, 1973), pp. 10; 9.
13 Ibid., pp. 15, 243.

14 Naipaul, *Enigma*, pp. 156, 309; V.S. Naipaul, Foreword, Seepersad Naipaul, *The Adventures of Gurudeva and Other Stories* (Deutsch, 1976), p. 18.

15 Naipaul, *Enigma*, p. 145.

16 A. Sivanandan, 'The enigma of the colonized: reflections on Naipaul's arrival', *Race and Class*, 32, 1 (1990), pp. 35, 43. And see Rob Nixon, *London Calling: V.S. Naipaul, Postcolonial Mandarin* (Oxford University Press, 1992).

17 Naipaul, *Enigma*, pp. 52, 131–2.

18 Nixon, *London Calling*, pp. 41–2.

19 Naipaul, *In a Free State*, pp. 226–8.

20 Naipaul, *Enigma*, pp. 190, 250, 301, 309, 315; V.S. Naipaul, 'East Indian' (1965), *The Overcrowded Barracoon* (Penguin, 1976), pp. 35–8.

21 See Adewale Maja-Pearce, 'The Naipauls in Africa: an African view', *Journal of Commonwealth Literature*, 20, 1 (1985), pp. 111–15; David Dabydeen, 'Race and community in anglophone Caribbean fiction', *Cambridge Journal of Education*, 14, 3 (1984), p. 13.

22 V.S. Naipaul, *The Middle Passage*, 1962 (Penguin, 1975), p. 88.

23 V.S. Naipaul, *A Million Mutinies Now* (Minerva, 1990), pp. 517–18, 399.

24 Naipaul, *Enigma*, pp. 317, 315–18.

25 Naipaul, *Middle Passage*, p. 29; V.S. Naipaul, *Finding the Centre*,1984 (Penguin, 1985), p. 11; *Enigma*, pp. 156–7.

26 Francis Bacon, 'Of goodness and goodness of nature', 1612, in *Francis Bacon: The Essays*, ed. J. Pitcher (Penguin, 1985), p. 98.

27 Homi Bhabha, 'Representation and the Colonial Text', in *The Theory of Reading*, ed. F. Gloversmith (Harvester Press, 1984), pp. 114–19.

28 Harriet Lane, 'Mr Motivator', *Observer Life Magazine* (9 March 1997), p. 22.

29 Jeanne Delbaere, ' "Only *re*-connect": temporary pacts in Michael Ondaatje's *The English Patient*,' in *The Contact and the Culmination: Essays in Honour of Hena Maes-Jelinek*, eds Marc Delrez and Benedicte Ledent (University of Liège, 1997), pp. 45–56 (p. 45).

30 Ibid., p. 52.

31 Sandra Hall, 'Hot sand and shimmering sensuality', *Sydney Morning Herald* (6 March 1997), p. 15.

32 Michael Ondaatje, *The English Patient* (Bloomsbury, 1992), pp. 299, 176.

33 Ibid., p. 139.

34 Caryn James, 'Any novel can be shaped into a movie', *New York Times* (17 November 1996), p. 17; 'Michael Ondaatje responds', *The Globe and Mail* (7 December 1996), p. C3.

35 'Ondaatje responds', p. C3.

36 Ondaatje, *English Patient*, pp. 283–4.

37 See Anthony Minghella, *The English Patient: A Screenplay* (Methuen, 1997), pp. 74–5.

38 Ondaajte, *English Patient*, p. 301.

39 Ibid., p. 261.

# Select Bibliography

## Literary Works

Chinua Achebe, *Things Fall Apart,* 1958 (Heinemann, 1986).

——, *Anthills of the Savannah* (Heinemann, 1987).

Louise Bennett, *Jamaica Labrish* (Sangster's, 1966).

James Berry, ed., *News for Babylon: The Chatto Book of Westindian–British Poetry* (Chatto, 1984).

Edward Kamau Brathwaite, *The Arrivants: A New World Trilogy* (Oxford University Press, 1973).

——, *Mother Poem* (Oxford University Press, 1977).

——, *X/Self* (Oxford University Press, 1987).

Stewart Brown, Mervyn Morris and Gordon Rohlehr, eds, *Voiceprint: An Anthology of Oral and Related Poetry from the Caribbean* (Longman, 1989).

Dennis Brutus, *A Simple Lust: Collected Poems of South African Jail and Exile* (Heinemann, 1973).

Joyce Cary, *Mister Johnson*, 1939 (Penguin, 1965).

J.M. Coetzee, *Dusklands* (Ravan, 1974).

Joseph Conrad, *Heart of Darkness*, 1899, ed. Joseph Kimborough (Norton, 1988).

David Dabydeen, *Slave Song* (Dangaroo, 1984).

Tsitsi Dangarembga, *Nervous Conditions* (Women's Press, 1988).

Keki Daruwalla, *The Keeper of the Dead* (Oxford University Press, 1982).

Ariel Dorfman, *Death and the Maiden*, tr. Ariel Dorfman, 1990 (Nick Hern Books, 1991).

Nissim Ezekiel, *Collected Poems 1952–1988*, intro. Gieve Patel (Oxford

India Paperbacks, 1992).

Athol Fugard, John Kani, Winston Ntshona, *Sizwe Bansi is Dead*, 1972; *The Island*, 1973; in Dennis Walder, ed., *Athol Fugard: The Township Plays* (Oxford University Press, 1993).

Nadine Gordimer, *The Lying Days*, 1953 (Virago, 1983).

———, *The Conservationist*, 1974 (Penguin, 1978).

Stephen Gray, ed, *The Penguin Book of Southern African Verse* (Penguin 1989).

Mafika Pascal Gwala, *Jol'iinkomo* (Donker, 1977).

Linton Kwesi Johnson, *Dread Beat an' Blood* (Bogle-L'Ouverture, 1975)

E.A. Markham, ed, *Hinterland: Caribbean Poetry from the West Indies and Britain* (Bloodaxe, 1989).

Gcina Mhlophe, Marilin Vanrenen and Thembi Mtshali, *Have You Seen Zandile?* 1988 (Heinemann/Methuen, 1990).

Anthony Minghella, *The English Patient: A Screenplay* (Methuen, 1997).

Rohinton Mistry, *A Fine Balance* (Faber and Faber, 1996).

Oswald Joseph Mtshali, *Sounds of a Cowhide Drum*, foreword by Nadine Gordimer (Renoster Books, 1971).

Bharati Mukherjee, *Darkness* (Penguin Canada, 1985).

V.S. Naipaul, *In A Free State*, 1971 (Penguin, 1973).

———, *The Enigma of Arrival* (Penguin, 1987).

———, *A Way in the World*, 1994 (Minerva, 1995).

R.K. Narayan, *The English Teacher*, 1946 (Indian Thought Publs., 1955).

———, *The Man-Eater of Malgudi*, 1961 (Penguin, 1983).

———, *The Painter of Signs*, 1976 (Penguin, 1982).

Grace Nichols, *i is a long-memoried woman* (Karnak House, 1983).

Okot p'Bitek, *Song of Lawino & Song of Ocol*, 1966, 1967 (Heinemann, 1984).

Michael Ondaatje, *The English Patient* (Bloomsbury, 1992).

Sol T. Plaatje, *Mhudi*, 1930 (Heinemann, 1978).

Raja Rao, *Kanthapura*, 1934 (Orient Books, 1971).

Victor J. Ramraj, ed., *Concert of Voices: An Anthology of World Writing in English* (Broadview Press, 1995).

Salman Rushdie, *Midnight's Children* (Jonathan Cape, 1981).

Nayantara Sahgal, *Rich Like Us*, 1983 (Sceptre, 1987).

Mongane Wally Serote, *Yakhal'inkomo* (Renoster Books, 1972).

John Thieme, ed, *The Arnold Anthology of Post-Colonial Literatures in English* (Arnold, 1996).

Derek Walcott, *Collected Poems 1948-1984* (The Noonday Press: Farrar, Straus & Giroux, 1986).

———, *Omeros* (Faber & Faber, 1990).

## Critical, Historical and Theoretical Works

Chinua Achebe, 'The African writer and the English language' (1964); 'The novelist as teacher' (1965); 'Named for Victoria, Queen of England' (1973); 'Colonialist criticism' (1974), reptd in *Morning Yet on Creation Day: Essays* (Heinemann, 1975), pp. 55–64, 42–5, 65–70, 3–18.

——, 'An image of Africa: racism in Conrad's *Heart of Darkness*', in Joseph Kimborough, ed., *Heart of Darkness* (Norton, 1988), pp. 251–62.

Aijaz Ahmad, *In Theory: Classes, Nations, Literatures* (Verso, 1992).

Jacques Alvarez-Péreyre, *The Poetry of Commitment in South Africa*, transl. Clive Wake (Heinemann, 1984).

Benedict Anderson, *Imagined Communities: Reflections on the Origin and Spread of Nationalism*. rev. edn (Verso, 1991).

Bill Ashcroft, Gareth Griffiths and Helen Tiffin, *The Empire Writes Back* (Routledge, 1989).

William Baer, 'An interview with Derek Walcott' (1993), in *Conversations with Derek Walcott*, ed. William Baer (University Press of Mississippi, 1996), pp. 194–206.

Ursula Barnett, *A Vision of Order: A Study of Black South African Literature in English* (Sinclair Browne, 1983).

Geoffrey Barraclough, *An Introduction to Contemporary History*, 1964 (Pelican, 1967).

Homi Bhabha, 'A Brahmin in the bazaar', *Times Literary Supplement* (8 April 1977), p. 421.

——, 'Representation and the colonial text: a critical exploration of some forms of mimeticism', *The Theory of Reading*, ed. Frank Gloversmith (Harvester, 1984), pp. 93–122.

——, *The Location of Culture* (Routledge, 1994).

——, 'Postcolonial criticism', in *Redrawing the Boundaries: The Transformation of English and American Literary Studies*, eds Stephen Greenblatt and Giles Gunn (Modern Languages Association, 1992), pp. 437–65.

Elleke Boehmer, *Colonial and Postcolonial Literature* (Opus, 1995).

Edward Kamau Brathwaite, *History of the Voice: The Development of Nation Language in Anglophone Caribbean Poetry* (New Beacon, 1984).

Annamarie Carusi, 'Post, Post and Post. Or, Where is South African Literature in All This?', in *Past the Last Post: Theorizing Post-Colonialism and Post-Modernism*, eds Ian Adam and Helen Tiffin (Harvester/Wheatsheaf, 1993), pp. 95–108.

Aimé Césaire, *Discourse on Colonialism*, 1955, tr. Joan Pinkham (Monthly Review Press, 1972).

Michael Chapman, *Southern African Literatures* (Longman, 1996).

Shirley Chew, 'Searching voices: Anita Desai's *Clear Light of Day* and Nayantara Sahgal's *Rich Like Us*', in *Motherlands: Black Women's Writing from Africa, the Caribbean and South Asia*, ed. Susheila Nasta (Women's Press, 1991), pp. 43–63.

Chinweizu, Onwuchekwa Jemie and Ihechukwu Madubuike, *Toward the Decolonization of African Literature: African Fiction and Poetry and Their Critics* (KPI Ltd, 1985).

Stephen Clingman, *The Novels of Nadine Gordimer: History from the Inside* (Allen & Unwin, 1986).

J. M. Coetzee, *White Writing: On the Culture of Letters in South Africa* (Yale University Press, 1988).

David Crystal, *The English Language* (Penguin, 1990).

David Dabydeen, 'Race and community in anglophone Caribbean fiction', *Cambridge Journal of Education*, 14, 3 (1984).

——, 'On not being Milton', in *The State of the Language*, eds Christopher Ricks and Leonard Michaels, 1990 (Faber and Faber, 1991), pp. 3–14.

David Dabydeen and Nana Wilson-Tagoe, eds, *Reader's Guide to West Indian and Black British Literature* (Hansib/Rutherford, 1989).

J. Michael Dash, 'Edward Kamau Brathwaite', *West Indian Literature*, ed. Bruce King, 2nd edn (Macmillan, 1995), pp. 194–208.

Basil Davidson, *Black Mother: Africa and the Atlantic Slave Trade* (Pelican, 1980).

Jeanne Delbaere, ' "Only re-connect": temporary pacts in Michael Ondaatje's *The English Patient*', in *The Contact and the Culmination: Essays in Honour of Hena Maes-Jelinek*, eds Marc Delrez and Benedicte Ledent (University of Liège, 1997), pp. 45–56.

Anita Desai, 'A secret connivance', *Times Literary Supplement* (14-20 September 1990), p. 973.

Ariel Dorfman, 'Silence is the enemy of a free press', *Observer* (3 May 1992).

Dorothy Driver, 'M'a-Ngoana O Tsoare Thipa ka Bohaleng - The child's mother grabs the sharp end of the knife: women as mothers, women as writers', in *Rendering Things Visible: Essays on South African Literary Culture*, ed Martin Trump (Ravan, 1990), pp. 225–55.

Carole and Jean-Pierre Durix, *The New Literatures in English* (Longman France, 1993).

Terry Eagleton, *Literary Theory: An Introduction*, 2nd edn (Blackwell, 1996).

Frantz Fanon, *The Wretched of the Earth*, 1961, transl. C. Farrington, intro by Jean-Paul Sartre (Penguin, 1967).

——, *Black Skin, White Masks*, 1952, transl. C.L. Markmann 1967, foreword by Homi Bhabha (Pluto Press, 1986).

Elaine Savory Fido as she then was, 'Macho Attitudes and Derek Walcott' (1986), in *Literature in the Modern World*, ed. Dennis Walder (Oxford University Press, 1990), pp. 288–94.

D.K. Fieldhouse, *The Colonial Empires: A Comparative Survey from the Eighteenth Century*, 2nd edn (Macmillan, 1982).

Peter Fryer, *Staying Power: The History of Black People in Britain* (Pluto Press, 1984).

Henry Louis Gates Jr., *Figures in Black: Words, Signs and the 'Racial' Self* (Oxford University Press, 1989).

Helen Gilbert and Joanne Tompkins, *Post-Colonial Drama: Theory, Practice, Politics* (Routledge, 1996).

Paul Gilroy, *The Black Atlantic: Modernity and Double Consciousness* (Verso, 1993).

Nadine Gordimer, 'The novel and the nation in South Africa' (1961), in *African Writers on African Writing*, ed. G.D. Killam (Heinemann, 1973), pp. 32–52.

——, 'Living in the interregnum' (1982); 'The essential gesture' (1984), reptd in *The Essential Gesture: Writing, Politics and Places*, ed. Stephen Clingman (Cape, 1988), pp. 262–84, 285–300.

Stephen Gray, *Southern African Literature: An Introduction* (David Philip/ Rex Collings, 1979).

Andrew Gurr, ed., *The Yearbook of English Studies*, vol. 27 (1997): *The Politics of Postcolonial Criticism Special Number* (W.S. Maney for the Modern Humanities Research Association, 1997).

Mafika Gwala, 'Black writing today' (1979), in *Soweto Poetry*, ed. Michael Chapman (McGraw-Hill, 1982), pp. 169–75.

Stuart Hall, 'Cultural identity and diaspora', *Identity: Community, Culture, Difference*, ed Jonathan Rutherford (Lawrence & Wishart, 1990), reptd in *Colonial Discourse and Post-Colonial Theory*, eds Patrick Williams and Laura Chrisman (Harvester Wheatsheaf, 1993), pp. 392–403.

——, 'When was "the post-colonial"'? Thinking at the limit', *The Post-Colonial Question*, eds Iain Chambers and Lidia Curti (Routledge, 1996), p. 255.

Robert D. Hamner, *Derek Walcott: Updated Edition*, Twayne's World Authors Series (Twayne, 1993).

Peter Huline, *Colonial Encounters: Europe and the Native Caribbean 1492–1797* (Methuen, 1986).

C.I. Innes, *Chinua Achebe* (Cambridge University Press, 1990).

K.R. Srinivasa Iyengar, *Indian Writing in English*, 1962, rev. edn (Sterling Publishers, 1990).

Maya Jaggi, 'Mi revalueshanary fren', *Guardian* (24 September 1996), p. 13.

C.L.R. James, *The Black Jacobins: Toussaint L'Ouverture and the San Domingo Revolution,* 1938 (Allison & Busby, 1991).

——, 'From Toussaint L'Ouverture to Fidel Castro' (1962), in *The C.L.R. James Reader,* ed. Anna Grimshaw (Blackwell, 1992), pp. 296–314.

Lawrence James, *The Rise and Fall of the British Empire* (Abacus, 1995).

Louis James, 'Brathwaite and jazz', in *The Art of Kamau Brathwaite,* ed. Stewart Brown (seren/Poetry Wales Press, 1995), pp. 62–74.

Abdul JanMohamed, *Manichean Aesthetics: The Politics of Literature in Colonial Africa,* 1983 (University of Massachusetts Press, 1988).

Rosemary Jolly, 'Rehearsals of liberation: contemporary postcolonial discourse and the new South Africa', *PMLA,* 110, 1 (January 1995), 17–29.

Denis Judd, *Empire: The British Imperial Experience from 1765 to the Present* (Fontana, 1997).

Victor Kiernan, *The Lords of Human Kind: European Attitudes to the Outside World in the Imperial Age* (Pelican, 1972).

Bruce King, ed., *Literatures of the World in English* (Routledge & Kegan Paul, 1974).

F.W. Knight and C.A. Palmer, 'Nationalism, nation and ideology: trends in the emergence of Caribbean literature', in F.W. Knight and C.A. Palmer, eds, *The Modern Caribbean* (University of North Carolina Press, 1989), pp. 293–340.

Devindra Kohli, ed., *Indian Writers at Work* (B.R. Publishing, 1991).

Bartolomé de Las Casas, *A Short Account of the Destruction of the Indies,* 1552, ed. and tr. Nigel Griffin (Penguin, 1992).

Douglas Livingstone, 'The poetry of Mtshali, Serote, Sepamla and others in English: notes towards a critical evaluation' (1976), in *Soweto Poetry,* ed. Michael Chapman (McGraw-Hill, 1982) pp. 157–61.

Thomas Macaulay, *Minute on Indian Education,* 1835, in *Imperialism: the Documentary History of Western Civilization,* ed. Philip Curtin (Walker & Co., 1971), pp. 178–91.

Adewale Maja-Pearce, 'The Naipauls in Africa: an African view', *Journal of Commonwealth Literature,* 20, 1 (1985), pp. 111–15.

Oscar Mannoni, *Prospero and Caliban: The Psychology of Colonization,* 1956 (Ann Arbor Paperbacks, University of Michigan Press, 1990).

Arthur Marwick, *British Society Since 1945,* 3rd edn (Penguin, 1996).

Barbara Masekela, 'We are not returning empty-handed', *Die Suid-Afrikaan,* 28 (August 1990), pp.38–40.

Anne McClintock, 'The angel of progress: pitfalls of the term "post-colonialism"', *Social Text* (Spring 1992), pp. 1–15, reptd in *Colonial Discourse and Post-Colonial Theory,* eds Patrick Williams and Laura Chrisman (Harvester Wheatsheaf, 1993), pp. 291–304.

Jane Miller, *Seductions: Studies in Reading and Culture* (Virago, 1990).

J. Hillis Miller, *Hawthorne and History: Defacing It* (Blackwell, 1991).

Sara Mills, *Discourses of Difference: An Analysis of Women's Travel Writing and Colonialism* (Routledge, 1993).

Trinh T. Minh-Ha, *Woman, Native, Other: Writing, Postcoloniality and Feminism* (Indiana University Press, 1989).

Vijay Mishra and Bob Hodge, 'What is post(-)colonialism?', *Textual Practice*, 5, 3 (1991), pp. 399–414, reptd in *Colonial Discourse and Post-Colonial Theory: A Reader*, eds Patrick Williams and Laura Chrisman (Harvester Wheatsheaf, 1993), pp. 276–90.

Bart Moore-Gilbert, *Postcolonial Theory: Contacts, Practices, Politics* (Verso, 1997).

Jan (then James) Morris, *Pax Britannica: The Climax of an Empire*, 1968 (Penguin, 1979).

Mervyn Morris, 'Walcott and the audience for poetry', reptd in *Critical Perspectives on Derek Walcott*, ed. Robert D. Hamner (Three Continents Press, 1993), pp. 174–92.

Arun Mukherjee, 'The ideology of form: notes on the third world novel', *Journal of Commonwealth Literature*, 26, 1 (1991), pp. 19–32.

Vrinda Nabar, *Caste as Woman* (Penguin India, 1995).

M.K. Naik, 'Towards an Aesthetic of Indian English Literature', *Studies in Indian English Literature* (Oriental University Press, 1987), pp. 158–74.

V.S. Naipaul, *The Middle Passage,* 1962 (Penguin, 1975).

——, 'Jasmine' (1964), 'East Indian' (1965), *The Overcrowded Barracoon* (Penguin, 1976), pp. 24–31, 32–41.

——, *An Area of Darkness*, 1964 (Penguin, 1968).

——, 'Images', *New Statesman*, 24 Sept. 1965, reptd in *Critical Perspectives on V.S. Naipaul*, ed. Robert D Hamner (Heinemann, 1979), pp. 26–7.

——, Foreword, Seepersad Naipaul, *The Adventures of Gurudeva and Other Stories* (Deutsch, 1976).

——, *India: A Wounded Civilization*, 1977 (Penguin, 1979).

——, *Finding the Centre*, 1984 (Penguin, 1985).

——, *India: A Million Mutinies Now* (Minerva, 1990).

Ashis Nandy, *The Intimate Enemy: Loss and Recovery of Self under Colonialism* (Oxford University Press, 1983).

R.K. Narayan, 'Indian English', *A Writer's Nightmare: Selected Essays 1958–1988* (Penguin, 1988), p. 197.

——, *My Days* (Penguin, 1989).

Njabulo Ndebele, *Rediscovery of the Ordinary: Essays on South African Literature and Culture* (Congress of South African Writers, 1991).

Judie Newman, *Nadine Gordimer* (Routledge, 1988).

Ngugi wa Thiong'o, *Decolonising the Mind: The Politics of Language in African Literature* (James Currey, 1986).

Grace Nichols, 'The battle with language', in *Caribbean Women Writers: Essays from the First International Conference*, ed. Samuel R. Cudjoe (Calaloux Publications, 1990), pp. 283–9.

Rob Nixon, *London Calling: V.S. Naipaul, Postcolonial Mandarin* (Oxford University Press, 1992).

Lewis Nkosi, *Tasks and Masks: Themes and Styles of African Literature* (Longman, 1981).

'Michael Ondaatje responds', *The Globe and Mail*, Toronto (7 December 1996), p. C3.

Martin Orkin, *Drama and the South African state* (Manchester University Press, 1991).

Benita Parry, 'Problems in current theories of colonial discourse', *Oxford Literary Review*, 1, 1–2 (1987), pp. 27–58.

Kirsten Holst Petersen, 'First things first: problems of a feminist approach to African literature', *Kunapipi* 6, 3 (1984), reptd in *The Post-Colonial Studies Reader*, eds Bill Ashcroft, Gareth Griffiths and Helen Tiffin (Routledge, 1995), pp. 251–4.

Sadhana Puranik, '*The Painter of Signs*: breaking the frontier', in *R.K. Narayan: Contemporary Critical Practices*, ed. Geoffrey Kain (Michigan State University Press, 1993), pp. 125–39.

Rajeswari Sunder Rajan, *Real and Imagined Women: Gender, Culture and Postcolonialism* (Routledge, 1993).

Kenneth Ramchand, *The West Indian Novel and Its Background* (Faber, 1970).

Gordon Rohlehr, ''Blues and rebellion: Edward Brathwaite's *Rights of Passage*' (1971), in *Critics on Caribbean Literature*, ed. Edward Baugh (George Allen & Unwin, 1978), pp. 63–74.

Salman Rushdie, *Imaginary Homelands* (Penguin/Granta, 1992).

Albie Sachs, 'Preparing ourselves for freedom', in *Spring is Rebellious*, eds Ingrid de Kok and Karen Press (buchu books, 1990), pp. 19–21.

Nayantara Sahgal, 'The schizophrenic imagination', in *From Commonwealth to Post-Colonial*, ed. Anna Rutherford (Dangaroo, 1992), pp. 30–6.

Edward Said, *Orientalism: Western Conceptions of the Orient*, 1978 (Penguin, 1995), with afterword.

——, *Nationalism, Colonialism and Literature*, Field Day Pamphlet no. 15 (1988), reptd in *Literature in the Modern World*, ed. Dennis Walder (Oxford, 1990), pp. 34–41.

——, 'Representing the colonized: anthropology's interlocutors', *Critical Inquiry*, 15, 2 (Winter 1989), pp. 205–25.

——, 'Figures, configurations, transfigurations', in *From Commonwealth to Post-Colonial*, ed Anna Rutherford (Dangaroo, 1992), pp. 3–17.

——, *Culture and Imperialism*, 1993 (Vintage, 1994).

Elaine Savory [Fido], 'Macho attitudes and Derek Walcott', in *Literature and the Modern World*, ed. Dennis Walder (Oxford University Press, 1990), pp. 288–94.

A. Sivanandan, *A Different Hunger: Writings on Black Resistance* (Pluto, 1982).

——, 'The enigma of the colonized: reflections on Naipaul's arrival', *Race and Class*, 32,1 (1990), pp. 33–43.

Leif Sjoberg, 'An Interview with Derek Walcott' (1983), in *Conversations with Derek Walcott*, ed William Baer (University Press of Mississippi, 1996).

Stephen Slemon, 'Unsettling the Empire: resistance theory for the second world', *World Literature Written in English*, 30, 2 (1990), pp. 30–41.

Angela Smith, *East African Writing in English* (Macmillan, 1989).

Allister Sparks, *The Mind of South Africa* (Heinemann, 1990).

Gayatri Chakravorty Spivak, 'Can the subaltern speak?'(1988), reptd in *Colonial Discourse and Post-Colonial Theory*, eds Patrick Williams and Laura Chrisman (Harvester Wheatsheaf, 1993), pp. 66–111.

——, *The Post-Colonial Critic: Interviews, Strategies, Dialogues*, ed. Sarah Harasym (Routledge, 1990).

Florence Stratton, *Contemporary African Literature and the Politics of Gender* (Routledge, 1994).

Sara Suleri, 'Woman skin deep: feminism and the postcolonial condition', *Critical Inquiry* 18 (Summer 1992), pp. 756–69.

Leonard Thompson, *A History of South Africa*, rev. edn (Yale University Press, 1995).

Tzvetan Todorov, *The Conquest of America: The Question of the Other*, first publ. 1982, tr. Richard Howard (HarperPerennial, 1992).

Harish Trivedi, *Colonial Transactions: English Literature and India*, 1993 (Manchester University Press, 1995).

Michael Vaughan, '*Staffrider* and directions within contemporary South African Literature', in *Literature and Society in South Africa*, ed. Landeg White and Tim Couzens (Longman, 1984), pp. 196–212.

Gauri Viswanathan, *Masks of Conquest: Literary Study and British Rule in India* (Faber and Faber, 1990).

Jean-Philippe Wade, 'Introduction: disclosing the nation', *Rethinking South African Literary History*, eds J.A. Smit, Johan van Wyk and Jean-Philippe Wade (Y Press, 1996), pp. 1–9.

Michael Wade, *Nadine Gordimer* (Evans Brothers Ltd, 1978).

Derek Walcott, 'The muse of history', in *Critics on Caribbean Literature*, ed. Edward Baugh, (George Allen & Unwin, 1978), pp. 38–43.

William Walsh, *Commonwealth Literature* (Oxford University Press, 1973).

——, *Indian Literature in English* (Longman, 1990).

Jonathan White, ed., *Recasting the World: Writing after Colonialism* (Johns Hopkins University Press, 1993).

Patrick Williams and Laura Chrisman, eds, *Colonial Discourse and Post-Colonial Theory: A Reader* (Harvester Wheatsheaf, 1993).

Raymond Williams, *Problems in Materialism and Culture: Selected Essays* (Verso, 1980).

Stanley Wolpert, *A New History of India*, 5th edn (Oxford University Press, 1997).

Robert J.C. Young, *White Mythologies: Writing, History and the West* (Routledge, 1990).

——, *Colonial Desire: Hybridity in Theory, Culture and Race* (Routledge, 1995).

# Index